SPANISH

LANGUAGE
SURVIVAL
GUIDE

HarperCollins*Publishers*

HarperCollins Publishers
Westerhill Rd, Bishopbriggs, Glasgow, G64 2QT

www.collins.co.uk

First published 2001

© HarperCollins Publishers, 2001

Reprint 10 9 8 7 6 5 4 3 2

ISBN 0 00 710164 3

A catalogue reference for this book is available from The British Library

Consultants: Carole Robinson & Barry Grossmith

Photography: Carole Robinson & Barry Grossmith
  With additional photography/material from: Teresa Alvarez, Robert
  Grossmith, The Printer's Devil
  Spanish National Tourist Office (F Ontañón: pp 92[tr], 93[tr], 94[bl],
  96[bl], 97[ml], 101[bl] & [mr], 103[br], 105[tr]; Juan José Pascual: pp
  93[bl], 95[tr], 100[tr]; Mario Brossa: p 96[tr]; Garrrido 102[tl]; De la
  Puente: [101[tl])
  Artville (pp 91, 92, 94, 95, 96, 97, 98, 99, 100, 102, 103, 104, 105,
  106)
  Wine guide: Andrea Gillies
  Map: Heather Moore
Layout & Origination: The Printer's Devil, Glasgow

Other titles in the Collins Language Survival Guide series:
  France (0 00 710161 9)
  Italy (0 00 710163 5)
  Germany (0 00 710162 7)
These titles are also published in a CD pack containing a 50-minute CD
and Language Survival Guide.

Printed in Italy by Amadeus SpA

CONTENTS

USEFUL WEBSITES

TOURIST INFORMATION SITES

Currency Converters
www.oanda.com
www.x-rates.com

Foreign Office Advice
www.fco.gov.uk/travel/
  countryadvice.asp

Passport Office
www.ukpa.gov.uk

Health advice
www.thetraveldoctor.com
www.doh.gov.uk/traveladvice

Pets
www.defra.gov.uk/animalh/
  quarantine

SPANISH SITES

Hotels
www.hostels.com/es.html *(Hostel accommodation)*
www.parador.es
  (Parador listings)

Transport
www.renfe.es *(National rail network)*
www.iberia.es *(National airline)*
www.aseta.es *(Spanish motorways)*
www.metromadrid.es
 (Madrid metro)

Tourism
www.spaintour.com *(National Tourist Office site: links to national parks, what's on, etc.)*
www.okspain.org *(To Spain from the US)*
www.goski.com *(Skiing information for Pyrenees & Andalucia)*

Internet Cafés
www.netcafes.com

Culture
www.surinenglish.com *(Costa del Sol news in English)*
www.gomadrid.com *(What's on in Madrid)*
www.cyberspain.com
www.webmadrid.com
  (Information on the capital)

INTRODUCTION

As technology sweeps across the world, travellers aren't just faced with the prospect of speaking a foreign language – they also have foreign machines to contend with. Machines for parking, for dispensing cash, for buying tickets and food. Often there is nobody about to ask how they work. *Collins Language Survival Guides* address this problem by showing photographically signs and situations you might come across.

The things that throw you are often the ones that look familiar – such as buses, trains or phones – but which operate slightly differently.

There are usually codes to how things operate, and though you might not think you are aware of them, you are probably using them every day: the colour-coding for roads (blue for motorways, green for major roads, yellow for temporary signs) or when buying milk (generally blue for whole milk, green for semi-skimmed and red for skimmed). It's when these familiar codes don't work in the same way, that you feel slightly at a loss and probably more unsure than you need be. By making a note of how these types of things work and knowing a few keywords, you will feel much more confident.

The unique combination of practical information, photos and phrases found in this book provides the key to hassle-free travel and the colour-coding below shows how information is presented and how to access it as quickly as possible.

i   *General, practical information which will provide useful tips on getting the best out of your trip*

◄ keywords

a la derecha
a la de-re-cha
right

a la izquierda
a la eeth-kyer-da
left

these are words that are useful to know both when you see them written down or when you hear them spoken

key talk ►

short, simple phrases that you can change and adapt to suit your own situation

excuse me!
¡oiga por favor!
oy-ga por fa-bor

do you know where ... is?
¿sabe dónde está...?
sa-be don-de es-ta...

can you help me?
¿me puede ayudar?
me pwe-de a-yoo-dar

The **Food Section** allows you to choose more easily from what is on offer, both for snacks and at restaurants.

The practical 5000-word English–Spanish, Spanish–English **Dictionary** means that you will never be stuck for words.

SPEAKING SPANISH

We've tried to make the pronunciation under the phrases as clear as possible. We've broken the words up to make them easy to read, but don't pause between syllables. The syllable to be stressed is shown in **heavy type**. *Spanish isn't really hard to pronounce and once you learn a few basic rules, it shouldn't be too long before you can read straight from the Spanish.*

Most letters are pronounced as in English: **b**, **ch**, **d**, **f**, **k**, **l**, **m**, **n**, **p**, **s**, **t**, **y** *and (usually)* **w** *and* **x**.

As for the vowels, **a** *is always as in* **tap** *(never as in* **tape***);* **e** *is always as in* **pet** *(never as in* **Pete***);* **i** *is always 'ee';* **o** *is always as in* **hop** *(never as in* **hope***);* **u** *is always 'oo' rather than the English sound* **hut***. They keep their sound even in combination with other letters, so 'au' (eg* **autobús** *ow-to-***boos***) is like English 'ow', not like English* **automatic***.*

The letter **h** *is always silent, and* **r** *is always rolled (even more strongly when double r). Spanish* **v** *and* **b** *are pronounced exactly the same, something like English* **b***, while* **q** *is like English* **k***.*

The letter **c** *before* **e** *or* **i** *and the letter* **z** *are pronounced like the* **th** *in* **thin***. The letter* **g** *before* **e** *or* **i** *and the letter* **j** *have the guttural sound you hear in the Scottish word* **loch** *and which we show as* **kh***.*

Basic rules to remember are:

spanish		sounds like	example	pronunciation
ll		million	**calle**	**kal**-ye
ñ		onion	**mañana**	man-**ya**-na
c		cat	**comer**	ko-**mer**
c	(before **e/i**)	**th**ink	**hacer**	a-**ther**
g		**g**ot	**gafas**	**ga**-fas
g	(before **e/i**)	lo**ch**	**hijo**	**ee**-kho
z		**th**ink	**zapatos**	tha-**pa**-tos
j		lo**ch**	**hijo**	**ee**-kho
q		**k**ick	**quiero**	**kyer**-o

EVERYDAY TALK

*There are two forms of address in Spanish, formal (**Usted**, often written **Vd**) and informal (**tu**). You should always stick with the formal until you are on a first name basis. For the purposes of this book, we will use the formal.*

yes
sí
see

no
no
no

ok/that's fine
¡vale!
ba-le

please
por favor
por fa-bor

thank you
gracias
grath-yas

thanks very much
muchas gracias
moo-chas grath-yas

don't mention it
de nada
de na-da

that's very kind
muy amable
mwee am-ab-le

hello
hola
o-la

goodbye
adiós
ad-yos

good day/morning
buenos días
bwe-nos dee-as

good evening
buenas tardes
bwe-nas tar-des

good night
buenas noches
bwe-nas no-ches

see you later
hasta luego
as-ta lwe-go

excuse me!
¡oiga por favor!
oy-ga por fa-bor

sorry!
¡perdón!
per-don

I am sorry
lo siento
lo syen-to

I don't understand
no entiendo
no en-tyen-do

I don't know
no sé
no se

Addressing People

Friends and acquaintances usually greet each other with a kiss on each cheek if one of the people is female. Greetings between men involve a simple shake of the hand. Even if you are introduced to someone for the first time, the same rules apply. In more formal situations or if there is uncertainty, wait and see how the other person addresses you. In shops and offices, it is usual to say *Buenos días* or *Buenas tardes* to the people around you, with no physical contact.

how are things?
¿qué tal?
ke tal

fine thanks
muy bien gracias
mwee byen grath-yas

and you?
¿y usted?
ee oo-sted

hi, Teresa
¡hola Teresa!
o-la te-re-sa

bye, Pedro
¡adiós Pedro!
ad-yos ped-ro

see you on Saturday
hasta el sábado
as-ta el sa-ba-do

*Asking for something in a shop or bar, you would ask for what you want, adding **por favor**.*

1	**uno**
	oo-no
2	**dos**
	dos
3	**tres**
	tres
4	**cuatro**
	kwat-ro
5	**cinco**
	theen-ko
6	**seis**
	seyss
7	**siete**
	syet-e
8	**ocho**
	o-cho
9	**nueve**
	nwe-be
10	**diez**
	dyeth

a ... please
un/una ... por favor
oon/oo-na ... por fa-bor

a white coffee
un café con leche
oon ka-fe kon le-che

a beer
una cerveza
oo-na ther-be-tha

a tea and 2 beers please
un té y dos cervezas por favor
oon te ee dos ther-be-thas por fa-bor

the ... please
el/la ... por favor
el/la ... por fa-bor

the menu please
la carta por favor
la kar-ta por fa-bor

the bill please
la cuenta por favor
la kwen-ta por fa-bor

another...
otro/otra...
o-tro/o-tra...

that is everything
nada más
na-da mas

another beer
otra cerveza
o-tra ther-be-tha

another tea
otro té
o-tro te

2 more beers
otras dos cervezas
o-tras dos ther-be-thas

2 more coffees
otros dos cafés
o-tros dos ka-fes

To catch someone's attention

In a shop/ bar, you would say **por favor**. In the street, for example if you want directions, you would say *disculpe*. A lot of young people speak basic English, particularly on the coast and in the big cities. Don't assume older people will have the same ability. Assume a lack of English knowledge in small villages. Apart from the *Costas* and international hotels, airports and major tourist attractions, almost all signs will be in Spanish only.

excuse me!
¡disculpe!
dee-skool-pe

can you help me?
¿puede ayudarme?
pwe-de a-yoo-dar-me

do you know where ... is?
¿sabe dónde está...?
sa-be don-de es-ta...

how do I get to...?
¿cómo voy a...?
ko-mo boy a...

By combining key words and phrases you can build up your language and adapt the phrases to suit your own situation.

¿tiene...? **do you have...?**	**do you have a map?** ¿tiene un mapa? *tyen-e oon ma-pa*	**do you have a room?** ¿tiene una habitación? *tyen-e oo-na a-bee-tath-yon*
¿cuánto? **how much?**	**how much is the cheese?** ¿cuánto cuesta el queso? *kwan-to kwes-ta el ke-so*	**how much is the ticket?** ¿cuánto es el billete? *kwan-to es el beel-ye-te*
quería... **I'd like...**	**I'd like a red wine** quería un vino tinto *ke-ree-ya oon bee-no teen-to*	**I'd like an ice-cream** quería un helado *ke-ree-ya oon e-la-do*
necesito... **I need...**	**I need a taxi** necesito un taxi *neth-e-see-to oon tak-see*	**I need a receipt** necesito un recibo *neth-e-see-to oon re-thee-bo*
¿cuándo? **when?**	**when does it open?** ¿cuándo abren? *kwan-do a-bren*	**when does it close?** ¿cuándo cierran? *kwan-do thyerr-an*
	when does it leave? ¿cuándo sale? *kwan-do sa-le*	**when does it arrive?** ¿cuándo llega? *kwan-do lyeg-a*
¿dónde? **where?**	**where is the bank?** ¿dónde está el banco? *don-de es-ta el ban-ko*	**where is the hotel?** ¿dónde está el hotel? *don-de es-ta el o-tel*
¿hay? **is there?**	**is there a market?** ¿hay mercado? *aee mer-ka-do*	**where is there a market?** ¿dónde hay un mercado? *don-de aee oon mer-ka-do*
no hay... **there is no...**	**there is no bread** no hay pan *no aee pan*	**is there no train?** ¿no hay tren? *no aee tren*
¿puedo...? **can I...?**	**can I smoke?** ¿puedo fumar? *pwe-do foo-mar*	**can I go by train?** ¿puedo ir en tren? *pwe-do eer en tren*
	where can I buy milk? ¿dónde puedo comprar leche? *don-de pwe-do kom-prar le-che*	
¿está...? **is it...?**	**is it near?** ¿está cerca? *es-ta ther-ka*	**is it far?** ¿está lejos? *es-ta le-khos*
me gusta... **I like...**	**I like red wine** me gusta el vino tinto *me goos-ta el bee-no teen-to*	**I don't like cheese** no me gusta el queso *no me goos-ta el ke-so*

These are a selection of small but very useful words to know.

keywords keywords keywords keywords keywords

grande
gran-de
large

pequeño
pe-ken-yo
small

un poco
un po-ko
a little

basta
bas-ta
enough

más próximo
mas prok-see-mo
nearest

lejos
le-khos
far

demasiado caro
de-mas-ya-do ka-ro
too expensive

y
ee
and

con/sin
kon/seen
with/without

para
pa-ra
for

mi
mee
my

esto/aquello
es-to/a-kel-yo
this one/that one

ahora enseguida
a-or-a en-se-gee-da
straightaway

más tarde
mas tar-de
later

a large car
un coche grande
oon ko-che gran-de

a small car
un coche pequeño
oon ko-che pe-ken-yo

a little please
un poco por favor
oon po-ko por fa-bor

that's enough thanks
basta gracias
bas-ta grath-yas

where is the nearest bank?
¿dónde está el banco más próximo?
don-de es-ta el ban-ko mas prok-see-mo

it is too expensive
es demasiado caro
es de-mas-ya-do ka-ro

it is too big
es demasiado grande
es de-mas-ya-do gran-de

is it full?
¿está lleno?
es-ta lyen-o

is it free?
¿está libre?
es-ta lee-bre

a tea and a coffee
un té y un café
oon te ee oon ka-fe

a beer and a dry sherry
una cerveza y un fino
oo-na ther-be-tha ee oon fee-no

with sugar
con azúcar
kon a-thoo-kar

with cream
con nata
kon na-ta

without sugar
sin azúcar
seen a-thoo-kar

without cream
sin nata
seen na-ta

for me
para mí
pa-ra mee

for her/him
para ella/él
pa-ra el-ya/el

my passport
mi pasaporte
mee pa-sa-por-te

my keys
mis llaves
mees lya-bes

I'd like this one
quería esto
ke-ree-ya es-to

I'd like that
quería aquello
ke-ree-ya a-kel-yo

I need a taxi straightaway
necesito un taxi ahora enseguida
neth-es-ee-to oon tak-see a-or-a en-se-gee-da

is it far?
¿está lejos?
es-ta le-khos

I'll call you later
le llamo más tarde
le lya-mo mas tar-de

It is always good to be able to say a few words about yourself to break the ice, even if you won't be able to tell your life story. Remember there are different endings for male and female.

my name is...
me llamo...
me lya-mo...

I am from...
soy de...
soy de...

I am on holiday
estoy de vacaciones
es-toy de ba-ka-thyo-nes

I am here on business
estoy aquí por razones de trabajo
es-toy a-kee por ra-tho-nes de tra-ba-kho

I am single
estoy soltero/a
es-toy sol-te-ro/a

I am married
estoy casado/a
es-toy ka-sa-do/a

I have a boyfriend
tengo novio
ten-go nob-yo

I have a girlfriend
tengo novia
ten-go nob-ya

I am a widow
soy viuda
soy byoo-da

I am a widower
soy viudo
soy byoo-do

I am divorced
estoy divorciado/a
es-toy dee-bor-thya-do/a

I am separated
estoy separado/a
es-toy se-pa-ra-do/a

I have a child
tengo un hijo
ten-go oon ee-kho

I have ... children
tengo ... hijos
ten-go ... ee-khos

I work
trabajo
tra-ba-kho

I am retired
estoy jubilado/a
es-toy khoo-bee-la-do/a

I am a student
soy estudiante
soy es-tood-yan-te

this is a beautiful place
es un lugar precioso
es oon loo-gar preth-yo-so

I love Spanish food
me encanta la comida española
me en-kan-ta la ko-mee-da es-pan-yo-la

people are very kind
la gente es muy amable
la khen-te es mwee am-ab-le

I hope to come back soon
espero volver pronto
es-per-o bol-ber pron-to

thank you very much for your kindness
muchas gracias, muy amable
moo-chas grath-yas mwee am-ab-le

I've enjoyed myself very much
lo he pasado muy bien
lo e pa-sa-do mwee byen

we will be back
volveremos
bol-ber-em-os

you will write?
me escribirá ¿no?
me es-kree-bee-ra no

can I have your address?
¿me da su dirección?
me da soo dee-rek-thyon

People on the street and in bars are generally helpful. Don't be afraid to ask for assistance should you need help with any problem. There can, however, be a difference between ordinary people and 'officialdom'. There is, on occasion, a lack of flexibility with regard to standard rules and regulations.

excuse me!
¡oiga por favor!
oy-ga por fa-bor

can you help me?
¿puede ayudarme?
pwe-de a-yoo-dar-me

I don't speak Spanish
no hablo español
no ab-lo es-pan-yol

I am sorry, I did not know
lo siento, no lo sabía
lo syen-to no lo sa-bee-a

I am lost
me he perdido
me e per-dee-do

we are lost
nos hemos perdido
nos e-mos per-dee-do

I have lost...	**my money**	**my tickets**	**my passport**
he perdido...	el dinero	los billetes	el pasaporte
e per-dee-do...	*el dee-ne-ro*	*los beel-ye-tes*	*el pa-sa-por-te*

I have left...	**in the restaurant**		**on the train**
me he dejado...	en el restaurante		en el tren
me e de-kha-do...	*en el rest-ow-ran-te*		*en el tren*

I have missed...	**my flight**	**the train**	**the coach**
he perdido...	el vuelo	el tren	el autocar
e per-dee-do...	*el bwe-lo*	*el tren*	*el ow-to-kar*

I need to get to...
tengo que ir a...
ten-go ke eer a...

how can I get there today?
¿cómo puedo ir allí hoy?
ko-mo pwe-do eer al-yee oy

my luggage hasn't arrived
no ha llegado mi equipaje
no a lyeg-a-do mee e-kee-pa-khe

my case has been damaged
me han estropeado la maleta
me an es-tro-pe-ya-do la ma-le-ta

someone has stolen...
me han robado...
me an ro-ba-do...

this is my address
esta es mi dirección
es-ta es mee dee-rek-thyon

my bag	**my purse**	**my wallet**	**I have no money**
la bolsa	el monedero	la cartera	no tengo dinero
la bol-sa	*el mo-ne-de-ro*	*la kar-te-ra*	*no ten-go dee-ne-ro*

I need to go to hospital
tengo que ir al hospital
ten-go ke eer al os-pee-tal

my son/daughter is missing
mi hijo/hija se ha perdido
mee ee-kho/ee-kha se a per-dee-do

go away!	**that man is following me**
¡váyase!	ese hombre me está siguiendo
ba-ya-se	*e-se om-bre me es-ta seeg-yen-do*

The British might have a reputation for not complaining, but the Spanish complain even less. Complaining does sometimes work, but don't expect miracles as it is not a major part of Spanish culture. However, if you insist on your rights, you'll be more likely to be satisfied. This is obviously easier if you're in a part of the country where English is understood.

there is no...
no hay...
no aee...

there is no soap
no hay jabón
no aee kha-bon

it is dirty
está sucio
es-ta sooth-yo

they are dirty
están sucios
es-tan sooth-yos

it is broken
está roto
es-ta ro-to

they are broken
están rotos
es-tan ro-tos

the ... does not work
el/la ... no funciona
el/la ... no foonth-yo-na

the ... do not work
los/las ... no funcionan
los/las ... no foonth-yo-nan

it is very noisy
hay mucho ruido
aee moo-cho rwee-do

the room is too small
la habitación es demasiado pequeña
la a-bee-tath-yon es de-mas-ya-do pe-ken-ya

it is too hot
hace demasiado calor
a-the de-mas-ya-do kalor

it is too cold
hace demasiado frío
a-the de-mas-ya-do free-yo

it is too expensive
es demasiado caro
es de-mas-ya-do ka-ro

you are charging too much
me está cobrando demasiado
me es-ta kob-ran-do de-mas-ya-do

I want to complain
quiero hacer una reclamación
kyer-o a-ther oo-na rek-la-math-yon

where is the manager?
¿dónde está el gerente?
don-de es-ta el kher-en-te

we want to order
queremos pedir
ke-rem-os pe-deer

the service is very bad
el servicio es muy malo
el ser-beeth-yo es mwee ma-lo

it is cold *(food, drink)*
está frío
es-ta free-yo

this coffee is cold
el café está frío
el ka-fe es-ta free-yo

this isn't what I ordered
esto no es lo que he pedido
es-to no es lo ke e pe-dee-do

please take it off the bill
quítelo de la cuenta
kee-te-lo de la kwen-ta

there is a mistake
hay un error
aee oon er-ror

please check the bill
compruebe la cuenta
kom-prwe-be la kwen-ta

EVERYDAY SPAIN

The next four pages should give you an idea of the type of things you will come across in Spain.

▲ OPEN

CLOSED ▼

▲ OPENING HOURS

Opening hours for smaller shops are generally 10 am–1.30 pm, reopening 5–8 pm. Shops usually stay closed on Sat afternoons.

▲ INFORMATION

▲ PUSH

PULL ▼

CASH DESK/PAY HERE ▲

► Kiosks marked *ONCE* sell lottery tickets. Draws take place 3 or 4 times a week, with big prizes at the weekend. The lottery is organised by the national organisation for the blind.

---

talking

do you sell...?	**stamps**	**phonecards**
¿vende...?	sellos	tarjetas telefónicas
ben-de...	*sel-yos*	*tar-khe-tas te-le-fo-nee-kas*
where can I buy...?	**plasters**	**a map**
¿dónde puedo comprar...?	tiritas	un mapa
don-de pwe-do kom-prar...	*tee-ree-tas*	*oon ma-pa*

◀ Paying machines are becoming more and more widespread.

importe exacto
exact amount
no devuelve cambio
no change given

cancelar to cancel

◀ Postboxes are yellow. There are also red postboxes for priority mail and these take a different tariff.

for sale

for hire/rent

EXIT ▶ **Salida ✓**

ENTRADA
▲ ENTRANCE

▼ OUT OF SERVICE

▲ Tobacconists are known as *estancos,* state-licensed shops which sell tobacco products, stamps, bus tickets, postcards and basic stationery. Some offer a photocopy service. Look out for the maroon sign with the yellow script and the leaf logo. If you want stamps it is much easier to buy them here. Post offices are not as easy to come across.

excuse me!
¡oiga por favor!
oy-ga por fa-bor

what do I have to do?
¿qué tengo que hacer?
ke ten-go ke a-ther

how does this work?
¿cómo funciona esto?
ko-mo foonth-yo-na es-to

what does this mean?
¿qué significa esto?
ke seeg-nee-fee-ka es-to

talking

◀ **SERVICE NOT INCLUDED**

Tipping in Spain is not all that common. Service is generally not included and a tip of between 5 and 10% is normal.

AIRE ACONDICIONADO ◀ **AIR CONDITIONED**

Smoking is still popular in Spain and you will sometimes see people smoking on TV. However it is prohibited on public transport, in hospitals and government offices. Smokers in bars or restaurants are unlikely to give much thought to non-smokers.

ZONA NO FUMADORES

▲ NO SMOKING ZONE

SMOKING ZONE ▼

ZONA FUMADORES

PROHIBIDO FUMAR

▲ NO SMOKING

ESTA PROHIBIDO
sobre los pasamanos y escalones,
objetos entre los peldaños,
sobre las escaleras, etc.

◀ WARNING IT IS FORBIDDEN

The word *prohibido* means forbidden. Things which might seem quite innocent to us, may not be allowed in Spain.

can I smoke?	**do you mind if I smoke?**
¿puedo fumar?	¿le importa que fume?
pwe-do foo-mar	*le eem-por-ta ke foo-me*
I don't smoke	**please don't smoke**
no fumo	no fume por favor
no foo-mo	*no foo-me por fa-bor*
an ashtray please	**a non-smoking area please**
un cenicero por favor	una zona de no fumadores por favor
oon then-ee-ther-o por fa-bor	*oo-na tho-na de no foo-ma-dor-es por fa-bor*

Toilets in Spain are free but vary considerably. The cleanest will be found in department stores and hotels, for which you rarely need to ask for a key. Disabled and baby-changing facilities here are generally good, but not so elsewhere. It is possible to use bar toilets, even if you are not a customer, but sometimes you need to ask the barman for a key. It is very rare to have to pay to use a toilet, or leave a tip, although occasionally there are coin operated doors.

◀ Automatic toilets are becoming more common.

AGUA NO POTABLE

▲ NOT DRINKING WATER

red
out of service
yellow
occupied
green
free

Aseos and *Servicios*
▼ are both toilets.

ASEOS

▲ TOILETS ▼

SERVICIOS

CABALLEROS

GENTS ▲

LADIES ▼

SEÑORAS

OCUPADO

▲ OCCUPIED

FREE ▼

LIBRE

Don't be fooled by the letters on the taps. *C* is for *caliente* which means hot and *F* is for *frío* which means cold.

excuse me! where is the toilet?
¡por favor! ¿dónde están los servicios?
*por fa-**bor** don-de es-**tan** los ser-**beeth**-yos*

do you have a key for the toilet?
¿tiene llave del servicio?
***tyen**-e **lya**-be del ser-**beeth**-yo*

is there a disabled toilet?
¿hay servicio para minusválidos?
*aee ser-**beeth**-yo **pa**-ra mee-noos-**ba**-lee-dos*

is there somewhere to change the baby?
¿hay algún sitio para cambiar al niño?
*aee al-**goon** **seet**-yo **pa**-ra kamb-**yar** al **neen**-yo*

ASKING THE WAY

Most towns and cities provide local maps free of charge from the Tourist Information Office. Town plans are also prominently displayed, even in some of the smaller villages. Sectional street maps are particularly good in Madrid and can be found at street level outside every metro station (look for the red and blue metro sign). If you need directions, try to ask for help providing your own map. It's a lot easier! People on the street and the Police are generally willing to assist.

▲ Most towns and villages have maps on display.

In Madrid street maps are displayed outside every metro station. ▶

▲ YOU ARE HERE

Plaza is the name for square. ▼

Calle and *Paseo* both mean street.

talking talking talking

excuse me!
¡oiga por favor!
oy-ga por fa-bor

do you know where... is?
¿sabe dónde está...?
sa-be don-de es-ta...

how do I get to...?
¿cómo se va a...?
ko-mo se ba a...

is this the right way to...?
¿se va por aquí a...?
se ba por a-kee a...

do you have a map of the town?
¿tiene un plano del ciudad?
tyen-e oon pla-no del thyoo-dad

can you show me on the map?
¿puede indicarmelo en el mapa?
pwe-de een-dee-kar-me-lo en el ma-pa

we're looking for...
estamos buscando...
es-ta-mos boos-kan-do...

where are...?
¿dónde están...?
don-de es-tan...

is it far?
¿está lejos?
es-ta le-khos

a street directory
un callejero
oon kal-ye-khe-ro

9

ASKING THE WAY

YOU ARE ON THE TOP FLOOR (VD. is short for *Usted*)

toilets phones multi-cinema up to information
complex parking

◀ CITY/TOWN CENTRE

ACCESS ▶
TO
BEACHES
Acceso a Playas→

Red roads are national roads, often dual carriageways (**autovía**).

Local streets are signposted in green (**glorieta** is a roundabout).

Places of interest to travellers (e.g. stations, hotels) are signposted in yellow.

Places of interest (e.g. museums) are signposted in maroon.

▲ EL LIDO BEACH
Brown signs are places of geographic or ecological interest, while burnt orange (left) is for sport and recreational places.

▼ FOOTBALL GROUND
campo de futbol

- mercado — market
- Policía Local / Guardia Civil — police station
- urgencias — A & E
- centro urbano — town centre
- ayuntamiento — town hall

---

a la derecha *a la de-re-cha* to the right

a la izquierda *a la eeth-kyer-da* to the left

recto *rek-to* straight ahead

vaya *ba-ya* go

gire *khee-re* turn

calle *kal-ye* road

plaza *pla-tha* square

semáforo *se-ma-fo-ro* traffic lights

iglesia *ee-gles-ya* church

primera *pree-me-ra* first

segunda *se-goon-da* second

lejos *le-khos* far

cerca de *ther-ka de* near to

al lado de *al la-do de* next to

enfrente de *en-fren-te de* opposite

hasta *as-ta* until

BANKS & MONEY

There is no shortage of banks, but check opening times as most close around 2 pm. Some banks are open-plan and easy to enter, but many operate a double-door system, allowing one person in at a time. You usually have to press a green button to enter, the door slides open and you go in. There is usually a metal detector so it is advisable to leave keys, mobile phones, etc. in the lockers provided in the lobby area. If you don't, you may hear a recorded voice asking you to do so. The second sliding door will then open, allowing you to pass into the bank. Don't assume that bank staff will be fluent in English, although some have basic skills. There is not always a special counter for changing money, but if in doubt, ask the security guard who will normally be very helpful.

▲ Most banks can be identified by the word *Banco* or *Caja*. The big banks in Spain include *BBVA*, *Banco de Santander*, *Caixa de Cataluña* and *Caja España*.

▼ BUSINESS HOURS

This bank opens 8.30am–2.30pm Mon–Fri. It is shut on Sat and Sun.

◄ There are cash dispensers everywhere.

24 HOUR CASH ▼

▲ Check that cash dispensers will accept your card. There will probably be a handling fee. If you use a non-Spanish card, they will automatically give you a choice of languages in which to carry out the transaction. You should be able to use a Switch card (check for the Cirrus sign).

►

Some cash dispensers ▶ are accessed by swiping your card in the door. Either the green light will flash for you to enter (*accesso libre*) or the red light will flash to indicate out of service (*fuera de servicio*).

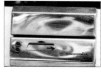

The euro is the currency of Spain. It breaks down into 100 euro cents.

◀ Notes: 5, 10, 20, 50, 100, 200, 500.

Coins: 2 euro, 1 euro, 50 cent, 20 cent, 10 cent, 5 cent, 2 cent, 1 cent. ▼

Although coins are officially *cent*, you find that Spanish people call them *céntimo*, a more familiar term for them. Euro notes are the same throughout Europe. The backs of coins carry different designs from each of the member European countries.

where is there...?
¿dónde está...?
don-de es-ta...

a bank
un banco
oon ban-ko

a bureau de change
una oficina de cambio
oo-na o-fee-thee-na de kam-byo

where can I change money?
¿dónde se puede cambiar dinero?
don-de se pwe-de kam-byar dee-ne-ro

I would like small notes
quería billetes pequeños
ke-ree-ya beel-ye-tes pe-ken-yos

where is the nearest cash dispenser?
¿dónde esté el cajero más próximo?
don-de es-ta el ka-khe-ro mas prok-see-mo

I want to change these travellers' cheques
quiero cambiar estos cheques de viaje
kyer-o kam-byar es-tos che-kes de bya-khe

the cash-dispenser has swallowed my card
el cajero se ha tragado la tarjeta
el ka-khe-ro se a tra-ga-do la tar-khe-ta

talking talking talking

WHEN IS...?

 The 24-hour clock is used in timetables and for train announcements in stations and for television programmes.

keywords keywords keywords

mañana
man-**ya**-na
morning

tarde
tar-de
afternoon

esta tarde
es-ta **tar**-de
this evening

hoy
oy
today

mañana
man-**ya**-na
tomorrow

ayer
a-**yer**
yesterday

más tarde
mas **tar**-de
later

ahora enseguida
a-**o**-ra en-seg-**ee**-da
straightaway

ahora
a-**o**-ra
now

a las ... menos cuarto
a las ... **me**-nos **kwar**-to
at a quarter to...

a las ... y media
a las ... ee **med**-ya
at half past ...

a las veinticuatro ho
a las bey-tee-**kwa**-tro o-

a las veintitrés horas
a las beyn-tee-**tres** o-ras

a las once
a las **on**-the

a las veintidós horas
a las beyn-tee-**dos** o-ras

a las diez
a las dyeth

a las veintiuno horas
a las beyn-tee-**oo**-no o-ras

a las nueve
a las **nwe**-be

a las veinte horas
a las **beyn**-te o-ras

a las ocho
a las **o**-cho

a las diecinueve horas
a las dyeth-ee-**nwe**-be o-ras

a las siete
a las **syet**-e

a las dieciocho hor
a las dyeth-ee-**o**-cho o-

a las ... menos veinte
a las ... **me**-nos be-**een**-te
at twenty to...

talking talking talking

when is the next...?
¿cuándo es el próximo...?
kwan-do es el **prok**-see-mo...

train
tren
tren

bus
autobús
ow-to-**boos**

boat
barco
bar-ko

when is...?
¿a qué hora es...?
a ke **o**-ra es...

breakfast
el desayuno
el de-sa-**yoo**-no

lunch
la comida
la ko-**mee**-da

dinner
la cena
la **then**-a

when does it leave?
¿cuándo sale?
kwan-do **sa**-le

when does it arrive?
¿cuándo llega?
kwan-do **lyeg**-a

when does it open?
¿cuándo abren?
kwan-do **a**-bren

when does it close?
¿cuándo cierran?
kwan-do **thyerr**-an

a medianoche
*a med-ya-**no**-che*
at midnight

a las ... y cuarto
*a las ... ee **kwar**-to*
at quarter past...

as doce
*as **doth**-e*

a la una
*a la **oo**-na*

a las trece horas
*a las **threth**-e o-ras*

a las dos
a las dos

a las catorce horas
*a las ka-**torth**-e o-ras*

a las tres
a las tres

a las quince horas
*a las **keenth**-e o-ras*

a las cuatro
*a las **kwat**-ro*

a las dieciséis horas
*a las dyeth-ee-**seyss** o-ras*

a las cinco
*a las **theen**-ko*

a las diecisiete horas
*a las dyeth-ee-**syet**-e o-ras*

las seis
las seyss

a las dieciocho horas y cuarenta minutos
*a las dyeth-ee-**o**-cho o-ras ee kwa-**ren**-ta mee-**noo**-tos*
at 18.40

lunes
loo-nes
Monday

martes
mar-tes
Tuesday

miércoles
mee-yer-ko-les
Wednesday

jueves
khoo-wev-es
Thursday

viernes
byer-nes
Friday

sábado
sa-ba-do
Saturday

domingo
do-meen-go
Sunday

keywords keywords keywords

have you the time please?
¿tiene hora por favor?
tyen-e o-ra por fa-bor

it's one o'clock
la una
la oo-na

it's five o'clock
las cinco
las cheen-ko

what is the date?
¿qué fecha es hoy?
ke fe-cha es oy

it is the 8th of May
(es) ocho de mayo
(es) o-cho de ma-yo

it is the 16th of September 2003
(es) dieciséis de septiembre del dos mil tres
(es) dyeth-ee-seyss de set-yemb-re del dos meel treds

which day?
¿qué día?
ke dee-ya

which month?
¿qué mes?
ke mes

talking talking talking

Timetables all use the 24-hour clock. Bus and train timetables usually change once a year and boat and ferry timetables tend to follow peak Summer season schedules. You can pick up timetables for coaches, trains and ferries/boats at the relevant offices/departure halls.

Lun. *Mon*
Mart. *Tues*
Mierc. *Wed*
Juev. *Thur*
Viern. *Fri*
Sab. *Sat*
Dom. *Sun*

◀ ARRIVALS

LLEGADAS

DEPARTURES ▶

SALIDAS

RETRASADO **◀ DELAYED**

information   origin of train

Train ▶
timetable

train

(1) No service on Sundays

(2) Lince train (type of train) runs on Fridays

Tren	Observaciones	Origen	Valladolid C. Grande	Valladolid Univ.	Cabezón de Pisuerga	Corcos-Aguilarejo	Cubillas de S. Marta	Dueñas	Venta
CLE (1)			7.30	7.34	7.40	–	–	7.51	7.59
R			13.00	13.04	13.09	13.13	13.18	13.24	13.33
CLE		MADRID CH. (11.30)	14.01	–	–	–	–	–	14.25
CLE		MADRID CH (14.30)	17.01	–	–	–	–	–	17.25
R			17.50	17.54	–	–	18.05	18.12	18.20
L	(2)	MADRID AT. (15.45)	18.40	–	–	–	–	–	19.04
CLE		MADRID CH. (18.30)	21.01	–	–	–	–	–	21.25

(1) No circula los domingos.
(2) Tren Lince. Circula los viernes.

CLE = Castile and Leon Express with free seat reservations and tickets can be purchased 15 days before the date of travel.▼

CLE = Tren Castilla y León Exprés con reserva de plazas gratuita y venta anticipada desde 15 dias antes de la fecha del viaje.

Hydrofoil ▶
timetable for
Málaga to North
Africa

BUQUEBUS

HORARIOS
MALAGA-CEUTA-MALAGA

	LUNES	MARTES	MIÉRCOLES	JUEVES	VIERNES	SABADO	DOMINGO
SALIDAS DE CEUTA	07.00 19.00 .	07.00 19.00 .	07.00 19.00 .	07.00 12.00 19.00	07.00 15.30 20.30	10.30 19.00 .	07.00 19.00 .
SALIDAS DE MALAGA	09.30 21.30 .	09.30 21.30 .	09.30 21.30 .	09.30 16.30 21.30	09.30 18.00 21.30	08.00 13.00 21.30	09.30 21.30 .

INFORMACIÓN Y RESERVAS: O EN SU AGENCIA DE VIAJES

Málaga: Tels.: **952 227 905** · Fax: **952 212 836**
Ceuta: Tels.: **956 505 353** · Fax: **956 501 505**

Los precios y horarios están sujetos a cambios sin previo aviso.
Les recordamos su presentación al embarque 30 minutos antes de la salida.

Prices and times subject to change without warning.

We remind you to present yourself for boarding half an hour before departure.

Bus timetable ▶
for Madrid–Barcelona ▼

departures arrivals frequency

Salidas Barcelona Nord	Llegadas Madrid	Frecuencias
01:00	08:30	Diario (*)
07:00	14:30	Diario (*)
08:30	**16:00**	Diario (**)
09:00	16:30	Diario (*)
10:00	**17:30**	Diario (**)
10:30	18:30	Diario (***)
11:30	19:00	Diario (*)
12:30	20:00	Diario (**)
13:00	20:30	Diario (*)
14:00	21:30	Diario (*)
15:00	23:00	Diario (***)
15:30	**23:00**	Diario (**)
17:00	00:30	Diario (*)(1)
17:30	01:00	Diario (*)
21:30	05:00	Diario (*)
22:00	**05:30**	Diario (**)
23:00	**06:30**	Diario (**)
24:00	**07:30**	Diario (**)

HORARIOS 1999

MADRID • BARCELONA

Nuevo Servicio

grupo ENATCAR
ARATESA

daily

(1) Para en Calatayud

▲ **Para en Calatayud**
stops at Calatayud

Aranjuez to Atocha timetable and key ▼

Aranjuez	Ciempozuelos	Valdemoro	Pinto	Getafe Industrial	San Cristobal Industrial	San Cristobal de los Ángeles	Villaverde Bajo	Atocha
x. 16.00	16.10	16.15	16.20	16.25	16.28	16.30	16.33	16.42
16.30	16.40	16.45	16.50	16.55	16.58	17.00	17.03	17.12
17.00	17.10	17.15	17.20	17.25	17.28	17.30	17.33	17.42
17.30	17.40	17.45	17.50	17.55	17.58	18.00	18.03	18.12
a. 17.50	18.00	18.05	18.10	18.15	18.18	10.20	18.23	18.32
d. 17.58	18.08	18.13	18.18	18.23	18.26	18.28	18.31	18.40

a.: Laborables excepto sábados.
d.: Sábados y festivos.
x.: Efectúa parada en Seseña 5 min. después de Aranjuez.
(1): No circula del 01/08/00 al 01/09/00 ambos inclusive.
(2): Circula diario del 01/08/00 al 01/09/00 ambos inclusive.

a.: Weekdays except Saturdays
d.: Saturdays and holidays
x.: Stops at Seseña 5 minutes after Aranjuez
(1): No service from 01/08/00 to 01/09/00 inclusive
(2): Daily service from 01/08/00 to 01/09/00 inclusive

TICKETS

*Tickets for transport are **billetes**. Tickets for cinema, theatre and museums are **entradas**.*

◄
Automatic ticket machines are becoming increasingly common. This one is for train tickets.

If you don't have the correct amount, make sure the machine indicates that change is given (**devuelve cambio** or **compto**). ▼

Seleccione ── *choose*

1 - Destino ── *destination*

── **sencillo** *single*

── **ida y vuelta/ ida y regreso** *return*

2 - Tipo de Billete

type of ticket

You can buy bus and metro tickets at the **estanco** or **tabacos**. ►

Train ticket ▼

| | | | class | date | | seat no. (P = aisle V = window) | |
| from | ticket no. | to | | ticket & reservation | | | date and time |

| 71 | N.º K 511494 | | | | BILLETE + RESERVA | | EL | 0054 C55E0323 00000000 2162 21/08/00 10:08 |

GRANDES LINEAS RENFE
D.I.F.:Q-2802074N
032323421612 40114

DE ──────► A	CLASE	FECHA	HORA SALIDA	TIPO DE TREN	COCHE	Nº PLAZA	DEPARTAMENTO	Nº TREN
MALAGA	BOBADILLA	T	21.08	14.00	TRD	1	58P	NO FUMA	3905
	HORA DE LLEGADA-->: 14.46					CLIMATIZ.			

Tarifa D10 TARIFA GENERAL
Forma de pago METALICO

FUR:****3,94 ── *price*

── *class/section*

── *train no.*

method of payment   *departure time*   *train type*   *carriage*

▲ Renfe local train ticket

10-journey bus ticket known as a **bono-bus**. It goes into the bus's validating machine in the direction of the arrow. ▶

◀ Renfe local ticket: one-journey bus ticket

10-journey ▶ (*10 Viajes*) metro and bus ticket (you must validate it on the bus in the machine by the driver).

The Malaga–Almeria via Melilla timetable, with ▼ discounted and concessionary fares (below).

▲

Return fare: 8% of passenger fare (except residents)
Young people's card, Retired and EU citizens over 60 years:
20% of passenger fare
Military conscripts (non-professional) who are posted in Melilla:
20% of passenger fare
Groups: 20% for over 11 people
Coaches with a minimum of 11 people: 50% for return, 25% for single journeys.

billete
beel-**ye**-te
ticket

bono-bus
bo-no-**boos**
10-journey ticket

entrada
en-**tra**-da
entry ticket

ida
ee-da
single

ida y vuelta
ee-da ee **bwel**-ta
return

adulto
a-**dool**-to
adult

niño
neen-yo
child

joven
kho-ben
young person

jubilado
khoo-bee-**la**-do
over 60

tercera edad
ter-**ther**-a ed-**ad**
over 60

minusválido
mee-noos-**ba**-lee-do
disabled

suplemento
soo-ple-**men**-to
supplement

ventanilla
ven-ta-**neel**-ya
window seat

pasillo
pas-**eel**-yo
aisle seat

keywords keywords keywords keywords

PUBLIC TRANSPORT

*Bus services vary from town to town. Generally speaking, you can buy single-journey tickets on the bus from the driver. You can also get a 10-journey ticket from **tabacos** or **estancos** and some kiosks which works out a little cheaper. These have to be validated in the ticket machine on the bus by putting them arrow down into the machine next to the driver (see p. 27). Under-4s normally travel free. Senior citizens and students can get discounts on multi-journey tickets but not on single tickets.*

▲ BUS STATION

METRO
BUS
TICKETS
ON SALE
HERE
▶

METRO BUS
de venta aquí

◀ Bus stops indicating the number of service and the stops en route. It is advisable to flag down the buses at the bus stop as they don't always stop automatically.

▶

Number and destination are normally shown on the front of the bus.

instructions ———

1. *Press the button to get a line (a recorded message will ask you to wait while the connection is made)*

2. *Once you get through talk normally* ———

If it doesn't work (there may be lots of calls) after a few seconds a new message will tell you that it is impossible to answer your query for the moment ———

Wait a few minutes and repeat the whole process ———

Business hours for the public from 9 am to 9 pm ———

PUNTO DE INFORMACIÓ
(SOLO SOBRE TRANSPORTES
URBANOS DE LA E.M.T.S.A.M.)

INSTRUCCIONES:

1 - PULSE EL BOTÓN PARA SOLICITAR LLAMADA
(Un mensaje le invitará a le espera mientras se establece la conexión).

2 - HABLE NORMALMENTE CUANDO LA COMUNICACIÓN SE ESTABLEZCA

EN CASO CONTRARIO
(Saturación de línea por otras llamadas) TRANSCURRIDOS UNOS SEGUNDOS, UN NUEVO MENSAJE LE INDICARÁ LA IMPOSIBILIDAD DE ATENDERLE EN ESE MOMENTO

ESPERE UNOS MINUTOS
Y REPITA LOS PASOS ANTERIORES

HORARIO DE ATENCIÓN AL PÚBLICO:
de 9 a 21 horas

Local bus information point ▶

There is a comprehensive long-distance coach network which is usually cheaper than travelling by train. All towns and cities have a central bus/coach station with information on routes, prices, times, etc. This is the best place to get information and buy tickets. Many coach companies run different routes and there is usually a board with a list of companies and destinations, showing the window number for specific routes. You need to go to the relevant window for information on prices and times. Advance booking is recommended especially at weekends and in high season. You can buy tickets up to 2 months in advance. Return tickets tend to be slightly more economical. Most coaches have toilets on board but few other facilities.

◀ The bus station is usually quite central.

▲ COACH STANDS 1–60
Check which stand your bus leaves from.

▼ COACH STAND

▲ Coach departure board. *Empresa* (in the second column) indicates the operator.

where do I catch a bus to...?
¿dónde se coge el autobús para...?
don-de se ko-khe el ow-to-boos pa-ra...

which number goes to...?
¿qué número va a...?
ke noo-me-ro ba a...

is there a coach to...?
¿hay algún autocar que vaya a...?
aee al-goon ow-to-kar ke ba-ya a...

which bus goes to the centre?
¿qué autobús va al centro?
ke ow-to-boos ba al then-tro

does this coach go to...?
¿este autocar va a...?
es-te ow-to-kar ba a...

please tell me when to get off
¿por favor me dice cuándo tengo que bajarme?
por fa-bor me dee-the kwan-do ten-go ke ba-khar-me

excuse me! I'm getting off!
¡por favor! me bajo aquí
por fa-bor me ba-kho a-kee

this is my stop
esta es mi parada
es-ta es mee pa-ra-da

talking talking

*Metro systems run in Madrid, Barcelona and Bilbao. Each operate their own ticket and travelcard system. In Madrid and Barcelona you can buy single tickets or tickets for 10 journeys which cover both the metro and bus system. These are valid for the central zone. It is possible to get a monthly pass (**abono mensual**) which covers the same system, but it is only worth getting one of these if you plan to spend 3 weeks of a calendar month in the city. For this option, you need to provide passport number and a photo. All types of tickets can be bought at metro station booths. Using the Metro is cheap and efficient. It is busy from 8.30 to 10 am and the evening rush hour can start as early as 3.30 pm and can go on till 8 pm. Most journeys will be within the central zone, but trips to the suburbs, for example, may require a supplement.*

Madrid metro maps ▶ are available from metro station booths. The Madrid metro operates from 6 am to 2 am daily. Their website is www.metromadrid.com

▲ Metro sign

Station name ▲
platform 2

The name of the station and the lines it serves; these are colour-coded ▼ (3, yellow and 5, green).

▲ Ticket machines
If you don't have the exact amount, check that the machine gives change (**devuelve cambio**).

end stops for line 2 (colour-coded red)

end stops for line 3 (colour-coded yellow)

▲ When planning a journey, look for the final destination for your particular line and follow signs to it.

Access to metro (line 6) and suburban trains ▼ (*Cercanías*).

▲ You must put your ticket through the barrier.

▲ DON'T FORGET TO TAKE YOUR TICKET

a single
un billete
oon beel-ye-te

a 10-journey ticket
un billete de diez viajes
oon beel-ye-te de dyeth bya-khes

a monthly ticket
un abono mensual
oon a-bo-no men-swal

have you a map of the metro?
¿tiene un plano del metro?
tyen-e oon pla-no del me-tro

where is the nearest metro station?
¿dónde está la estación de metro más próxima?
don-de es-ta la es-ta-thyon de me-tro mas prok-see-ma

I want to go to...
quiero ir a...
kyer-o eer a...

do I have to change?
¿tengo que cambiar de línea?
ten-go ke kamb-yar de lee-ne-ya

where?
¿dónde?
don-de

which line is it for...?
¿qué línea es para...?
ke lee-ne-ya es pa-ra...

in which direction?
¿en qué dirección?
en ke dee-rek-thyon

which station is it for...?
¿cuál es la estación de metro para...?
kwal es la es-ta-thyon de me-tro pa-ra...

please let me off
me deja salir por favor
me de-kha sa-leer por fa-bor

talking talking talking talking talking

*The national rail network is called RENFE. Train tickets can be bought at: train stations at the **taquilla**, RENFE agencies in large cities, travel agencies displaying the RENFE sign, or over the internet on the RENFE website, www.renfe.es. You can then pick up your tickets at the station. Tickets can be bought up to 2 months in advance. A high-speed train service called AVE (**Alta Velocidad España**) exists linking Madrid with Seville (a good link with local trains for the Costa del Sol). AVE also offers high-speed train services called TALGO 200 which are as good as AVE but cheaper (the only difference is that it takes 15 minutes longer to reach your destination). The AVE network's base is at the RENFE Atocha station in Madrid.*

▼ Ticket office

Taquillas

estación de **RENFE**

▲ Road sign for the train station

exit — **Salida**
customer service — **Atención al Cliente**

▶ Ticket machine for regional trains

AVE
Venta de Billetes
Trenes Regionales

BILLETES

REGIONALES RENFE

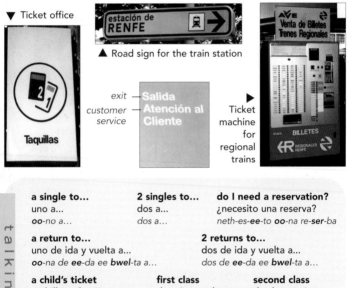

talking talking

a single to...	**2 singles to...**	**do I need a reservation?**
uno a...	dos a...	¿necesito una reserva?
oo-no a...	*dos a...*	*neth-es-ee-to oo-na re-ser-ba*

a return to...	**2 returns to...**
uno de ida y vuelta a...	dos de ida y vuelta a...
oo-na de ee-da ee bwel-ta a...	*dos de ee-da ee bwel-ta a...*

a child's ticket	**first class**	**second class**
un billete de niño	de primera clase	de clase turista
oon beel-ye-te de neen-yo	*de pree-me-ra kla-se*	*de kla-se too-rees-ta*

I booked my ticket on the internet	**where do I collect it?**
he reservado el billete por internet	¿dónde lo recojo?
e re-ser-ba-do el beel-ye-te por een-ter-net	*don-de lo re-ko-kho*

I want to book...	**2 seats**	**window/aisle**
quiero reservar...	dos asientos	ventanilla/pasillo
kyer-o re-ser-bar...	*dos as-yen-tos*	*ven-ta-neel-ya/pas-eel-yo*

a couchette	**smoking**	**non-smoking**
una litera	fumador	no fumador
oo-na lee-te-ra	*foo-ma-dor*	*no foo-ma-dor*

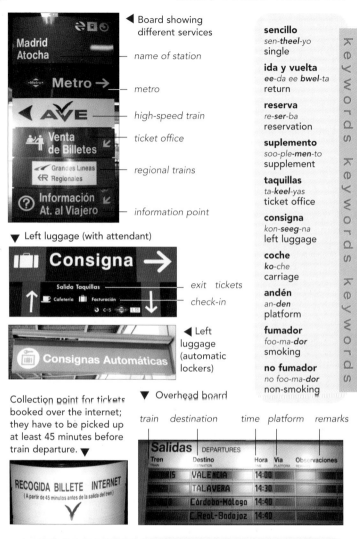

◀ Board showing different services

name of station

metro

high-speed train

ticket office

regional trains

information point

▼ Left luggage (with attendant)

Consigna →

exit   tickets

check-in

◀ Left luggage (automatic lockers)

Collection point for tickets booked over the internet; they have to be picked up at least 45 minutes before train departure. ▼

RECOGIDA BILLETE INTERNET
(A partir de 45 minutos antes de la salida del tren)

▼ Overhead board

train   destination   time   platform   remarks

keywords keywords keywords keywords

sencillo
sen-theel-yo
single

ida y vuelta
ee-da ee bwel-ta
return

reserva
re-ser-ba
reservation

suplemento
soo-ple-men-to
supplement

taquillas
ta-keel-yas
ticket office

consigna
kon-seeg-na
left luggage

coche
ko-che
carriage

andén
an-den
platform

fumador
foo-ma-dor
smoking

no fumador
no foo-ma-dor
non-smoking

Salidas DEPARTURES				
Tren TRAIN	Destino DESTINATION	Hora TIME	Via PLATFORM	Observaciones REMARKS
...15	VALENCIA	14:00		
	TALAVERA	14:30		
	Córdoba-Málaga	14:40		
	C.Real-Badajoz	14:40		

the train to...
el tren para...
el tren pa-ra...

is this the train for...?
¿es este el tren para...?
es es-te el tren pa-ra...

which platform does it leave from?
¿de qué andén sale?
de ke an-den sa-le

this is my seat
este es mi asiento
es-te es mee as-yen-to

talking

TAXI

In most places taxis are plentiful, reliable and not particularly expensive. It is, however, difficult (though not impossible) to order taxis in advance. It's quite easy to simply hail them in the street. Taxis can take a maximum of 4 passengers. Should you wish to make a complaint it's best to try to sort the matter out with the driver. Failing that, all taxis carry an identification number on the door which you can use to report the taxi to the town hall (**Ayuntamiento**). *In each town there is usually a fleet of taxis specifically designed to take wheelchairs. These have to be ordered, either by hailing a normal taxi and getting the driver to radio for one or by telephoning the taxi company.*

◀ Taxi stand with prices displayed.

Taxis to and from airports or stations often carry a supplement which can considerably increase the fare. Tipping is not common but it is normal to round up the total cost.

Taxis are generally ▶ white. If a taxi is free it shows a green light and the word *libre*. If it has passengers it usually shows a red light with the word *ocupado*.

where is the taxi stand?
¿donde está la parada de taxis?
*don-de es-**ta** la pa-**ra**-da de **tak**-sees*

to ... please
a ... por favor
*a ... por fa-**bor***

how much is it to...?
¿cuánto cuesta hasta...?
*kwan-to **kwes**-ta **as**-ta...*

please order me a taxi
¿por favor me pide un taxi?
*por fa-**bor** me **pee**-de oon **tak**-see*

for ... o'clock
para las ...
pa-ra las...

I need a receipt
necesito un recibo
*neth-e-**see**-to oon re-**theeb**-o*

keep the change
quédese con la vuelta
*ke-de-se kon la **bwel**-ta*

is there a special rate for the airport?
¿hay una tarifa especial para el aeropuerto?
*aee **oo**-na ta-**ree**-fa es-peth-**yal** pa-ra el aee-ro-**pwer**-to*

CAR HIRE

Car hire is not difficult to find and isn't too expensive (except in the Balearics and Canaries). You must provide a full driving licence and identification (passport). You need to be 21 and have had a driving licence for at least a year. Check what is included in the price, particularly insurance. The better-known companies will be able to provide baby seats, etc. Most if not all companies will also provide you with instructions of what to do in case of an accident or breakdown (see also pp. 37–38). This information is often in English.

◄ VEHICLE HIRE

I want to hire a car
quiero alquilar un coche
kyer-o al-kee-lar oon ko-che

for one day
para un día
pa-ra oon dee-ya

for ... days
para ... días
pa-ra ... dee-yas

I want...
quiero...
kyer-o...

a small car
un coche pequeño
un ko-che pe-ken-yo

a large car
un coche grande
un ko-che gran-de

an automatic
uno automático
oo-no ow-to-mat-ee-ko

a people carrier
un monovolumen
oon mo-no-vo-loo-men

how much is it?
¿cuánto es?
kwan-to es

is there a kilometre charge?
¿hay que pagar kilometraje?
aee ke pa-gar kee-lo-me-tra-khe

I am ... old
tengo ... años
ten-go ... an-yos

here is my driving licence
este es mi carnet de conducir
es-te es mee kar-ne de kon-doo-theer

what does the insurance cover?
¿qué cubre el seguro?
ke koob-re el se-goo-ro

does it take unleaded petrol?
¿usa gasolina sin plomo?
oo-sa ga-so-lee-na seen plo-mo

how do the controls work?
¿cómo funcionan los mandos?
ko-mo foonth-yo-nan los man-dos

where are the documents?
¿dónde está la documentación?
don-de es-ta la do-koo-men-tath-yon

what do we do if we have a breakdown?
¿qué hay que hacer si tenemos una avería?
ke aee ke a-ther see te-ne-mos oo-na ab-er-ee-a

can we have a child's seat?
¿nos deja un asiento de niño?
nos de-kha oon as-yen-to de neen-yo

how is it fitted?
¿cómo se pone?
ko-mo se po-ne

talking talking talking talking talking

DRIVING

The most noticeable aspect of Spanish driving is the overuse of the car horn. Although in general driving standards are quite good, drivers do tend to be impatient, particularly in traffic jams. The minimum age for driving in Spain is 18. There are strict laws on drink-driving. If bringing your car into Spain, you will need your vehicle registration document and driving licence. You may also need a Green Card, available from your insurer in the UK for a small fee. Within the EU your general UK car insurance covers you. You may want to take out extra breakdown cover (AA or RAC).

Speed restrictions

built up area	50 km/h
ordinary roads	90 km/h
dual carriageway	120 km/h
motorway	120 km/h

▲ **CITY CENTRE**

Spanish ▶ numberplate
E is for *España*.

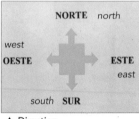

▲ Direction indicators

Colour-coding for Spanish road signs ▼

Green and E- is a European route and a main road.

Red with N- is a dual carriageway (autovía; these function also as motorways).

Blue with A- is a motorway, autopista.

Orange with C- is a primary road.

Green with C- is a secondary road.

Yellow with C- is a third-class road.

Orange with a D- indicates a deviation; follow this to rejoin your original route.

▲ **SPEED LIMIT CONTROLLED BY RADAR**

There are on-the-spot fines for traffic offences, notably speeding and drink-driving – and credit cards are accepted!

▼ In cities and towns, the colour-coding on road signs changes.

white: major route signposted from a town

yellow: places of interest to visitors; the port

green: street names

major route signposted from a town; to the **Autovía**

a place of interest to visitors; parking

▲ **FORBIDDEN TO ALL VEHICLES PEDESTRIAN ZONE**

◄ **PEDESTRIAN ZONE**

▲ *Vía Preferente* indicates a bus and taxi lane.

▼ **LORRY EXIT**

◄ **END OF PEDESTRIAN ZONE**

▲ Few drivers stop at zebra crossings. An oncoming driver flashing their lights does NOT mean 'after you'; it will probably mean 'I'm coming through'.

we are going to...
vamos a...
ba-mos a...

is the road good?
¿está bien la carretera?
es-*ta* byen la kar-re-*te*-ra

is the pass open?
¿está abierto el puerto?
es-*ta* a-*byer*-to el **pwer**-to

which is the best route?
¿cuál es la mejor ruta?
kwal es la me-**khor** *roo*-ta

can you show me on the map
¿puede indicarmelo en el mapa?
pwe-de een-dee-**kar**-me-lo en el **ma**-pa

do we need snow chains?
¿hace falta usar cadenas?
a-the **fal**-ta oo-*sar* ka-*de*-nas

talking

*Some motorways (**autopistas**) are free and some carry toll
charges (which can be expensive). Look out for the sign **peaje**
(toll). Payment is due on completion of each sector covered.
You do not receive tickets. These toll motorways are similar to UK
motorways but aren't usually as busy. Non-toll motorways, however,
are more like dual carriageways with numerous exits. They offer a
great number of possibilities for stopping, ranging from simple
café/bars to restaurants, hotels and petrol stations. There are also
big service stations with full facilities (cash dispensers, mini-markets,
play areas, etc.), but they are few and far between.*

▲
Spanish motorways are
signposted in blue.
The speed limit is 120kph.
Motorway info website is
www.aseta.es

motorway (A-7)

European
route (E-15)

national
road (N-340)

motorway exit
500 m on the right;
exit number 214

TOLL ▼

▶
Before you
reach the toll
booth there
will be a sign
showing which
cards are
accepted for
payment.

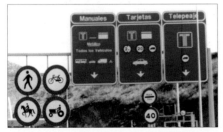

◀
At the toll stop you have a
choice of payment: either
cash (**Manuales**) for all
vehicles (**metálico** means
cash), card (**Tarjetas**) or
prepaid (**Telepeaje**).

▲ Card-only lane for payment

▲ The amount will be displayed at the booth. The front passenger will be closest in a right-hand drive car.

Services are available on taking the 162 exit. Service stations are known as *Areas de Servicio.* ▼

◀ ▲
Roadside SOS phones have instructions in English, French and German as well as Spanish.

If you break down on the motorway

There is a very small or no hard shoulder on Spanish motorways. If you have to stop or you break down, you must pull over as far as you can, put on your hazard lights and place your warning triangle 50 metres behind the vehicle. (It should be visible for at least 100 metres). Both *autopistas* and *autovías* have SOS emergency phones located at about 1500-metre intervals. You simply press the button and wait for assistance.

my car has broken down
se me ha averiado el coche
se me a a-ber-ya-do el ko-che

what should I do?
¿qué hago?
ke a-go

I am on my own
estoy sola
es-toy so-la

my children are in the car
los niños están en el coche
los neen-yos es-tan en el ko-che

the car is...
el coche está...
el ko-che es-ta...

before junction...
antes de la salida...
an-tes de la sa-lee-da...

after junction...
después de la salida...
des-pwes de la sa-lee-da...

registration number...
matrícula...
mat-ree-koo-la...

it is a blue fiat
es un fiat azul
es oon fee-yat a-thool

Spanish drivers will often park their car wherever their fancy takes them. Be warned that whilst this is common, it is still illegal. In general, parking can be a problem almost everywhere. The safest option is to find a multi-storey or pay-and-display area. There are restrictions regarding parking and these are clearly indicated. Cars may be towed away if parked in a restricted area. This is more common than clamping. If your car has been towed away you will have to pick it up from the local council compound, give details of the car and pay the fine. Police or traffic wardens will know where the local compound is. Semi-official parking attendants will often assist you in finding parking spaces on the street. A small tip of around 1 euro is expected.

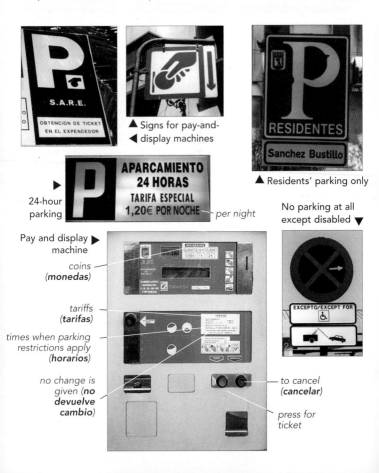

S.A.R.E.

OBTENCION DE TICKET EN EL EXPENDEDOR

▲ Signs for pay-and-
◀ display machines

RESIDENTES

Sanchez Bustillo

▲ Residents' parking only

▶
24-hour parking

P APARCAMIENTO 24 HORAS
TARIFA ESPECIAL
1,20€ POR NOCHE ← *per night*

No parking at all except disabled ▼

EXCEPTO/EXCEPT FOR

Pay and display ▶ machine

*coins (**monedas**)*

*tariffs (**tarifas**)*

*times when parking restrictions apply (**horarios**)*

*no change is given (**no devuelve cambio**)*

← *to cancel (**cancelar**)*

← *press for ticket*

Charges ▶

first half hour or part of

each further half hour or part of

maximum 24 hours

TARIFAS APARCAMIENTO	
PRIMERA HORA Ó FRACCION	1,00 €
CADA HORA RESTANTE Ó FRACCION	0,75 €
MÁXIMO 24 HORAS	15,00 €

IVA INCLUIDO
EN VIGOR A PARTIR DEL DÍA 1 DE ENERO DEL 2.002

*(including VAT)
in force from 1 January 2002*

▲ Be careful: *libre* means 'spaces' not 'free of charge'. *Completo* means full. ▼

Laborables de 9 a 14 h. y 16 a 20 h. excepto carga y descarga

▲ NO PARKING WEEKDAYS 9 AM–2 PM AND 4 PM–8 PM EXCEPT FOR LOADING AND UNLOADING

▼ Pay point

P CAJA CASH

PARKING ▶ PROHIBITED WE WILL CALL A TOW TRUCK

PROHIBIDO APARCAR LLAMAMOS GRUA

No parking on Thursdays from 8 am–3 pm for a street market. ▼

parking only for cars and motorbikes

caravans and lorries forbidden

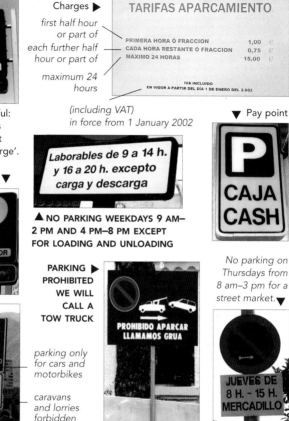

JUEVES DE 8 H. - 15 H. MERCADILLO

where is the best place to park?
¿cuál es el mejor sitio para aparcar?
kwal es el me-khor seet-yo pa-ra a-par-kar

where is there a car park?
¿dónde hay un aparcamiento?
don-de aee oon a-par-ka-myen-to

can I park here?
¿se puede aparcar aquí?
se pwe-de a-par-kar a-kee

how long for?
¿cuánto tiempo?
kwan-to tyem-po

the ticket machine doesn't work
no funciona el parquímetro
no foonth-yo-na el par-kee-met-ro

talking

*Petrol stations are essentially the same as those in the UK. Although self-service (**autoservicio**) is common, many petrol stations still have pump attendants. Most accept credit cards. Be aware that leaded petrol still exists in Spain and you must ask for unleaded petrol (**sin plomo**) which is always coloured green. Many petrol stations offer a lot of services other than just providing petrol (car wash, air, water, etc.). Car washes are very similar in style and format all over Spain. Valet cleaning is generally not available. You will probably have to pay for air and sometimes water.*

Super Diesel | Super Plus | Euro Super | Super

98 95 97

▲ Colour-coded pumps: black for diesel (**gasóleo**), green for unleaded (**sin plomo**) and red for leaded (**super**).

LAVADO MANUAL Y CAMBIO DE ACEITE 4ª PLANTA
HORARIO LUNES A VIERNES de 8 a 20 h

— hand wash &
— oil change
— 4th floor

Aspirador

▲ VACUUM

◀ AIR

AIRE

¡NO TIENE DINERO! ESTA MAQUINA SE RECAUDA DIARIAMENTE

AUTOMATICO

bar

MANUAL

+

−

no money!
This machine is emptied daily.

automatically balanced and inflated pressure (choose button for precise bar pressure measurement)

bar counter (to measure pressure manually)

manually balanced and inflated pressure (adjust using buttons)

where is there a petrol station?
¿dónde hay una gasolinera?
don-de aee oo-na ga-so-lee-ne-ra

...worth of unleaded petrol
...de gasolina sin plomo
...de ga-so-lee-na seen plo-mo

the card for the carwash
la tarjeta para el autolavado
la tar-khe-ta pa-ra el ow-to-la-ba-do

fill it up please
lleno por favor
lyen-o por fa-bor

pump number...
surtidor número...
soor-tee-dor noo-me-ro...

how much is that?
¿cuánto es?
kwan-to es

talking

If you are a member of a motoring organisation, such as the AA or RAC, you will have access to R.A.C. de E (Real Automobil Club de España), Spain's national motoring organisation. This round-the-clock national emergency call-out service is based in Madrid. You can contact them on 91 593 33 33. You may need to contact your cover organisation in the UK to check if you have to pay a supplement for this or not. Kwik-Fit type fitters are few and far between in Spain but look out for 'Feu–Vert' signs (French-owned equivalent).

◀ Garage for repairs. This one offers 24-hour pick-up truck and tyre service for cars.

I have broken down
tengo una avería
ten-go oo-na a-be-ree-ya

the car won't start
el coche no arranca
el ko-che no ar-ran-ka

the battery is flat
la batería está descargada
la ba-te-ree-ya es-ta des-kar-ga-da

I have a flat tyre
tengo una rueda pinchada
ten-go oo-na rwe-da peen-cha-da

I need new tyres
necesito neumáticos nuevos
neth-es-ee-to ne-oo-ma-tee-kos nwe-bos

I have run out of petrol
me he quedado sin gasolina
me e ke-da-do seen ga-so-lee-na

where is there a garage?
¿dónde hay un garaje?
don de aee ôn ga-ra-khe

something is wrong with...
algo le pasa a(l)...
al-go le pa-sa a(l)...

the ... is not working
el/la ... no funciona
el/la ... no foonth-yo-na

the ... are not working
los/las ... no funcionan
los/las ... no foonth-yo-nan

can you repair it?
¿puede arreglarlo?
pwe-de ar-re-glar-lo

how long will it take?
¿cuánto tardan en arreglarlo?
kwan-to tar-dan en ar-re-glar-lo

when will it be ready?
¿para cuándo estará?
pa-ra kwan-do es-ta-ra

how much will it cost?
¿cuánto me costará?
kwan-to me kos-ta-ra

can you replace the windscreen?
¿me puede cambiar el parabrisas?
me pwe-de kamb-yar el pa-ra-bree-sas

please change...	**the oil**	**the tyres**
¿me cambia...?	el aceite	los neumáticos
me kamb-ya...	*el a-they-te*	*los ne-oo-ma-tee-kos*

SHOPPING

In Spain there is a tendency to use small, local shops more (on a daily basis), particularly for bread, meat and fish. Many shops are closed during the 'siesta' hours of 2 pm–5 pm and remain closed on Saturday afternoons. They are, however, often open later in the evening than is usual in the UK. Very large department stores and supermarkets stay open all day. Sunday opening is not common.

keywords keywords keywords

panadería
pa-na-de-ree-a
baker's

carnicería
kar-nee-the-ree-a
butcher's

pescadería
pes-ka-de-ree-a
fish shop

tienda de comestibles
tyen-da de ko-mes-tee-bles
grocer's

pastelería
pas-te-le-ree-a
cake shop

supermercado
soo-per-mer-ka-do
supermarket

estanco
es-tan-ko
tobacconist's

bodega
bo-de-ga
wine merchant's

▲ Main shopping area

▼ Off-license

Check out the local markets, particularly for fresh products. They are busy, lively and well worth visiting. Most large towns have a daily market, smaller towns a weekly one. ▼

There are several types of lottery. The national lottery (3 times a week) is similar to the UK's, with a 6-number pick. Buy the tickets from kiosks and shops with this sign. ▼

▲ GIFTS

Bookshop ▶
Tienda means shop.

General grocer's ▲
Small shops' opening hours are 10 am–2 pm and 5 pm–8.30 pm.

▼ FISH SHOP

fresh & frozen

BAKER'S ▶

*Smaller supermarkets can be found within the city limits and larger ones on the outskirts of town. Big supermarkets or hypermarkets are **Pryca**, **Eroski** and **Alcampo**. In these, you can find everything you need, normally including petrol. Out-of-town supermarkets provide free parking. By and large, all supermarkets offer a good range of products. You usually have to get someone to weigh the fruit for you at the fruit & veg section. Plastic bags are free. Larger supermarkets have cash dispensers.*

▲ Supermarket sign

Locker- and present-wrapping area
You must leave bags in a locker at the entrance or with an attendant who will give you a token to return as you leave. ▼

◀ Trolleys generally take a 1 euro coin

◀ Scanner to check prices

10 items or less checkout ▶

where can I buy...?
¿dónde puedo comprar...?
*don-de **pwe**-do kom-**prar**...*

do you have...?
¿tiene...?
***tyen**-e...*

I am looking for...
estoy buscando...
*es-**toy** boos-**kan**-do...*

is there a market?
¿hay mercado?
*aee mer-**ka**-do*

have you change for the trolley?
¿tiene cambio para el carro?
***tyen**-e **kamb**-yo **pa**-ra el **kar**-ro*

batteries
pilas
***peel**-as*

how much is it?
¿cuánto es?
***kwan**-to es*

a present
un regalo
*oon re-**ga**-lo*

which day?
¿qué día?
*ke **dee**-ya*

can I pay with this card?
¿puedo pagar con esta tarjeta?
***pwe**-do pa-**gar** kon **es**-ta tar-**khe**-ta*

a tin-opener
un abrelatas
*oon a-bre-**la**-tas*

a good wine
un buen vino
*oon bwen **bee**-no*

talking talking talking

Weights and measures are all in metric. At, for example, a deli counter you would ask for the number of grams required (e.g. 250 g); for wine or water, the number of bottles or litres. You can also buy cheap wine in cartons. Almost all products other than fresh ones are prepacked so you only need to ask for the product by name.

▲ Baker's sell fresh bread, milk, juice and other basic items.

When asking for bread, ask for *una barra* (similar to French stick) or the number of rolls (*bollos*) you want. For a more rounded country loaf, ask for *un pan.* ▼

◀ You can ask for cheese or meat by a number of slices (*lonchas*) rather than by weight. *Jamón serrano* is cured ham; cooked ham is known as *jamón de York.*

◀ ▲ Health foods (*Productos Dietéticos*) are available in large supermarkets and specialist shops (*Herbolisterías*) but they are not very widespread.

◀ whole milk (*leche entera*)

Milk is almost always UHT. To get the type you want, go by the wording, not the carton colour, as these may vary.

skimmed milk (*leche desnatada*) ▼

semi-skimmed milk (*leche semidesnatada*) ▼

▲ Eggs are sold by the dozen and half-dozen (*dozena y media dozena*). It may be difficult to get free-range (*huevos de campo*).

▲ FAT-FREE

▲ Gluten-free flour (*harina*) for bread and pastry

nutrition

no added sweetener (*sacarosa*) or salt (*sal*)

low in sodium

unsaturated vegetable fat

NO SUGAR ▶

◀ *Bio* generally indicates organic produce

Valor nutricional medio por 100g
Average nutritional value per 100g ▼

	Valor	
energy	energético	Kcal 42 / KJ 177
protein	Proteínas	1,3g
fat	Grasos	1,6g
carbo-hydrates	Hidratos de Carbono	0,1g

a piece of that cheese
un trozo de ese queso
oon **tro**-tho de **e**-se **ke**-so

a little more please
un poco más por favor
oon **po**-ko mas por fa-**bor**

a little less please
un poco menos por favor
oon **po**-ko **me**-nos por fa-**bor**

that's enough thanks
basta gracias
bas-ta **grath**-yas

10 slices of cooked ham
diez lonchas de jamón de York
dyeth **lon**-chas de kha-**mon** de york

200 grams of chorizo
doscientos gramos de chorizo
dos-**thyen**-tos **gra**-mos de cho-**ree**-tho

a carton of milk
un cartón de leche
oon kar-**ton** de **le**-che

a bottle of mineral water
una botella de agua mineral
oo-na bo-**tel**-ya de **a**-gwa mee-ne-**ral**

still
sin gas
seen gas

fizzy
con gas
kon gas

a tin of...
una lata de...
oo-na **la**-ta de...

a roll of...
un rollo de...
oon **rol**-yo de...

a jar of...
un tarro de...
oon **tar**-ro de...

a bottle of...
una botella de...
oo-na bo-**tel**-ya de...

a packet of...
un paquete de...
oon pa-**ke**-te de...

that's everything thanks
nada más gracias
na-da mas **grath**-yas

talking talking talking talking talking talking talking talking

Everyday Foods comestibles *ko-mes-teeb-les*

biscuits	las galletas *ga-lye-tas*
bread	el pan *pan*
bread roll	el panecillo *pa-ne-theel-yo*
bread *(sliced)*	el pan de molde *pan de mol-de*
butter	la mantequilla *man-te-kee-lya*
cereal	los cereales *the-re-a-les*
cheese	el queso *ke-so*
chicken	el pollo *pol-yo*
coffee	el café *ka-fe*
cream	la nata *na-ta*
cottage cheese	el requesón *re-ke-son*
crisps	las patatas fritas *pa-ta-tas free-tas*
eggs	los huevos *we-bos*
fish	el pescado *pes-ka-do*
flour	la harina *a-ree-na*
ham *(cooked)*	el jamón de York *kha-mon de york*
ham *(cured)*	el jamón serrano *kha-mon ser-ra-no*
herbal tea	la infusión *een-foo-syon*
honey	la miel *myel*
jam	la mermelada *mer-me-la-da*
juice	el zumo *thoo-mo*
margarine	la margarina *marga-ree-na*
marmalade	la mermelada de naranja *mer-me-la-da de na-ran-kha*
meat	la carne *kar-ne*
milk	la leche *le-che*
mustard	la mostaza *mos-ta-tha*
oil	el aceite *a-the-ee-te*
orange juice	el zumo de naranja *thoo-mo de na-ran-kha*
pasta	la pasta *pas-ta*
pepper	la pimienta *pee-myen-ta*
rice	el arroz *ar-roth*
salt	la sal *sal*
sausage	la salchicha *sal-cheech-a*
sugar	el azúcar *a-thoo-kar*
stock cubes	las pastillas de caldo *pas-teel-yas de kal-do*
tea	el té *te*
tomatoes *(tin)*	la lata de tomates *la-ta de tom-a-tes*
tuna *(tin)*	el atún *a-toon*
vinegar	el vinagre *bee-na-gre*
yoghurt	el yogur *yo-goor*

Fruit	fruta *froo-ta*
apples	las manzanas *man-tha-nas*
apricots	los albaricoques *al-ba-ree-ko-kes*
bananas	los plátanos *pla-ta-nos*
cherries	las cerezas *the-re-thas*
figs	los higos *ee-gos*
grapefruit	el pomelo *po-me-lo*
grapes	las uvas *oo-bas*
lemon	el limón *lee-mon*
melon	el melón *me-lon*
nectarines	las nectarinas *nek-ta-ree-nas*
oranges	las naranjas *na-ran-khas*
peaches	los melocotones *melo-ko-to-nes*
pears	las peras *pe-ras*
pineapple	la piña *peen-ya*
plums	las ciruelas *thee-rwe-las*
raspberries	las frambuesas *fram-bwe-sas*
strawberries	las fresas *fre-sas*
watermelon	la sandía *san-dee-ya*

Vegetables	verduras *ver-doo-ras*
artichokes	las alcachofas *al-ka-cho-fas*
aubergines	las berenjenas *be-ren-khen-as*
asparagus	los espárragos *es-par-ra-gos*
carrots	las zanahorias *tha-na-o-ryas*
cauliflower	la coliflor *ko-lee-flor*
celery	el apio *a-pee-o*
courgettes	los calabacines *kala-ba-thee-nes*
cucumber	el pepino *pe-pee-no*
french beans	las judías verdes *khoo-dee-yas ber-des*
garlic	el ajo *a-kho*
leeks	los puerros *pwer-ros*
lettuce	la lechuga *le-choo-ga*
mushrooms	los champiñones *cham-peen-yo-nes*
onions	las cebollas *the-bol-yas*
peas	los guisantes *gee-san-tes*
peppers	los pimientos *pee-myen-tos*
potatoes	las patatas *pa-ta-tas*
radishes	los rábanos *ra-ba-nos*
spinach	las espinacas *espee-na-kas*
spring onions	las cebolletas *theb-ol-ye-tas*
tomatoes	los tomates *to-ma-tes*
turnip	el nabo *na-bo*

*Spain's most famous department store is **El Corte Inglés**. It is not the cheapest place to shop, but it has the advantage of being open on Sundays, and there is a branch in all major towns.*

keywords keywords keywords

grandes almacenes
gran-des al-ma-**then**-es
department store

sótano
so-ta-no
basement

planta baja
plan-ta ba-kha
ground floor

primera planta
pree-me-ra plan-ta
first floor

departamento
de-par-ta-men-to
department

aparatos eléctricos
a-pa-ra-tos e-lek-tree-kos
electrical goods

joyas
kho-yas
jewellery

señoras
sen-yo-ras
ladies'

caballeros
ka-bal-ye-ros
men's

Spain's most famous department store ▲

HORARIO de VERANO — summer opening
DE LUNES A SABADO — Monday to Saturday

—ABIERTO— open
de 10 de la mañana from 10 in the mornin
a 10 de la noche to 10 at night
DOMINGOS Y FESTIVOS CERRADO TODO EL DIA

MERCANCIA PROTEGIDA ELECTRONICAMENTE — Sundays and holidays closed all day

CAJA

▲ PAY HERE

SOLD OUT ▼

AGOTADO

REBAJAS

Sales usually take place in Jan/Feb and ◀ again in Jul/Aug.

talking

which floor is the...?
¿en qué planta está...?
en ke plan-ta es-ta...

food department
alimentación
a-lee-men-tath-yon

shoe department
zapatería
tha-pa-te-ree-ya

can I try this on?
¿puedo probarme esto?
pwe-do pro-bar-me es-to

where is the changing room?
¿dónde está el probador?
don-de es-ta el pro-ba-dor

There is a good selection of clothes and shoe shops in Spain. It is essential to produce your receipt if you want a refund and you may well be offered another product or credit note instead of getting your money back. Neither customers nor shop staff seem to be particularly aware of consumer legislation on this issue. The legislation itself is unclear.

Ascensores a: 2ª, 3ª y 4ª Planta — lifts to the 2nd, 3rd and 4th floors

Aseos — toilets

ESTA USTED EN LA PLANTA 1ª — you are on the 1st floor

▲ In-store guide

PROBADORES
▲ CHANGING ROOMS

ZAPATOS
▲ SHOES

CLOTHES ▼

CONFECCIONES

100 % Seda
▲ 100% SILK

50%
TODO A MITAD DE PRECIO
▲ EVERYTHING AT HALF PRICE

70 % lana
30 % algodon

70% WOOL 30% COTTON ▶

do you have size...?
¿tiene talla...?
tyen-e tal-ya...

do you have this in my size?
¿tiene esto en mi talla?
tyen-e es-to en mi tal-ya

it is too big
es demasiado grande
es de-mas-ya-do gran-de

I need a larger/smaller size
necesito una talla más grande/pequeña
ne-thes-ee-to oo-na tal-ya mas gran-de/pe-ken-ya

do you have this...?
¿lo tiene...?
lo tyen-e...

do you have shoe size...?
¿tiene el número...?
tyen-e el noo-me-ro...

I take shoe size 40...
uso el cuarenta...
oo-so el kwa-ren-ta...

it is too small
es demasiado pequeño
es de-mas-ya-do pe-ken-yo

in black/brown
en negro/marrón
en neg-ro/mar-ron

in other colours
en otros colores
en o-tros ko-lo-res

talking talking talking

*If you simply want to buy stamps, it is easier to buy them from tobacconists (**estancos**) or kiosks. A few of the big hypermarkets have post offices on site, which have the same opening times as the supermarket. Within the European Union, the rate for sending postcards is the same as a standard-sized letter. They go by air automatically, but postcards do generally take a little longer than letters, perhaps up to a week. For destinations outside the EU, check at the Post Office.*

◀ Spanish Post Office logo

For letters and parcels, go to a window marked *Admisión Polivalente*; there you can also buy envelopes, phonecards and send telegrams and faxes. For sending something big, go to the section marked *Admisión Masiva*.

◀ When sending normal letters or cards, find a yellow post-box. If you have a choice, use the slot marked *EXTRANJERO* (Overseas).

Red boxes are for urgent mail with a different tariff. ▶

◀ Collection times

HORARIO LIMITE DE RECOGIDA
Lunes a Viernes : 17 h.
Sábados : 13 h.

*Mon-Fri 5 pm
Sat 1 pm*

where is the post office?
¿dónde está Correos?
don-de es-ta kor-re-os

do you have stamps?
¿tiene sellos?
tyen-e sel-yos

10 stamps please
diez sellos por favor
dyeth sel-yos por fa-bor

for postcards
para postales
pa-ra po-sta-les

for letters
para cartas
pa-ra kar-tas

to Europe
para Europa
pa-ra e-oo-ro-pa

to America
para América
pa-ra a-me-ree-ka

to Australia
para Australia
pa-ra ows-tral-ya

I want to send this registered
quiero mandar esto certificado
kyer-o man-dar es-to ther-tee-fee-ka-do

I want to send this parcel
quiero mandar este paquete
kyer-o man-dar es-te pa-ke-te

priority mail
correo urgente
kor-re-o oor-khen-te

surface
por correo normal
por kor-re-o nor-mal

airmail
por avión
por a-byon

Horario de Apertura
Lunes a Viernes:
de 8:30 a 20:30 h.
Sábados:
de 9:30 a 14:00 h.
Domingos y Festivo :
ERRADO

◀ Opening hours of a main post office
The quietest time to visit is 2 pm–5 pm. In smaller towns they often open only in the mornings.

BUZONES

▲ Letterboxes

You can also buy stamps at *estancos* and kiosks. The *timbres* sign means stamps. ▼

◀ Buy films in specialist photographic shops for the best prices. In tourist areas, outlets doing fast developing sell films at much higher prices. For camcorder equipment, go to good photographic shops, as the choice will be better and prices lower.

◀ As a rule, you can't take photos in art galleries, museums, etc.

keywords

carrete
kar-re-te
film

pila
pee-la
battery

en mate
en ma-te
matt

en brillo
en breel-yo
glossy

video-cámara
bee-de-o-ka-ma-ra
camcorder

cintas
theen-tas
tapes

copias
kop-yas
prints

talking

where can I buy film?
¿dónde venden carretes?
don-de ben-den kar-re-tes

a colour film
un carrete en color
oon kar-re-te en ko-lor

with ... pictures
de ... fotos
de ... fo-tos

can you develop this film?
¿me pueden revelar este carrete?
me pwe-den re-be-lar es-te kar-re-te

can you take a picture of us?
¿podría hacernos una foto?
pod-ree-ya a-ther-nos oo-na fo-to

tapes for the camcorder
cintas para esta video-cámara
theen-tas pa-ra es-ta bee-de-o-ka-ma-ra

a slide film
un carrete de diapostivas
oon kar-re-te de dee-a-po-see-tee-bas

24
veinticuatro
beyn-tee-kwat-ro

36
treinta y seis
treyn-ta-ee-seyss

when will the photos be ready?
¿para cuándo estarán las fotos?
pa-ra kwan-do es-ta-ran las fo-tos

can I video here?
¿puedo usar la cámara de vídeo aquí?
pwe-do oo-sar la-ka-ma-ra de bee-de-yo a-kee

PHONES

*Mobile phones are extremely popular, particularly with young people. There are, however, sufficient public telephone boxes which take coins, phonecards and occasionally credit cards. You can buy a range of phonecards in post offices, tobacconist's (**tabacos**), kiosks and some small supermarkets. There are a range of phonecards. Shops selling phonecards have a sign displayed.*

Phonecards (**tarjetas telefónicas**) come in denominations of 6 and 12 euros.

▼

▲
Where you see this sign, you can buy phonecards.

talking talking talking talking

do you have phonecards?
¿tiene tarjetas telefónicas?
tyen-e tar-khe-tas te-le-fo-nee-kas

a phonecard	**6 euros**	**12 euros**
una tarjeta telefónica	de seis euros	de doce euros
oo-na tar-khe-ta te-le-fo-nee-ka	*de seyss e-oo-ros*	*de doth-e e-oo-ros*

Mr Alvarez please
con el Señor Alvarez por favor
kon el sen-yor al-ba-rez por fa-bor

hello (anwering the phone)
diga
dee-ga

can I speak to Maria?
¿puedo hablar con María?
pwe-do a-blar kon ma-ree-a

this is Caroline
soy Caroline
soy caroline

can I have an outside line please
¿me da línea por favor?
me da lee-ne-a por fa-bor

extension...
extensión...
es-tens-yon...

I'd like to make a reverse charge call
quiero hacer una llamada a cobro revertido
kyer-o a-ther oo-na lya-ma-da a ko-bro re-ber-tee-do

what is your phone number?
¿cuál es su número de teléfono?
kwal es soo noo-me-ro de te-le-fo-no

my phone number is...
mi número es...
mee noo-me-ro es...

*If you see lit up on the display **solo llamadas gratuitas** it means free calls only, i.e. emergency numbers or the operator.*

keywords

tarjeta telefónica
tar-**khe**-ta
te-le-**fo**-nee-ka
phonecard

móvil
mo-beel
mobile

código
ko-dee-go
code

información telefónica
een-for-math-**yon**
te-le-**fo**-nee-ka
directory enquiries

páginas amarillas
pa-khee-nas
a-ma-**reel**-yas
yellow pages

Most bars have a public phone, which usually only takes coins. ▼

▲
There is no shortage of public phones.

TELEFONO
☏ PUBLICO

Larger cities usually have a phone centre (*locutorio*) where you phone from a booth and pay afterwards (by credit card or cash). ▶

I will call back...
le volveré a llamar...
le bol-be-**re** a lya-**mar**...

later
más tarde
mas **tar**-de

tomorrow
mañana
man-**ya**-na

do you have a mobile?
¿tiene móvil?
tyen-e **mo**-beel

is it switched on?
¿está encendido?
es-**ta** en-then-**dee**-do

what is your mobile number?
¿cuál es su número de móvil?
kwal es soo **noo**-me-ro de **mo**-beel

my mobile number is...
mi número de móvil es...
mee **noo**-me-ro de **mo**-beel es...

talking

There are a lot of internet cafés in Spain, particularly in student and tourist areas. Rates vary but typically you can expect to pay around 2 euros an hour. Staff are quite likely to have some knowledge of English and are generally quite helpful.

keywords

sala de charla
sa-la de char-la
chat-room

pantalla
pan-tal-ya
screen

ratón
ra-ton
mouse

teclado
tek-la-do
keyboard

anexo
a-neks-o
attachment

descargar
des-kar-gar
download

▲ Internet café sign

National and local tourist and what's-on information can be accessed via the internet. ▼

◀ Many places offer deals where you buy a number of hours in advance, which works out cheaper. However, check how many days you have to use up your hours – some offers are not as good as they look.

talking

what is your e-mail address?
¿cuál es su dirección de email?
kwal es soo dee-rekth-yon de ee-meyl

my e-mail address is...
mi dirección de email es...
mee dee-rekth-yon de ee-meyl es...

caroline.smith@anycompany.co.uk
caroline punto smith arroba anycompany punto co punto uk
caroline poon-to smith ar-ro-ba anycompany poon-to co poon-to uk

can I send an e-mail?
¿puedo mandar un email?
pwe-do man-dar oon ee-meyl

did you get my e-mail?
¿le llegó mi email?
le lyeg-o mee ee-meyl

can I send and receive e-mail here?
¿puedo mandar y recibir email aquí?
pwe-do man-dar ee reth-ee-beer ee-meyl a-kee

how much does an hour of netsurfing cost?
¿cuánto es una hora de internet?
kwan-to es oo-na o-ra de een-ter-net

Main post offices offer fax services. The cost is around 2 euros per page within Spain, and 6 euros to Europe. Faxes to North America can cost 12 euros per page. You usually also have to pay to receive a fax (around 50 cents a page). It is worth checking out internet cafés and shops and offices which carry the FAX PUBLICO signs. These outlets would almost certainly be cheaper.

Precios ◀ PRICES

inicio
ee-neeth-yo
begin

ayuda
a-yoo-da
help

buscar
boos-kar
search

todos los sitios
to-dos los seet-yos
all sites

mensaje
men-sa-khe
message

contraseña
kon-tra-sen-ya
password

keywords keywords keywords

date sent: ▶
time sent:
no. of pages including this:

| Fecha de envío: |
| Hora de envío: |
| Número de páginas incluida la portada: |

A   ◀ *to*

Nombre: *name*
Organización o depto.: *organisation or department*
CC: *copy*
Teléfono: *telephone no.*
Fax: *fax*

☐ Urgente *urgent*
☐ Para revisar *to view*
☐ Se ruega comentar *please comment*
☐ Se ruega contestación *please reply*

I want to send a fax
quiero mandar un fax
kyer-o man-dar oon faks

can I send a fax from here?
¿puedo mandar un fax desde aquí?
pwe-do man-dar oon faks des-de a-kee

how much is it to send a fax?
¿cuánto cuesta mandar un fax?
kwan-to kwes-ta man-dar oon faks

what is your fax number?
¿cuál es su número de fax?
kwal es soo noo-me-ro de faks

I'm trying to send a fax
estoy intentando mandar un fax
es-toy een-ten-tan-do man-dar oon faks

do you have a fax?
¿tiene fax?
tyen-e faks

can I receive a fax here?
¿puedo recibir un fax aquí?
pwe-do reth-ee-beer oon faks a-kee

it has ... pages
tiene ... hojas
tyen-e ... o-khas

please confirm your number
confirme su número por favor
kon-feer-me soo noo-me-ro por fa-bor

did you get my fax?
¿le llegó mi fax?
le lyeg-o mee faks

talking talking talking

OUT & ABOUT

Normally you have to pay to enter galleries and museums, but minors, the unemployed and senior citizens sometimes get free admission. There are 3 dates worth mentioning when admission in some museums is free. These are: May 18th (International Museum Day), October 12th (Spanish National Holiday), and December 6th (Constitution Day). You can sometimes also get a discount with an International Student Card.

Tourist information offices can help with accommodation, local attractions, transport, etc. There will usually be at least one English speaker in the office.

You can get ▶ free maps from tourist offices.

▲ There are no special deals to visit art galleries and museums except for the 3-gallery ticket to visit the Reina Sofía gallery, the Thyssen gallery and the Prado in Madrid.

Most museums close one day a week, normally Mon. In this sign the museum is closed Tue. ▼

Larger ▶ museums will have guided tours.

meeting point

In some larger museums, scanners are used to check bags. The large museums usually have cafeterias, gift shops and disabled access.

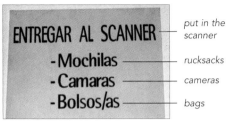

- *put in the scanner* — ENTREGAR AL SCANNER
- *rucksacks* — Mochilas
- *cameras* — Camaras
- *bags* — Bolsos/as

General signs ▼

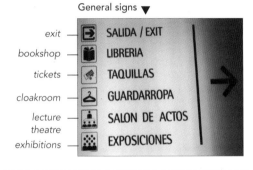

- *exit* — → SALIDA / EXIT
- *bookshop* — LIBRERIA
- *tickets* — TAQUILLAS
- *cloakroom* — GUARDARROPA
- *lecture theatre* — SALON DE ACTOS
- *exhibitions* — EXPOSICIONES

CONSERVE SU ENTRADA HASTA LA SALIDA

▲ KEEP YOUR ENTRY TICKET UNTIL YOU LEAVE

keywords keywords keywords

espectáculo
es-pek-**ta**-koo-lo
show

exposición
eks-po-seeth-**yon**
exhibition

excursión
eks-koors-**yon**
trek, ramble

cata de vinos
ka-ta de **bee**-nos
wine tasting

parque de atracciones
par-ke de at-rak-**thyo**-nes
fun fair

iglesia
ee-**gles**-ya
church

catedral
ka-ted-**ral**
cathedral

castillo
kas-**teel**-yo
castle

ayuntamiento
a-yoon-ta-**myen**-to
town hall

excuse me, where is the tourist office?
¡oiga por favor! ¿dónde está la oficina de turismo?
oy-ga por fa-bor don-de es-ta la o-fee-thee-na de too-rees-mo

do you have...?	**a map of the town**	**leaflets in English**
¿tiene...?	un mapa de la ciudad	folletos en inglés
tyen-e...	*oon ma-pa de la thyoo-dad*	*fol-ye-tos en een-gles*

we'd like to visit...
queríamos visitar...
ke-ree-ya-mos bee-see-tar...

how do we get there?
¿cómo se llega hasta allí?
ko-mo se lyeg-a as-ta al-yee

when can we visit the...?
¿cuándo se puede ir a ver el/la...?
kwan-do se pwe-de eer a ber el/la...

when does it close?
¿cuándo cierra?
kwan-do thyer-ra

is there a tour of the town?
¿se puede hacer una visita guiada a la ciudad?
se pwe-de a-ther oo-na bee-see-ta gee-a-da a la thyoo-dad

talking talking talking

Public sports facilities and accessibility are somewhat limited. On the coast, the possibilities are considerably greater than inland (e.g. hiring bikes, surfboards, pony trekking, etc.) National parks in Spain generally have walking and cycling trails. However, it is best not to leave the routes. If you are staying in a good hotel, you will probably have access to a swimming pool, tennis courts and a gym. Public swimming pools exist, but opening hours vary. You must wear a cap at all indoor pools, but usually don't have to in outdoor ones.

CHANGING ROOMS ▼

▲ **DIVING FORBIDDEN**

Most tourist beaches have a lifeguard and a flag system. They are cleaned regularly and have shower (but not changing) facilities. ▶

BUEN TIEMP
GOOD WEATH

PRECAUCIOI
PRECAUTIOI

PELIGRO
DANGER

PROFUNDIDAD
2.0 M

▲ **DEPTH 2 METRES**
It is not unusual for there to be no shallow end, so not all pools are suitable for children.

◀ Police beach patrols

◀ Restricted swimming areas

◀ Prices for renting a sunshade (*hamaca*) are per person per day.

where can we...?	**play tennis**	**play golf**
¿dónde se puede...?	jugar al tenis	jugar al golf
don-de se pwe-de...	*khoo-gar al te-nees*	*khoo-gar al golf*
	go windsurfing	**go waterskiing**
	hacer surfing	hacer esquí acuático
	a-ther soor-feeng	*a-ther e-skee a-kwa-tee-ko*
how much is it to...?	**hire bikes**	**go riding**
¿cuánto cuesta...?	alquilar bicis	montar a caballo
kwan-to kwes-ta...	*al-kee-lar bee-thees*	*mon-tar a ka-bal-yo*

is there a swimming pool?   **can we hire equipment?**
¿hay piscina?   ¿se puede alquilar el equipo?
aee pees-thee-na   *se pwe-de al-kee-lar el e-kee-po*

per hour/day   **where can we hire beach umbrellas?**
por hora/día   ¿dónde se alquilan sombrillas?
por o-ra/dee-ya   *don-de se al-kee-lan som-breel-yas*

Spain's national parks offer trekking. Walks are well signposted and graded according to difficulty. ▼

Golf facilities, particularly on the Costa del Sol, are good, but can be expensive. You usually do not need to be a club member to play a round.

◀ Signs are fairly easily understood and are given in English at the course (*campo de golf*).

VISITANTES

▲ AWAY SUPPORTERS

▼ SIDE ENCLOSURES

TRIBUNA

GOL

▲ ENCLOSURE BEHIND THE GOAL

▲ Local football stadium
Football is Spain's most popular spectator sport. The season runs Aug–May.

MALAGA C.F.
Tienda Oficial

▲ MALAGA FC CLUB SHOP

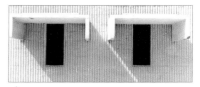

▲ The easiest way to buy tickets is direct from the stadium ticket booth an hour before kick-off. However, for big games you should try to buy a ticket in advance. Violence at matches is rare.

we'd like to see a football match
nos gustaría ver un partido de fútbol
nos goos-ta-ree-ya ber oon par-tee-do de foot-bol

who is playing?
¿quién juega?
kyen khwe-ga

where can we get tickets?
¿dónde se sacan las entradas?
don-de se sa-kan las en-tra-das

how much are they?
¿cuánto cuestan?
kwan-to kwes-tan

how do we get to the stadium?
¿como se va al estadio?
ko-mo se ba al es-tad-yo

what time is the match?
¿a qué hora es el partido?
a ke o-ra es el par-tee-do

talking

ACCOMMODATION

*Accommodation is divided into several different categories: hotels, **pensiones** and **hostales**. There is not much difference between the latter two. They are usually owned by a live-in proprietor, like very large guest-houses. They do not provide meals.*

RESERVAS HOTELES Y PENSIONES

◀ You can find booking agencies at larger railway stations and airports.

◀ The hotel star system goes from 1 to 5. For a 1 or 2 star *hostal*, accommodation will be basic, sometimes with shared wash and WC facilities, but usually clean. For 3-star, expect en-suite and probably TV. For facilities such as meals, mini-bars and sports facilities, you should choose a hotel.

In addition to hotels, *hostales* and *pensiones*, there is a network of *paradores*, good quality hotels, usually set in gardens or the hotel itself being a monument or listed building. ◀

Booking in advance

The Spanish Tourist Office will be able to provide information on different types of accommodation. You can either book through them or phone up yourself once you have decided on where you want to stay.

I want to book a room
quiero reservar una habitación
*kyer-o re-ser-**bar** oo-na a-bee-tath-**yon***

single/double
individual/doble
*een-dee-bee-**dwal**/**dob**-le*

for ... nights
para ... noches
*pa-ra ... **no**-ches*

from ... to...
del ... al...
del ... al...

my name is...
soy...
soy...

I will fax to confirm
se lo confirmaré por fax
*se lo kon-feer-ma-**re** por faks*

my credit card number is...
el número de mi tarjeta de crédito es...
*el **noo**-me-ro de mee tar-**khe**-ta de **kre**-dee-to es...*

please can you fax me to confirm my booking
¿puede mandarme un fax para confirmar la reserva?
***pwe**-de man-**dar**-me oon faks **pa**-ra kon-feer-**mar** la re-**ser**-ba*

Pensiones provide rooms and *hostales* are similar. Both tend to be family-run establishments. Price often only includes bed, not breakfast.

Sometimes there is also *HR*, a *Hostal/Hotel Residencial*, which has long-term guests. These are worth a try if you can find nothing else. ▼

◀ Registration form
When checking in to accommodation, show your passport. It may be kept overnight or even for the duration of your stay. If you need it back, just ask. Reception staff will often fill out the registration form for you and just ask you to sign it. If you do have to fill it out yourself, it will probably be in English as well as Spanish.

RECEPCION

▲ **RECEPTION**
You only get room service in hotels. There should be instructions in English by your room phone regarding room service.

do you have a ... room?
¿tiene una habitación...?
tyen-e oo-na a-bee-tath-yon...

can I see the room?
¿puedo ver la habitación?
pwe-do ber la a-bee-tath-yon

single
individual
een-dee-bee-dwal

double
doble
dob-le

double-bedded
de matrimonio
de mat-ree-mon-yo

family
familiar
fa-meel-yar

with ensuite bath
con baño
kon ban-yo

with shower
con ducha
kon doo-cha

for tonight
para esta noche
pa-ra es-ta no-che

for one night
para una noche
pa-ra oo-na no-che

for... nights
para ... noches
pa-ra ... no-ches

is breakfast included?
¿es con desayuno?
es kon de-sa-yoo-no

how much is half board?
¿cuánto cuesta con media pensión?
kwan-to kwes-ta kon med-ya pen-syon

full board?
¿con pensión completa?
kon pen-syon kom-ple-ta

can I have my passport back?
¿me puede devolver el pasaporte?
me pwe-de de-bol-ber el pa-sa-por-te

talking talking talking

In self-catering accommodation, if you are using gas it will probably be bottled rather than from a mains supply. It is a good idea to turn this off every night, by flicking the switch on the top of the bottle. Plugs are 2-pinned and 220 volt/50 Hz, the same as the rest of continental Europe. Be careful: some places still operate 125 or 110 volt (in such cases the sockets should be labelled). You will need a transformer for British appliances.

▲ If you arrive in Spain with no accommodation and want to go self-catering, look for the signs *Alquiler de apartamentos* (apartments to rent).

◀ Rubbish is collected from bins in the streets daily (usually at night). Recycling bins are often available. This one takes all kinds of glass (*vidrio*). There is no distinction between which colours.

▲ There are approaching 200 youth hostels in Spain. They vary greatly in quality and service. The best ones offer services from fax to solarium; others offer little. You can book in advance in most of them. Accommodation prices are per person and vary according to season.

◀ PAPER RECYCLING

◀ You can get leaflets about youth hostels from the local Spanish tourist office.

You can usually rent towels, sheets and duvets and will probably be able to drink alcohol on site. Curfews and day lockouts can exist in small hostels.

▼

towels for rent

toilet pack

eating hours

breakfast (desayuno)

lunch (almuerzo)

dinner (cena)

keywords keywords keywords

líquido lavavajillas
lee-kee-do la-ba-ba-kheel-yas
washing-up liquid

detergente
de-ter-khen-te
washing powder

jabón
kha-bon
soap

abrelatas
a-bre-la-tas
tin-opener

velas
be-las
candles

cerillas
ther-ee-lyas
matches

bombona de gas
bom-bo-na de gas
gas cylinder

---

there is/are no...
no hay...
no aee...

how does ... work?
¿cómo funciona ...?
ko-mo foonth-yo-na...

can you show us how this works?
¿nos enseña cómo funciona?
nos en-sen-ya ko-mo foonth-yo-na

the cooker
la cocina
la ko-thee-na

the washing machine
la lavadora
la la-ba-dor-a

the dishwasher
el lavavajillas
el la-ba-ba-kheel-yas

the microwave
el microondas
el meek-ro-on-das

who do I contact if there are problems?
¿a quién aviso si hay algún problema?
a kyen a-bee-so see aee al-goon prob-le-ma

when is the rubbish collected?
¿cuándo recogen la basura?
kwan-do re-ko-khen la ba-soo-ra

where do we leave the rubbish?
¿dónde se deja la basura?
don-de se de-kha la ba-soo-ra

can you give us another key?
¿nos puede dar otra llave?
nos pwe-de dar o-tra lya-be

talking talking talking

CAMPING

Campsites in Spain are given either 1st-class (1ª), 2nd-class (2ª) or 3rd-class (3ª) ratings. Even the third grade sites usually have hot showers, a cafeteria and electrical hook-ups. The first-grade sites often have heated swimming pools, laundry service, restaurants, etc. You usually pay per tent, per person and per car/caravan. Sites can get very busy in July and August, when it is advisable to book in advance. In tourist areas, staff will probably speak English. Prices in cafés and shops on sites can be a little on the high side.

◀ Tourist offices will have information on local campsites and should also be able to help with bookings.

Camping ▶ sign

Remember the limit is 10 km/h not 10 mph.

no sounding horn

no dogs

no vehicles between 11 pm and 7 am.

---

we are looking for a campsite
estamos buscando un camping
es-ta-mos boos-kan-do oon kam-peen

have you any vacancies?
¿tienen sitio?
tyen-en seet-yo

we want to stay for ... nights
queremos quedarnos ... noches
ke-re-mos ke-dar-nos ... no-ches

where should we pitch the tent?
¿dónde ponemos la tienda?
don-de se po-ne-mos la tyen-da

how much is it?
¿cuánto cuesta?
kwan-to kwes-ta

per tent
por tienda
por tyen-da

per caravan
por caravana
por ka-ra-ba-na

where are...?
¿dónde están...?
don-de es-tan...

the showers
las duchas
las doo-chas

the toilets
los servicios
los ser-bee-thee-os

is there a restaurant on the campsite?
¿hay restaurante en el camping?
a-ee res-tow-ran-te en el kam-peen

do you have a more sheltered site?
¿tienen algún sitio más resguardado?
tyen-en al-goon seet-yo mas res-gwar-da-do

can we camp here overnight?
¿podemos acampar aquí para pasar la noche?
po-de-mos a-kam-par a-kee pa-ra pa-sar la no-che

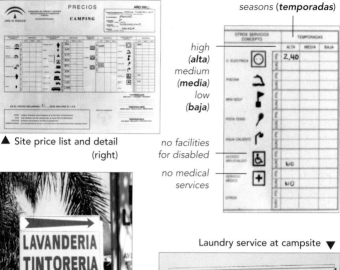

▲ Site price list and detail (right)

seasons (**temporadas**)

OTROS SERVICIOS CONCEPTO		TEMPORADAS		
		ALTA	MEDIA	BAJA
C. ELÉCTRICA	○	2,40		
PISCINA				
MINI-GOLF				
PISTA TENIS				
AGUA CALIENTE				
ACCESO MINUSVÁLIDO	👤	NO		
SERVICIO MÉDICO	✚	NO		
OTROS				

high (**alta**)
medium (**media**)
low (**baja**)

no facilities for disabled
no medical services

▲ LAUNDERETTE
DRY CLEANERS

Laundry service at campsite ▼

is there a launderette near here?
¿hay alguna lavandería automática por aquí cerca?
*aee al-**goo**-na la-ban-de-**ree**-ya ow-to-**ma**-tee-ka por a-**kee ther**-ka*

where can I do some washing?
¿dónde puedo lavar algo de ropa?
*don-de **pwe**-do la-**bar** al-go de **ro**-pa*

can I do some washing?
¿puedo lavar algo de ropa?
*pwe-do la-**bar** **al**-go de **ro**-pa*

can I borrow an iron?
¿me pueden dejar una plancha?
*me **pwe**-den de-**khar** **oo**-na **plan**-cha*

when will my things be ready?
¿para cuándo estarán mis cosas?
*pa-ra **kwan**-do es-ta-**ran** mees **ko**-sas*

talking talking talking

SPECIAL NEEDS

*Access for the disabled in Spain is poor and needs to be checked out carefully before your trip. The British organisation RADAR is worth contacting for their publication on travel abroad for disabled people. You can also visit their website **www.radar.org.uk**. It also has links to other useful sites. In Spain, wheelchair access to buses exists but the number of buses and routes covered is limited. Although public buildings may well have ramps, once you are inside, you may find that the toilet facilities are on the first floor only.*

▲ Large supermarkets usually have trolleys for the disabled.

► Ramp to get on to the beach

▲ Some buses have wheelchair access: check for the sign at the door.

◄ Disabled parking is clearly signed but once parked, you may find general accessibility difficult.

are there any disabled toilets?
¿hay aseos para minusválidos?
*aee a-**se**-os **pa**-ra mee-noos-**ba**-lee-dos*

is there a wheelchair-accessible entrance?
¿hay acceso para sillas de ruedas?
*aee ak-**the**-so **pa**-ra **seel**-yas de **rewd**-as*

is it possible to visit ... with a wheelchair?
¿se puede entrar en ... con silla de ruedas?
*se **pwe**-de en-**trar** en ... kon **seel**-ya de **rwed**-as*

is there a reduction for the disabled?
¿hay descuento para minusválidos?
*aee des-**kwen**-to **pa**-ra mee-noos-**ba**-lee-dos*

I need a bedroom on the ground floor
necesito una habitación en la planta baja
*neth-es-**ee**-to **oo**-na a-bee-ta-th**yon** en la **plan**-ta **ba**-kha*

I use a wheelchair
uso silla de ruedas
***oo**-so **seel**-ya de **rwe**-das*

where is the lift?
¿dónde está el ascensor?
don**-de es-**ta** el as-then-**sor

WITH KIDS

In Spain children are accepted almost everywhere. They will often be out with the family until very late at night. Children under 4 go free on trains and buses. On trains, they pay only 60% of the adult fare if between 4 and 11 years old. All children must be secured in the car at all times, using any of a variety of seatbelts/chairs, etc.

ALIMENTO INFANTIL

Baby Changing Station

▲ Hypermarkets and larger motorway services often have play areas and baby-changing facilities.

▲ The best place to buy baby food, nappies, etc., is in supermarkets, hyper-markets or chemists'.

Most large super-markets have little play trolleys for children (*carritos para niños*). ▼

CARRITOS
PARA NIÑOS

niño
neen-yo
child

asiento del bebé
as-yen-to del be-be
baby seat

silla alta
seel-ya al-ta
high chair

cuna
koo-na
cot

parque infantil
par-ke een-fan-teel
play park

pañales
pan-ya-les
nappies

keywords keywords keywords

where can I change the baby?
¿dónde puedo cambiar al niño?
don-de pwe-do kamb-yar al neen-yo

a child's ticket
un billete de niño
oon beel-ye-te de neen-yo

do you have...?
¿tiene...?
tyen-e...

a high chair
una silla alta
oo-na seel-ya al-ta

a cot
una cuna
oo-na koo-na

do you sell nappies?
¿vende pañales?
ben-de pan-ya-les

baby wipes
toallitas infantiles
to-al-yee-tas een-fan-tee-les

baby food
potitos
po-tee-tos

is there a children's menu?
¿hay un menú para niños?
aee oon me-noo pa-ra neen-yos

a small portion
una ración pequeña
oo-na rath-yon pe-ken-ya

is there a play park near here?
¿hay algún parque infantil por aquí cerca?
aee al-goon par-ke een-fan-teel por a-kee ther-ka

talking talking talking

HEALTH

Most people in Spain rely heavily on the national health service. When visiting Spain, as an EU citizen, it is advisable to take an E111 form (available from your local post office). This allows you temporarily to transfer your medical insurance/social security rights to a member state during your stay. It is unlikely that you will be charged for any service provided from the Public Health System but if this does happen, get a receipt and present it with the E111 to the relevant authorities back in the UK for reimbursement.

◀ If you need to see a doctor, simply visit the nearest clinic with your E111 and ask for an appointment. Make sure you are being treated as a National Health patient and not privately. You usually need to go in the morning (9 am) to get a ticket for an appointment later that day. It is not usual to phone or book from one day to the next. Many doctors speak some English, but don't take this for granted.

All dental provision is private. Simply book an appointment, but it is advisable to get a quote in advance for any work to be done.

▲ PHARMACY ▼

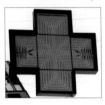

Chemist's sell medical items for which you often don't need a doctor's prescription. A chemist's is a good place to seek advice for minor ailments and suggested non-prescription medicines (including some antibiotics).

where is there a chemist?
¿dónde hay una farmacia?
don-de aee oo-na far-math-ya

have you something for...?
¿tiene algo para...?
tyen-e al-go pa-ra...

an upset stomach
la indigestión
la een-dee-khest-yon

sunburn
las quemaduras del sol
las ke-ma-doo-ras del sol

diarrhoea
la diarrea
la dee-ar-re-a

a headache
el dolor de cabeza
el do-lor de ka-be-tha

I have cystitis
tengo cistitis
ten-go thees-tee-tees

I need antibiotics
necesito antibióticos
neth-e-see-to an-tee-bee-yo-tee-kos

talking

FIRST
◀**AID**

ASISTENCIA SANITARIA

◀ Each town has a 'duty chemist'. Every chemist will list the duty chemist rota (*Farmacia de Guardia*) in their window or posted nearby. You can also find this list in local newspapers, including English language ones.

I am not well
me encuentro mal
*me en-**kwen**-tro mal*

he/she is not well
no se encuentra bien
*no se en-**kwen**-tra byen*

I need to see a doctor
necesito un médico
*neth-e-**see**-to oon **med**-ee-ko*

we need a doctor to come out
necesitamos que venga un médico
*neth-e-**see**-ta-mos ke **ben**-ga oon **med**-ee-ko*

please call the doctor
llame al médico por favor
*lyam-e al **med**-ee-ko por fa-**bor***

my child is ill
mi hijo está enfermo
*mee **ee**-kho es-**ta** en-**fer**-mo*

I have a pain here
me duele aquí
*me **dwe**-le a-**kee***

I am on this medication
estoy tomando estos medicamentos
*es-**toy** to-**man**-do **es**-tos me-dee-ka-**men**-tos*

I'm pregnant
estoy embarazada
*es-**toy** em-ba-ra-**tha**-da*

I am on the pill
estoy tomando la píldora
*es-**toy** to-**man**-do la **peel**-do-ra*

I'm breastfeeding
estoy dando de mamar
*es-**toy** **dan**-do de ma-**mar***

I have an infected finger
tengo el dedo infectado
*ten-go el **ded**-o een-fek-**ta**-do*

I'm diabetic
soy diabético/a
*soy dee-a-**be**-tee-ko/a*

I'm allergic to...
soy alérgico/a a...
*soy a-**ler**-khee-ko/a a...*

I've high blood pressure
tengo la tensión alta
***ten**-go la ten-**syon** **al**-ta*

is this covered by Social Security?
¿esto lo cubre la Seguridad Social?
*es-**to** lo **koob**-re la se-goo-ree-**dad** soth-**yal***

I need a receipt for my insurance
necesito un recibo para el seguro
*neth-e-**see**-to oon re-**thee**-bo **pa**-ra el se-**goo**-ro*

how much will it cost?
¿cuánto va a costar?
***kwan**-to ba a **kos**-tar*

I need a dentist
necesito un dentista
*ne-thes-**ee**-to oon den-**tees**-ta*

I have toothache
tengo dolor de muelas
***ten**-go do-**lor** de **mwe**-las*

can you repair my dentures?
¿puede arreglarme la dentadura postiza?
***pwe**-de ar-reg-**lar**-me la den-ta-**doo**-ra pos-**tee**-tha*

I need a temporary filling
necesito un empaste provisional
*neth-e-**see**-to oon em-**pas**-te pro-bee-syo-**nal***

I have an abscess
tengo un absceso
***ten**-go oon ab-**thes**-o*

*Accident and Emergency (**Urgencias**) operate pretty much the same as in the UK. You will need to complete a registration form at reception and this will be in Spanish only.*

▲ Road sign to hospital

▲ The ambulance service is private. Contact numbers are available in local phone directories, tourist information offices and chemist's. For the emergency ambulance, call 061.

▲ **ACCIDENT & EMERGENCY**

A TODAS LAS SALAS ↑

▲ **TO ALL WARDS**

▲ *Pabellón* means section

If you need to go to hospital

Make sure you take with you your E111 form and passport. If you do not do this, you will be charged as a private patient and will be unlikely to get your money back.

will he/she have to go to hospital?
¿tendrá que ir al hospital?
*ten-**dra** ke eer al os-pee-**tal***

where is the hospital?
¿dónde está el hospital?
don**-de es-**ta** el os-pee-**tal

I need to go to casualty
necesito ir a urgencias
*neth-s-**see**-to eer a oor-**khenth**-yas*

please take me to the nearest hospital
por favor ¿me lleva al hospital más cercano?
*por fa-**bor** me **lyeb**-a al os-pee-**tal** mas ther-**ka**-no*

when are visiting hours?
¿cuáles son las horas de visita?
*kwal-es son las **o**-ras de bee-**see**-ta*

which ward?
¿qué planta?
*ke **plan**-ta*

can you explain what is the matter?
¿me puede explicar qué pasa?
*me **pwe**-de eks-plee-**kar** ke **pa**-sa*

EMERGENCY

*The Spanish police is in 3 parts: **Guardia Civil** (for country-side, roads and borders), **Policia Nacional** (for provincial capitals and large towns) and **Policia Municipal/local** (for local bylaws). The **Guardia Civil** deal with traffic accidents and offences, but local parking offences fall to the **Policia Municipal**. All carry guns. Generally speaking, you may find the local police the easiest and most relaxed to deal with. The emergency number for the local police is 092. If you have to report an accident, etc., you will have to fill in a form at the local police station. This will be in Spanish.*

help!
¡socorro!
*so-**kor**-ro*

can you help me!
¿me puede ayudar?
*me **pwe**-de a-yoo-**dar***

please call...
por favor llame a...
*por fa-**bor** **lya**-me a...*

the police
la policía
*la po-lee-**thee**-ya*

an ambulance
una ambulancia
*oo-na am-boo-**lanth**-ya*

fire!
¡fuego!
***fwe**-go*

please call the fire brigade!
por favor llame a los bomberos
*por fa-**bor** **lya**-me a los bom-**be**-ros*

my ... has been stolen
me han robado...
*me an ro-**ba**-do...*

I want to report a theft
quiero denunciar un robo
***kyer**-o de-noon-**thyar** oon **ro**-bo*

here are my insurance details
aquí tienen mis datos del seguro
*a-**kee tyen**-en mees **da**-tos del se-**goo**-ro*

where is the police station/the hospital?
¿dónde está la comisaría/el hospital?
don**-de es-**ta** la kom-ee-sa-**ree**-ya/el os-pee-**tal

I would like to phone...
quería llamar a...
*kee-**ree**-ya lya-**mar** a...*

my car has been broken into
me han entrado en el coche
*me an en-**tra**-do en el **ko**-che*

please give me your insurance details
¿me puede dar sus datos del seguro?
*me **pwe**-de dar soos **da**-tos del se-**goo**-ro*

I need a report for my insurance
necesito un informe para el seguro
*neth-e-**see**-to oon een-for-me **pa**-ra el se-**goo**-ro*

talking talking talking talking talking

FOOD

AND

DRINK

SPANISH FOOD

It is very easy to find something to eat in Spain almost any time and anywhere. Food is not particularly expensive and eating snacks rather than full meals is common and popular. Breakfast is normally light, consisting of coffee/milk with bread and olive oil or butter. The main meal is still eaten at lunchtime (2–3 pm) and this is very much a family event. Lunches are usually 3-course meals, with the second course often being a piece of meat with no accompaniment. When people eat in the evening, either at home or out, their meal may not start until 10 pm or later. Food tends to be 'Mediterranean'-based, i.e., using lots of fresh produce, meat, salads, fish and olive oil. In the north and interior there is more emphasis on stews, using lentils, chickpeas and a lot of meat.

◀ Bars serve drinks, coffee and breakfasts Spanish-style. They may also offer **tapas**, **pinchos** (snacks) and **bocadillos** (sandwiches).

▲ A **Mesón** is a traditional-style tavern restaurant.

Cafeterías serve some dishes as well as toasted sandwiches and **pasteles** (cakes). **Platos combinados** consist normally of meat or fish with rice, potatoes or chips and vegetables, i.e. a full dish. If what you order isn't a **plato combinado** and you order, for example, a piece of fish, you will only get fish. The waiter will usually ask you if you want it with chips or vegetables.

▼

DINING ROOM ▲

▶ **BREAKFASTS AND MEALS**

At restaurants, be prepared to spend time at the table. You can order à la carte or opt for the set menu, in which case you will be served more quickly. But take into consideration the large portions generally served. In Spain salads and vegetable dishes are considered as separate items and normally brought to the table before the main dish. Bread is always provided but not butter. Flexibility is often the key here. For example, if you want boiled potatoes instead of chips, ask and they will probably be able to do it. ▼

RESTAURANTE EL ANCLA
PESCAITOS - PESCADOS - MARISCOS Y CARNES

fried fish   *fish*   *shellfish*   *meat*

Bodega means wine cellar. It is rather like a wine bar which would serve some food. ▼

BODEGAS QUITAPENAS

It is normal to pay for drinks as you leave the bar. However, in some outdoor cafés, the waiter will present you with the bill as he gives you the drink and you are expected to pay there and then.

where can we have a snack?
¿dónde se puede comer algo?
*don-de se **pwe**-de ko-**mer al**-go*

can you recommend a good local restaurant?
¿puede recomendarnos algún buen restaurante de aquí?
pwe**-de re-ko-men-**dar**-nos al-**goon** bwen rest-ow-**ran**-te de a-**kee

are there any vegetarian restaurants?
¿hay aquí algún restaurante vegetariano?
*aee a-**kee** al-**goon** rest-ow-**ran**-te be-khe-tar-**ya**-no*

do we need to book a table?
¿necesitamos reservar mesa?
*ne-thes-**ee**-ta-mos re-ser-**bar me**-sa*

what dishes do you recommend?
¿qué platos nos recomienda?
*ke **pla**-tos nos re-kom-**yen**-da*

how do we get to the restaurant?
¿cómo se va al restaurante?
***ko**-mo se ba al rest-ow-**ran**-te*

There is no shortage of places to eat, from restaurants to tapas bars and pizzerias to cafés. If you want international cuisine, you'll find foreign restaurants on the coast, in major cities and in large hotels; Italian food is widely available. A popular and inexpensive alternative is the tapas bar – you'll find these wherever you go. Many offer a Menú del Día which is a limited selection of basic fare in the form of a 3-course meal, often including bread and wine. At around 7 euros a head they are very good value. See pp. 80–81 for tapas.

▲ Beach bars/restaurants are called *Chiringuitos*.

Kiosks are good for soft drinks, crisps, sweets and ice-creams. ◀

Snacks are often sold on the street, especially in shopping areas and during fiestas ▶

ALMENDRAS	almonds
AVELLANAS	hazelnuts
PISTACHOS	pistachios
CONGUITOS	chocolate peanuts
PIPAS	sunflower seeds
PATATAS FRITAS	crisps (**bolsa**=bag)

talking talking talking

I'd like a ... please
quería un/una ... por favor
ke-**ree**-ya oon/**oo**-na ... por fa-**bor**

a white coffee
un café con leche
oon ka-**fe** kon **le**-che

an espresso
un café solo
oon ka-**fe** **so**-lo

a decaff coffee
un café descafeinado
oon ka-**fe** des-ka-feyn-**a**-do

a hot chocolate
un chocolate
oon cho-ko-**la**-te

a tea with milk
un té con leche
oon te kon **le**-che

an orange juice
un zumo de naranja
oon **thoo**-mo de na-**ran**-kha

an apple juice
un zumo de manzana
oon **thoo**-mo de man-**tha**-na

a red wine
un tinto
oon **teen**-to

a white wine
un vino blanco
oon **bee**-no **blan**-ko

a half lager
una caña
oo-na **kan**-ya

a bottle of mineral water
una botella de agua mineral
oo-na bo-**tel**-ya de **ag**-wa mee-ne-**ral**

fizzy
con gas
kon gas

still
sin gas
seen gas

ICE-CREAMS • ICED DRINKS
COLD SOFT DRINKS

◀ A popular breakfast dish is thick hot chocolate with *churros* (fried batter sticks) for dipping. It is also a popular snack in the late afternoon (*merienda*).

Ordering a tea with milk will ▶ often get you a teabag put into hot milk; tea with cold milk is *un té con leche fría aparte*. Coffee comes in many varieties; the most common is *café con leche* (coffee with milk); *café solo* (black coffee) is very strong and served in a very small cup. If you want decaffeinated coffee, be careful that you ask for *descafeinado de máquina* (from the espresso machine) or you are likely to get a cup of warm milk and a sachet of Nescafé.

Beer in Spanish means lager. Local brews are very good. You can order a bottle (*un botellín*) or a draft beer (*una caña*), normally quite a small measure. In major cities and tourist areas, you can find UK-style pubs where there is a larger selection of imported but expensive beers and wines. ▶

can we eat?
¿podemos comer?
po-**de**-mos ko-**mer**

what can we eat?
¿qué podemos comer?
ke po-**de**-mos ko-**mer**

do you have a dish of the day?
¿tiene un menú del día?
tyen-e oon me-**noo** del **dee**-ya

what is the dish of the day?
¿cuál es el plato del día?
kwal es el **pla**-to del **dee**-ya

what sandwiches do you have?
¿qué bocadillos tiene?
ke bo-ka-**deel**-yos **tyen**-e

what cakes do you have?
¿qué pasteles tiene?
ke pas-**te**-les **tyen**-e

I would like ice cream
quería un helado
ke-**ree**-ya oon e-**la**-do

what flavours are there?
¿qué sabores hay?
ke sa-**bor**-es aee

talking

*Sampling the many tastes and textures of Spanish food couldn't be easier: just stop at a bar (**bar**) and order **tapas**.*
Tapas *seem to have originated in Andalusia, but they are a way of life in the whole of Spain and have become fashionable even outside the country. They have the advantage of allowing you to taste lots of dishes at once, because, even though they can just be appetizers such as cured ham (**jamón serrano**) or cheese, they are often small portions of main dishes. In fact almost any dish can be served as a **tapa**: for instance, meat balls in sauce (**albóndigas**), squid rings fried in batter (**calamares fritos**), tripe (**callos**) and many more. Often each person orders two or three different **tapas**, so if you are eating with a group of friends you will have a dozen or so mini dishes to share. **Tapas** are ideal as a quick snack or light meal – often very welcome when you consider how late the meals are served in Spain.*

◀ In **tapas** bars, there are usually two sets of prices, the lower one for sitting at the bar and the other for sitting at a table. If you are at the bar, ordering **tapas** is simply a matter of pointing at what you want. If you only want a drink, particularly during the day, you may find you are asked if you want something to eat. Spaniards don't often drink without picking at some small **tapas** or snack. If you're unsure about anything on the menu, don't hesitate to ask – staff are often very helpful. In tourist centres many dishes are shown in picture form and you simply order by number. Be warned, however, that some bars can be quite cramped and don't have tables, so you have to eat and drink standing up, amid the hubbub of lively conversation.

▲ *Tortilla*
Spanish omelette cooked with fried sliced potatoes. This is often served as a **tapas**, but can also be ordered as a main dish. Variations can be cooked with tuna fish, asparagus and prawns.

A selection of **tapas**: toasted bread with sardines, tomatoes with anchovies and toasted bread with black pudding. ▼

A *tapa* is a small serving (which will probably be served on a saucer). It is really a means to be nibbling on something whilst you are drinking. A *ración* is a larger amount (served on a slightly bigger plate) which you might order if there were a group of you eating together. You will also see the word *pincho* which is another term for *tapa*. The word *pincho* actually means 'pierced through'; i.e. it is a bite on a cocktail stick.

Calamares fritos
deep fried squid in batter ▼

Tapas menu ▶

tapas and portions ———

			TAPA	RACIÓN
	Bar			**Mistral**
	Tapas y Raciones			
stew	1	**ESTOFADO**	2,85	4,30
lean meat and tomato	2	**MAGRO CON TOMATE**	2,20	4,30
meatballs	3	**ALBONDIGAS**	2,40	3,70
tripe	4	**CALLOS**	1,80	3,70
Russian salad	5	**ENSALADILLA RUSA**	1,30	2,85
lamb kebab	6	**PINCHITOS DE CORDERO**	1,80	——
sirloin kebab	7	**PINCHITOS DE SOLOMILLO**	1,50	——
mini-hamburgers	8	**CRESTAS**	1,80	——
Spanish omelette	9	**TORTILLA DE PATATAS**	1,00	
fresh anchovies	10	**BOQUERONES AL NATURAL**	2,40	——
fish, peppers, tomatoes, hardboiled eggs, onions	11	**PIPIRRANA**	1,30	2,85
snails	12	**CARACOLES**	2,40	4,30

do you have tapas?
¿tiene tapas?
tyen-e ta-pas

what tapas do you have?
¿qué tapas tiene?
ke ta-pas tyen-e

a portion of that and that
una ración de eso y eso
oo-na rath-yon de es-o ee es-o

what tapas do you recommend?
¿qué tapas nos recomienda?
ke ta-pas nos re-kom-yen-da

what is this?
¿qué es esto?
ke es es-to

talking

To get the bill, catch the waiter's attention either through eye contact or by slightly raising your hand. Service is rarely included and if sitting at a table, you are expected to add around 5%, something which is not automatic if you are at the bar.

Options are limited if you are vegetarian. Menus are predominantly meat- or fish-based and even 'vegetable' dishes, soups and salads need to be checked for ingredients. It's worth telling the waiter that you don't eat animal products (*no como productos animales*). Simply saying you are vegetarian may not help, as ham and chicken is often not considered meat. *Tapas* bars are probably your safest bet as you can see the food before you order it and there are often dishes which contain only one vegetable or item. In Madrid, Barcelona and some tourist areas you will find the occasional vegetarian restaurant.

Tomato salad with onions and olives ▼

jarra de rosado
(carafe of rosé)

pimiento (pepper)

sal (salt)

cuenta (bill)
propina (tip)

I would like to book a table
quería reservar una mesa
*ke-**ree**-ya re-ser-**bar oo**-na **me**-sa*

for tonight
para esta noche
*pa-ra **es**-ta **no**-che*

for lunch
para comer
*pa-ra **ko**-mer*

at 8.30
a las ocho y media
*a las **o**-cho ee **med**-ya*

in a non-smoking area
en la zona de non-fumadores
*en la **thon**-a de non foo-ma-**dor**-es*

for 4 people
para cuatro personas
*pa-ra **kwat**-ro per-**so**-nas*

for tomorrow night
para mañana por la noche
*pa-ra man-**ya**-na por la **no**-che*

at 2 o'clock
a las dos
a las dos

at 9 o'clock
a las nueve
*a las **nwe**-be*

in the name of Smith
a nombre de Smith
*a **nomb**-re de smith*

Paella has become a dish that is served all over Spain though it originated around Valencia. Different regions of Spain vary the *paella* according to the local produce. Vegetables, meat and chicken are found in the *paellas* of interior Spain. Valencia and Barcelona combine sea foods with chicken and vegetables. Saffron is another ingredient of the dish. The name comes from the iron frying pan with two handles in which the rice is cooked and served. You can generally only order it for a minimum of two people.

▼

the menu please
la carta por favor
la kar-ta por fa-bor

the wine list please
la carta de vinos por favor
la kar-ta de bee-nos por fa-bor

do you have a children's menu?
¿tienen menú para niños?
tyen-en me-noo pa-ra neen-yos

for a starter I will have...
de primero quiero...
de preem-er-o kyer-o...

for a main dish I will have...
de segundo quiero...
de se-goon-do kyer-o...

what vegetarian dishes do you have?
¿qué platos vegetarianos tienen?
ke pla-tos ve-khe-tar-ya-nos tyen-en

what desserts do you have?
¿qué postres tiene?
ke post-res tyen-e

some tap water please
¿me da agua del grifo?
me da ag-wa del gree-fo

some more bread please
más pan por favor
mas pan por fa-bor

the bill please
la cuenta por favor
la kwen-ta por fa-bor

we would like to pay separately
queremos pagar por separado
ke-re-mos pa-gar por se-pa-ra-do

*Some menus exist in the form of a blackboard on the wall of the restaurant for dish-of-the-day-type meals. Other menus (**cartas**) include different categories of food: **tapas y raciones**, **platos combinados**, etc.*

Menus ▼

breakfasts and Snacks

Infusiones Variadas
selection of herbal teas

DESAYUNOS Y MERIENDAS

Café, Descafeinado, Infusiones Varias	1,40
Chocolate	1,70
Vaso de Leche	1,30
Café Vienés	2,40
Café con Nata	1,80
Carajillo	2,10
Capuchino	2,40
Café Irlandés	5,30
Té Americano	2,00
Café o Te con Suizo	2,10
Café o Té con Tostadas	3,35
Borrachuelos	2,90
Croissant, Ensaimada, Torta o Suizo	1,95
Plum Cake	2,80
Desayuno Completo	7,80

glass of milk — Vaso de Leche
coffee with cream — Café con Nata
coffee with a dash of brandy — Carajillo
Tea — Té Americano
con suizo *with a bun* — Café o Te con Suizo
con tostadas *with toast* — Café o Té con Tostadas
sponge cake soaked in wine and syrup — Borrachuelos
ensaimada *spiral bun* **torta** *cake* *full breakfast*

SÁNDWICH	Vegetal	3,75
	Jamón y Queso	3,90
	J. York o Chorizo o Salchichón	4,20
BOCADILLO	Atún	3,90
	J. Serrano	4,75

jamón York *cooked ham* *jamón serrano* *cured ham*

TAPAS Y RACIONES

Pepito de Ternera	8,15
Tortilla Francesa	3,60
Tortilla Patatas	4,80
Tortilla de Atún	4,50
Tortilla de Espárragos	5,45
Tortilla de Gambas	7,25
Ensalada de Pimientos	3,90
Ensalada Mixta	5,70
Ensaladilla Rusa	3,60

veal with fried green pepper and sometimes with a slice of cured ham — Pepito de Ternera

Russian salad — Ensaladilla Rusa

Salmón Marinado al Eneldo	10,25
Jamón Ibérico de Bellota	13,50
Surtido de Quesos	6,85
Queso del día	4,80
Chorizo cular	3,90
Gambas a la Plancha	9,65
Gambas Orly (Rebozadas)	5,90
Boquerones Fritos	5,70
Calamares Fritos	5,90
Calamares Fritos	8,15

selection of cheeses — Surtido de Quesos

fried anchovies — Boquerones Fritos

La Carta

The menu will indicate the various types of dishes served, dividing them into categories, i.e. soups, starters, fish dishes, and so on, in more or less detail, according to the type of restaurant.

Entremeses *Starters (also **entrantes fríos** or **calientes** – starters, cold or hot)*

Sopas *Soups*

Plato del día *Dish of the day*

Primer plato *First course*

Ensalada *Salad*

Verduras *Vegetables*

Huevos *Egg dishes*

Revueltos *Scrambled eggs (generally cooked with something like mushrooms, asparagus or spinach)*

Pastas *Pasta dishes*

Arroz *Rice dishes. (Many rice dishes, such as paella, are normally only prepared for a minimum of two people.)*

Parrilladas *Grilled food*

Pescados *Fish dishes*

Carnes *Meats*

Postres *Desserts*

Quesos *Cheeses*

---

main meals (from 12.30 to 6 pm)

solomillo adobado
marinated sirloin

patatas a lo pobre
potatoes cooked in
garlic & parsley

filetes de rosada
rock fish

*cogollos de
lechugas*
lettuce hearts

pechugas de pollo
chicken breasts

huevos fritos
fried eggs

potaje del día
soup of the day

choice of smoked
meats with gherkins
& anchovies

dessert: cake, ice-
cream or fruit

PLATOS COMBINADOS (de 12'30 a 18'00 horas)

1. **Solomillo adobado, huevos fritos, patatas a lo pobre y pimientos** **9,05**
2. **Filetes de rosada a la parilla, cogollos de lechugas, espárragos verdes con vinagreta**..**8,45**
3. **Pechugas de pollo a la plancha, croquetas, patatas fritas y salsa de tomate**..**7,25**
4. **Salteado de verduras de temporada, espárragos y jamón en juliana**...**7,25**
5. **Ensalada de pimientos con frituras de boquerones y adobo de rosada**..**7,25**
6. **Entrecot de ternera a la plancha con arroz blanco y rodajas de tomate**..**10,85**
7. **Huevos fritos con bacon, salchichas y pimientos fritos** **7,25**
8. **Escalope de ternera con ensaladilla rusa y pimientos del Piquillo**...**10,25**
9. **Cucharon potaje del día** **6,00**
10. **Selección de ahumados con pepinillos y anchoas** **11,45**

POSTRE: Tarta, Helado o Fruta..**3,35**

WINE

In Britain when we think of Spanish wine we tend to think of Rioja, but there is far more to explore in Spain than big, beefy, powerfully alcoholic, oaky reds. No country is more diverse: there are wines to be found here that mirror those of Australia, California and Bordeaux, and many more with a unique character, totally Spanish. Quality is soaring as Spanish winemakers get to grips with new techniques and international taste. Dig deep and be adventurous.

◀ Rioja

The unoaked *sin crianza* style can be a revelation: silky, fruity, rich, modern, lacking the big oak attack of the *reserva* (3 years' ageing) and *gran reserva* (5 years). The *crianza* (1 year) is often the best bet. Watch out – Rioja quality is increasingly variable. Riojas are red blends, but single Tempranillo grape wines and Tempranillo/Cabernet blends can be delicious. Some good whites too, particularly those lower in oak.

There are now some very good Albariño whites under the Rias Baixas *DO*. Other wines to try are those from Navarra. An exciting but often pricey region: superb Tempranillos, Tempranillo/Cabernet and Tempranillo/Merlot blends. Some world-class Chardonnays are emerging and other good whites. Try the Garnacha-based pinks, the *rosados*. Also try wines from Ribera del Duero. Spain's smartest *DO* has some wonderful wine. Tempranillo is called

Tinto Fino here. Like Navarra, there are single varietals, but Tempranillo blended with Merlot or Cabernet Sauvignon is often more successful. Whites are less exciting. No other Castilla region wines come close, though Rueda whites are good. Bierzo *DO* is improving fast.

Priorato, Tarragona, Costers del Segre and Conca de Barberà *DO* are all good wines to try from the Penedès region. Look out for the following regions. Aragón: this is one of the up-and-coming names. Superb whites from Somontano, and improving reds from Cariñena, Campo de Borja and Calatayud. Valencia: wines are generally medium-mediocre in quality. Try the traditional sweet *moscatel de Valencia*. La Mancha: In the centre of Spain, this is traditionally the plonk zone, but modern approaches are improving quality. The best are everyday wines, not stars; Valdepeñas *DO* is the best of them.

cosecha
vintage

At 13% ABV, this quite a strong wine. A table wine would probably be about 11%; port is 20%.

The *DO* (*denominación de origen*) system is based on regions (in this case Penedès). *DOC* (adding the word *calificada*), supposedly a higher level of quality, thus far only applies to Rioja wines and merely reflects tighter growing and making controls. Stick to *DO* and *DOC*, and avoid the lowlier *vino de la tierra* and *vino de mesa*. The really exciting wine areas are in the north and east, particularly from Navarra and Ribera del Duero.

There are three sherry towns: Jerez, El Puerto de Santa María and Sanlúcar. Avoid the cheapies. *Fino*: dry, lean, subtle and lemony from Jerez. *Amontillado*: an aged *Fino*, rich and nutty. *Manzanilla*: briny, dry, yeasty. *Palo Cortado*: a halfway house between *Amontillado* and *Oloroso*. *Oloroso*: rich, spicy, christmassy. Once opened you should finish the bottle within a week.

the wine list please
la carta de vinos por favor
la *kar*-ta de *bee*-nos por fa-*bor*

what wines do you have?
¿qué vinos tiene?
ke *bee*-nos *tyen*-e

is there a local wine?
¿hay un vino típico de esta zona?
aee oon *bee*-no *tee*-pee-ko de *es*-ta *tho*-na

can you recommend a good wine?
¿puede recomendarnos un vino bueno?
pwe-de re-ko-men-*dar*-nos oon *bee*-no *bwen*-o

a glass of red wine please
un tinto por favor
oon *teen*-to por fa-*bor*

a glass of white wine please
un vino blanco por favor
oon *bee*-no *blan*-ko por fa-*bor*

a bottle of wine
una botella de vino
oo-na bo-*tel*-ya de *bee*-no

red wine
vino tinto
bee-no *teen*-to

white wine
vino blanco
bee-no *blan*-ko

a carafe of house wine
una jarra de vino de la casa
oo-na *khar*-ra de *bee*-no de la *ka*-sa

a dry sherry
un fino
oon *fee*-no

talking talking talking

FLAVOURS OF SPAIN

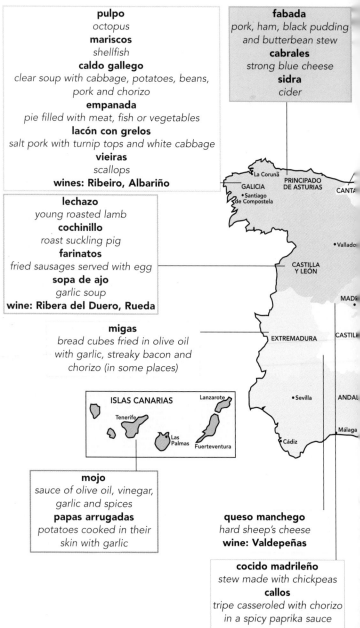

pulpo
octopus
mariscos
shellfish
caldo gallego
*clear soup with cabbage, potatoes, beans,
pork and chorizo*
empanada
pie filled with meat, fish or vegetables
lacón con grelos
salt pork with turnip tops and white cabbage
vieiras
scallops
wines: Ribeiro, Albariño

fabada
*pork, ham, black pudding
and butterbean stew*
cabrales
strong blue cheese
sidra
cider

lechazo
young roasted lamb
cochinillo
roast suckling pig
farinatos
fried sausages served with egg
sopa de ajo
garlic soup
wine: Ribera del Duero, Rueda

migas
*bread cubes fried in olive oil
with garlic, streaky bacon and
chorizo (in some places)*

ISLAS CANARIAS

La Coruña
GALICIA
Santiago
de Compostela
PRINCIPADO
DE ASTURIAS
CANTA

Vallado

CASTILLA
Y LEÓN

MADI

EXTREMADURA

CASTILI

Lanzarote
Tenerife
Las
Palmas
Fuerteventura

Sevilla

ANDAL

Cádiz

Málaga

mojo
*sauce of olive oil, vinegar,
garlic and spices*
papas arrugadas
*potatoes cooked in their
skin with garlic*

queso manchego
hard sheep's cheese
wine: Valdepeñas

cocido madrileño
stew made with chickpeas
callos
*tripe casseroled with chorizo
in a spicy paprika sauce*

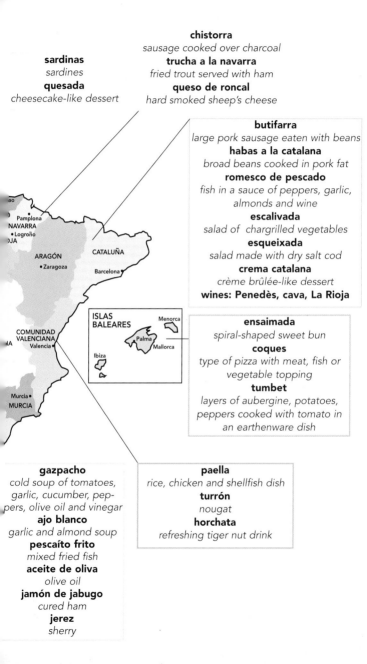

chistorra
sausage cooked over charcoal
trucha a la navarra
fried trout served with ham
queso de roncal
hard smoked sheep's cheese

sardinas
sardines
quesada
cheesecake-like dessert

butifarra
large pork sausage eaten with beans
habas a la catalana
broad beans cooked in pork fat
romesco de pescado
fish in a sauce of peppers, garlic, almonds and wine
escalivada
salad of chargrilled vegetables
esqueixada
salad made with dry salt cod
crema catalana
crème brûlée-like dessert
wines: Penedès, cava, La Rioja

ensaimada
spiral-shaped sweet bun
coques
type of pizza with meat, fish or vegetable topping
tumbet
layers of aubergine, potatoes, peppers cooked with tomato in an earthenware dish

gazpacho
cold soup of tomatoes, garlic, cucumber, peppers, olive oil and vinegar
ajo blanco
garlic and almond soup
pescaíto frito
mixed fried fish
aceite de oliva
olive oil
jamón de jabugo
cured ham
jerez
sherry

paella
rice, chicken and shellfish dish
turrón
nougat
horchata
refreshing tiger nut drink

If you cannot eat certain things, it is as well warning the waiter before making your choice.

talking talking talking talking talking talking

I'm vegetarian
soy vegetariano/a
soy ve-khe-tar-ya-no/a

I don't eat meat/pork
no como carne/cerdo
no ko-mo kar-ne/ther-do

I don't eat fish/shellfish
no como pescado/mariscos
no ko-mo pes-ka-do/ma-rees-kos

I'm allergic to shellfish
soy alérgico(a) al marisco
soy a-ler-khee-ko(a) al ma-rees-ko

I can't eat raw eggs
no puedo comer huevos crudos
no pwe-do ko-mer hwe-bos kroo-dos

I am on a diet
estoy a dieta
es-toy a dyet-a

I am allergic to peanuts
soy alérgico(a) a los cacahuetes
soy a-ler-khee-ko(a) a los ka-ka-we-tes

I can't eat liver
no puedo comer hígado
no pwe-do ko-mer ee-ga-do

I don't drink alcohol
no bebo alcohol
no be-bo al-kol

what is in this?
¿qué lleva esto?
ke lyeb-a es-to

is it raw?
¿está crudo?
es-ta kroo-do

is it made with unpasteurised milk?
¿está hecho con leche sin pasteurizar?
es-ta e-cho kon le-che seen past-e-oo-ree-thar

frito
free-to
fried

cocido
ko-thee-do
boiled

al vapor
al ba-por
steamed

asado
a-sa-do
roast/baked

pincho moruno
peen-cho mo-roo-no
kebab

relleno
rel-ye-no
stuffed

a la plancha
a la plan-cha
grilled

ahumado
a-oo-ma-do
smoked

guisado
gee-sa-do
stewed

adobado
a-dob-a-do
marinated

en escabeche
en es-ka-be-che
pickled

escalfado
es-kal-fa-do
poached

azucarado
a-thoo-ka-ra-do
sugared

salado
sa-la-do
salted

MENU READER

A

...a la/al in the style of
...a la **Navarra** stuffed with ham
...a la **parilla/plancha** grilled
...a la **Romana** fried in batter
...al **horno** baked/roast
aceite oil
  aceite de oliva olive oil
aceitunas olives
  aceitunas rellenas stuffed olives
acelgas Swiss chard
adobo, en marinated
agua water
  agua mineral mineral water
  agua con gas sparkling water
  agua sin gas still water
aguardiente a kind of clear
  grape brandy
ahumado smoked
ajetes garlic shoots
ajillo, ...al with garlic

ajo

ajo garlic
  ajo blanco garlic and almond
  soup served cold
  ajo de las manos sliced, boiled
  potatoes mixed with a garlic, oil
  and vinegar dressing, and
  flavoured with red chillies
albahaca basil
albaricoque apricot
albóndigas meat balls in sauce
alcachofas artichokes
  alcachofas a la vinagreta artichokes served with a strong
  vinaigrette

alcachofa

  alcachofas con jamón sautéed
  artichoke hearts with ham
  alcachofas rellenas stuffed
  artichokes
alcaparras capers
aliño dressing
alioli/all i oli olive oil and garlic
  mashed together into a creamy
  paste similar to mayonnaise.
  Served with meat, potatoes or
  fish
almejas clams
  almejas a la marinera steamed
  clams cooked with parsley, wine
  and garlic
almendras almonds
alubias large white beans found
  in many stews
amontillado medium-dry to dry
  sherry, very prized
ancas de rana frogs' legs
anchoa anchovy

apio

anguila eel

angulas baby eels (elvers)
  angulas al ajillo baby eels cooked with garlic
  angulas en cazuelita garlic-flavoured, fried baby eels seasoned with hot pepper

anís (seco or **dulce)** aniseed liqueur, dry or sweet, normally drunk as a long drink with water and ice

apio celery

arenque herring

arroz rice
  arroz a banda a dish of rice and fish. The dish is served in two courses: first the rice cooked with saffron is served and then the fish that has been cooked in it
  arroz a la cubana rice with fried eggs and tomato sauce
  arroz a la levantina rice with shellfish, onions, artichokes, peas, tomatoes and saffron
  arroz a la marinera rice with seafood
  arroz a la valenciana Valencian version of paella, sometimes with eel added
  arroz a la zamorana rice with pork, peppers and garlic
  arroz blanco boiled rice
  arroz con costra rice with chicken, rabbit, sausages, chick-peas and pork meatballs baked in the oven with an egg topping
  arroz con leche rice pudding flavoured with cinnamon
  arroz con pollo rice with chicken, garnished with peas and peppers
  arroz negro black rice (with squid in its own ink)
  arroz santanderino rice cooked with salmon and milk

asado roasted

asadillo roasted sliced red peppers in olive oil, tomatoes and garlic

atún tuna (usually fresh)
  atún con salsa de tomate tuna fish in tomato sauce

avellana hazelnut

azafrán saffron

azúcar sugar

B

bacalao al pil-pil

bacalao salt cod, cod
  bacalao a la vizcaína salt cod cooked with dried peppers, onions and parsley
  bacalao al ajo arriero salt cod fried with garlic to which is added vinegar, paprika and chopped parsley
  bacalao al pil-pil a Basque speciality – salt cod cooked in a creamy garlic and olive oil sauce
  bacalao con patatas salt cod slowly baked with potatoes, peppers, tomatoes, onions, olives and bay leaves
  bacalao de convento salt cod cooked with spinach and potato

bajoques farcides peppers stuffed with rice, pork, tomatoes and spices

bandeja de quesos cheese platter

barbacoa, ...a la barbecued

berenjena aubergine (eggplant)

berenjena

berenjenas a la catalana
aubergines with tomato sauce,
Catalan style
berenjenas rellenas stuffed
aubergines (usually with mince)
berenjenas salteadas
aubergines sautéed with
tomatoes and onions

besugo red bream

bistec steak

bizcocho sponge
bizcocho borracho sponge
soaked in wine and syrup

blanco y negro a milky coffee
with ice

bocadillo sandwich (French
bread)

bogavante lobster

bonito tunny fish, lighter than
tuna, good grilled

boquerones fresh anchovies
boquerones fritos fried
anchovies

brasa, ...a la brasa barbecued

butifarra

C

caballa mackerel

cabello de ángel sweet pumpkin
filling

cabrito kid (goat)
cabrito al horno roast kid

cacahuete peanut

cachelada chopped boiled
potatoes and cabbage with
garlic, red pepper and fried
bacon. Often served with *chorizo*

café coffee
café con leche milky coffee
(hot)
café cortado coffee with only a
little milk
café descafeinado decaffeinated
instant coffee
café helado coffee with ice
café solo black coffee

calabacines courgettes
calabacines rellenos stuffed
courgettes

calabaza guisada stewed
pumpkin

calamares squid
calamares a la romana fried
squid rings in batter
calamares en su tinta squid
cooked in its own ink
calamares fritos fried squid
calamares rellenos stuffed
squid

calçotada roasted spring onion
laced with olive oil and almonds

caldeirada fish soup from Galicia

caldereta stew/casserole

buñuelos

buñuelos type of fritter. Savoury
ones are filled with cheese, ham,
mussels or prawns. Sweet ones
can be filled with fruit
buñuelos de bacalao salt cod
fritters

butifarra special sausage from
Catalonia
butifarra blanca white sausage
containing pork and tripe
butifarra negra black sausage
containing pork blood, belly
and spices

calabacines

caldereta de cordero lamb casserole

caldereta de langosta lobster stew

caldereta de pescado fish stew

caldo clear soup

caldo de pescado fish soup

caldo gallego clear soup with green vegetables, beans, pork and *chorizo*

caliente hot

callos tripe

callos a la madrileña fried tripe casseroled in a spicy paprika sauce with tomatoes and *chorizo*

camarones shrimps

canela cinnamon

cangrejo crab

caracoles snails

caracoles de mar winkles

callos a la madrileña

caracolillos winkles

carajillo black coffee with brandy which may be set alight depending on regional customs

cardo cardoon, plant related to the artichoke

carne meat

carne de buey beef

carne picada minced meat

carnero mutton

cassolada pork and vegetable stew

castaña chestnut

cavas champagne-style sparkling wines from Catalonia

cazuela de fideos legumes, meat and noodle stew

cebolla onion

cebollas rellenas stuffed onions

cebollas rojas

centollo spider crab

cerdo pork

cerdo asado roast pork

cerezas cherries

cerveza beer

champán champagne

champiñones mushrooms

chanfaina a stew made from pig's liver and other parts such as the lungs

chilindrón, al sauce made with pepper, tomato, fried onions and meat (pork or lamb)

chistorra spicy sausage from Navarra

chocolate drinking chocolate (thickened)

chorizo spicy red sausage. The larger type is eaten like salami, the thinner type is cooked in various dishes

choto kid, calf
  choto albaicinero kid fried with garlic
chuleta chop
  chuleta de cerdo pork chop
  chuleta de ternera veal chop
  chuletas de cordero grilled lamb chops
chuletón large chop
churrasco barbecued steak
churros fried batter sticks sprinkled with sugar, usually eaten with thick hot chocolate
ciervo deer (venison)
cigalas king prawns
ciruelas plums

cordero asado

coca (coques) type of pizza with meat, fish or vegetables served in the Balearic Islands. They can also be sweet
cochinillo roast suckling pig
cocido stew made with various meats, vegetables and chickpeas. There are regional variations of this dish and it is worth trying the local version
  cocido de lentejas thick stew of lentils and *chorizo*
  cocido de pelotas a rich spicy stew with mince wrapped in cabbage leaves containing pork and chickpeas
coco coconut
cóctel de gambas prawn cocktail
codillo de cerdo pig's trotter
codornices asadas roast quail
codorniz quail
col cabbage
coles de Bruselas Brussel sprouts
coliflor cauliflower

coliflor

comino cumin
coñac brandy; it can be on the dry side or sweet and fragrant, as the Spaniards prefer
conchas finas large scallops
conejo rabbit
consomé consommé
  consomé al jerez consommé with sherry
  consomé de gallina chicken consommé
copa goblet
  copa de helado assorted ice cream served in a goblet
coques see **coca**
  coques de torró wafers filled with almonds, sold at Christmas in Majorca
cordero lamb
  cordero al chilindrón lamb in a spicy pepper sauce
  cordero asado roast lamb
  cordero asado a la mancha spit-roasted young lamb
  cordero relleno trufado lamb stuffed with truffles
costillas ribs
  costillas de cerdo pork ribs
crema cream soup/cream
  crema catalana similar to crème brûlée
  crema de espárragos cream of asparagus
  crema de tomate cream of tomato soup
crema generic name given to smooth liqueurs, i.e. *crema de naranja* (orange cream)

cremat coffee with brandy and rum, served in Catalonia

croquetas croquettes (made with thick bechamel sauce)
croquetas de camarones shrimp croquettes

crudo raw

cuajada cream-based dessert served with honey or sugar

cubalibre coca-cola mixed with rum or gin

culantro coriander

D

dátiles dates

descafeinado decaffeinated

dorada sea bream
dorada a la sal sea bream cooked in the oven, covered only with salt, forming a crust
dorada al horno baked sea bream

dulce sweet

ensalada de casa

tomato and onion salad (may include tuna)
ensalada de huevos salad with hard boiled eggs

ensaladilla rusa diced cooked vegetables in mayonnaise

entrecot entrecôte steak

entremeses starters
entremeses de fiambre cold meat hors d'œuvres
entremeses de pescado fish hors d'œuvres

escabeche, en pickled
escabeche de pescado fish marinated in oil and served cold

escalfado poached

escalivada salad of chargrilled vegetables such as peppers and aubergines soaked in olive oil

escalope de ternera veal escalope

escarola endive

escudella meat, vegetable and chickpea stew. Traditionally served as two courses: a soup and then the cooked meat and vegetables
escudilla de pages white bean, sausage, ham and pork soup

dorada a la sal

E

embutido sausage, cold meat

empanada pastry/pie filled with meat or fish and vegetables

empanadilla pasty/small pie filled with meat or fish

empanado breadcrumbed and fried

ensaimada sweet spiral-shaped yeast bun from Majorca

ensalada (mixta/verde) salad (mixed/green)
ensalada de la casa lettuce,

espárragos

espárragos asparagus
  espárragos con mahonesa asparagus with mayonnaise
espinacas gratinadas spinach au gratin
esqueixada salt cod salad
estofado braised, stewed
  estofado de cordero lamb stew
  estofado de ternera veal stew
estragón tarragon

F

fabada asturiana pork, cured ham, black pudding, large butter beans or sausage stew, *chorizo* and *morcilla*

fabada

faisán pheasant
farinatos fried sausages served with eggs
faves large white haricot beans
fiambre cold meat
  fiambre de tenera veal pâté
  fiambres surtidos assorted cold meats
fideos noodles/thin ribbons of pasta
  fideos a la cazuela noodles cooked with pork, sausages, ham and *sofrito* (fried onions, garlic and tomato)
fideuà amb marisc seafood dish with fine pasta (vermicelli)
filete fillet steak
  filete de ternera veal steak

fresa

filete a la plancha grilled fillet steak
filetes de lenguado sole fillets
fino the finest sherry, light and dry, equally good when young or after being aged
flan crème caramel
frambuesas raspberries
fresas strawberries
  fresas con nata strawberries and cream
frijoles beans (name used in the Canary Islands)
frío cold
frite pieces of lamb fried in olive oil and paprika
frito fried
fritura de pescado fried assortment of fish
fruta fruit
  fruta del tiempo fruit in season
frutos secos nuts (general term)

G

galleta biscuit
gallina hen
gambas prawns
  gambas a la plancha grilled prawns
  gambas al ajillo grilled prawns with garlic
  gambas pil-pil sizzling prawns cooked with chillies
ganso goose
garbanzos chickpeas
  garbanzos con espinacas chickpeas with spinach
garrotxa goat's cheese

guindillas

gazpacho traditional cold soup of southern Spain. There are many different recipes. Basic ingredients are water, tomatoes, garlic, cucumber, green pepper, fresh breadcrumbs, vinegar and olive oil. Should always be served chilled.
  gazpacho extremeño a version of gazpacho made with finely chopped green peppers and onions

ginebra gin

gofio toasted corn meal often rolled into balls and eaten as a bread substitute in the Canary Islands

gran reserva classification given to aged wines of exceptional quality

granada pomegranate

granizado fruit drink with crushed ice

guisantes

gratinado au gratin
grelos young turnip tops
guindilla chilli
guisado stew or casserole
guisantes peas
  guisantes a la española boiled peas with cured ham, lettuce, carrots and onions

H

habas broad beans
  habas a la catalana broad beans cooked in pork fat often served with *chorizo*
  habas con jamón broad beans with cured ham
hamburguesa hamburger
helado ice cream
hervido boiled
hígado liver
  hígado con cebolla fried calf's liver with onions

higos

higos figs
  higos secos dried figs
horchata de chufas cool drink made with tiger nuts
horno, ...al baked (in the oven)
huevos eggs
  huevos a la española stuffed eggs with a cheese sauce
  huevos a la flamenca baked eggs with tomatoes, peas, peppers, asparagus and *chorizo*
  huevos al plato eggs baked in butter
  huevos con jamón fried eggs and cured ham

I

infusión herbal tea
intxaursalsa whipped cream and
walnut pudding

J

jamón ham
  jamón de Jabugo Andalusian
  prime-quality cured ham
  jamón de York cooked ham
  jamón serrano cured ham
jengibre ginger
jerez sherry
jibia cuttlefish
judías beans
  judías blancas haricot beans
  judías verdes green beans
  **judías verdes a la
  castellana/española** boiled
  green beans mixed with fried
  parsley, garlic and peppers
jurel horse mackerel

judías verdes

K

kokotxas hake's cheeks usually
fried

L

lacón con grelos salted pork with
  young turnip tops and white
  cabbage
langosta lobster
  langosta a la catalana potatoes
  with a lobster filling served with
  mayonnaise
langostinos king prawns
  langostinos a la plancha grilled
  king prawns

langostinos a la vinagreta
casseroled crayfish with hard-
boiled eggs in vinaigrette sauce
laurel bay leaf
lechazo young lamb (roasted)
leche milk
  leche caliente hot milk
  leche fría cold milk
  leche frita very thick custard
  dipped into an egg and bread-
  crumb mixture, fried and served
  hot in squares
  leche merengada type of ice
  cream made with egg whites,
  sugar and cinnamon. Also
  served as a milkshake

lechuga

lechuga lettuce
legumbres fresh or dried pulses
lengua tongue
lenguado sole
  lenguado a la romana sole
  fried in batter
  lenguados fritos fried fillets of
  sole often served on a bed of
  mixed sautéed vegetables
  lenguados rellenos fillets of
  sole stuffed with shrimps or
  prawn
lentejas lentils (very popular in
  Spain)
licor liqueur
liebre hare
  liebre estofada stewed hare
limón lemon
limonada lemonade (normally
  canned and fizzy)
lomo loin of pork
longaniza spicy pork sausage

longaniza con judías blancas spicy pork sausage with white beans

lubina sea bass
lubina a la asturiana Asturian-style sea bass, with cider
lubina al horno baked sea bass with potatoes, onion, tomato and garlic

M

macarrones macaroni
macedonia de fruta fruit salad
magras con tomate slices of fried ham dipped into tomato sauce
mahonesa mayonnaise
maíz sweetcorn
majorero goat's cheese from Canary Islands
manitas de cerdo pig's trotters
mantequilla butter
manzana apple
manzanas rellenas stuffed baked apples
manzanilla camomile tea (not to be confused with *manzanilla* as a sherry)
manzanilla very dry special sherry
mariscada mixed shellfish
marisco shellfish
marmitako tuna fish and potato stew
mayonesa mayonnaise
mazapán marzipan
medallón thick steak, medallion
mejillones mussels

menestra

mejillones a la marinera mussels steamed in wine
mejillones al vapor mussels (steamed)
melocotón peach
melocotón en almíbar peaches in syrup
melón melon
melón con jamón melon and cured ham
membrillo quince jelly
menestra de verduras fresh vegetable stew often cooked with cured ham
merluza hake, one of the most popular fish in Spain
merluza a la asturiana boiled hake served with mayonnaise and garnished with hard boiled eggs
merluza a la sidra hake baked with clams, onions and cider
merluza en salsa verde hake with green sauce (with parsley)
mermelada jam
mero grouper
miel honey
migas cubes of bread (like croûtons) usually fried in garlic, olive oil with streaky bacon and *chorizo* (in some places)
migas con jamón ham with breadcrumbs
migas extremeñas breadcrumbs fried with egg and *chorizo*
mojama cured tuna fish

melocotón

migas

mojo a sauce made from olive oil, vinegar, garlic and different spices. Paprika is added for the red mojo. Predominantly found in the Canary Islands
  mojo verde *mojo* made with fresh coriander
  mojo picón spicy *mojo* made with chilli peppers
mollejas sweetbreads
  mollejas de ternera calves' sweetbread
morcilla black pudding
moros y cristianos boiled rice, black beans and onions served with garlic sausage
moscatel muscat grape wine, sweet and fragrant
mostaza mustard

mojo de tomate

N

nabo turnip
naranja orange
nata cream
natillas custard
navajas razor clams
nécora sea crab
nectarinas nectarines
nuez walnut
nuez moscada nutmeg

O

olla

olla stew made traditionally with white beans, beef and bacon
  olla gitana thick stew/soup made with chickpeas, pork and vegetables and flavoured with almonds and saffron
  olla podrida thick, ham, vegetable and chickpea stew/soup
oloroso sweet, darker sherry
oreja de cerdo a la plancha grilled pigs's ears
ostras oysters

P

paella one of the most famous of Spanish dishes. Paella varies from region to region but usually consists of rice, chicken, shellfish, vegetables, garlic and saffron. The dish's name derives from the large shallow pan in which it is cooked. The traditional paella Valenciana contains rabbit and chicken

paella

paella de mariscos a rice and shellfish paella

pan bread
pan de higos dried figs pressed together in the shape of a small cake

panades lamb pasties eaten at Easter in Balearics

panchineta almond and custard tart

panecillo bread roll

panelleta small cakes with pine nuts and almonds

papas arrugadas potatoes cooked in their skins with garlic

parrilla, ...a la grilled

parrillada mixed grill (can be meat or fish)
parrillada de mariscos mixed grilled shellfish

pasas raisins

pasta pasta

pastel cake/pastry
pastel de carne meat pie
pastel de ternera veal pie

patatas potatoes
patatas arrugadas potatoes cooked in their skins with garlic

patatas

patatas bravas sliced boiled potatoes mixed with a garlic, oil and vinegar dressing and flavoured with red chilli peppers
patatas con chorizo potatoes cooked with **chorizo**
patatas fritas chips/crisps
patatas nuevas new potatoes

pato duck
pato a la sevillana joints of wild duck cooked with sherry, onion, tomatoes, herbs and garlic, served in an orange and olive sauce

pavo turkey
pavo relleno stuffed turkey

pechuga de pollo chicken breast
pechugas en bechamel chicken breast in bechamel sauce

pedro ximénez sweet, rich sherry-type dessert wine

pepino cucumber

pepitoria de pavo/pollo turkey/chicken fricassée

pera pear

percebes goose-neck barnacle, a Galician shellfish

perdices con chocolate partridge with a chocolate sauce

perdiz partridge

perejil parsley

pescado fish

pescaíto frito mixed fried fish

pez espada swordfish

picada sauce made of chopped parsley, almonds, pine nuts and garlic

pichones young pigeon

pimienta pepper (spice)

pimientos red and green peppers, one of the typical Spanish flavours
pimientos de piquillo pickled red peppers
pimientos rellenos peppers stuffed with meat or fish

piña pineapple

pinchos small tapas
pinchos morunos meat grilled on a skewer

piperrada type of scrambled eggs with red and green peppers, tomato, onion, garlic and paprika

piña

pipirrana a salad of baked fish, peppers, tomatoes, hard-boiled eggs and onions

pisto manchego a mixture of sautéed peppers, onions, aubergines, tomatoes, garlic and parsley. Similiar to French ratatouille. Served hot or cold

plancha, ...a la grilled

plátano banana

platija plaice (flounder)

plato dish

plato del día dish of the day

platos combinados quick meal usually eaten in a bar; consists of assorted food served together on one plate

pollo chicken
  pollo al chilindrón chicken cooked with onion, ham, garlic, red pepper and tomatoes
  pollo asado roast chicken
  pollo con patatas chicken and chips
  pollo en pepitoria breaded chicken pieces fried, then casseroled with herbs, almonds, garlic and sherry
  pollo estofado chicken stewed with potatoes, mushrooms, shallots, bay leaves and mushrooms
  pollo relleno stuffed chicken

polvorones very crumbly cakes made with almonds and often eaten with a glass of *anís*

pomelo grapefruit

porras fried sticks of batter

postres desserts

potaje thick soup/stew often with pork and pulses
  potaje murciano red bean, french bean and rice soup

pote thick soup with beans and sausage which has many regional variations
  pote gallego thick soup made with cabbage, white kidney beans, potatoes, pork and sausage

primer plato first course

puchero hotpot made from meat or fish
  puchero canario salted fish and potatoes served with *mojo* sauce

puerros leeks

pulpo octopus

pulpo

puré de garbanzos thick chick-pea soup

puré de patatas mashed potatoes

Q

queimada warm drink made with *aguardiente* (clear brandy) sweetened with sugar and flamed, a speciality from Galicia

quesada dessert similar to cheesecake

queso cheese

queso de Burgos curd cheese from Burgos
queso de cabrales strong blue cheese from Asturias
queso de Idiazábal smoked sheep's milk cheese from the Basque country
queso de Mahón strong hard cheese from Menorca
queso de oveja mild sheep's cheese from León
queso de Roncal hard, smoked sheep's cheese
queso de tetilla soft, white cheese made in the form of a woman's breast
queso fresco green cheese
queso manchego hard sheep's curd cheese from La Mancha

R

rábanos radishes
rabo de toro bull's tail, usually cooked in a stew
rancio dry sweet wine for dessert
ración portion of tapas
rape monkfish
  rape a la marinera monkfish cooked with wine
raya skate
rebozado in batter
refresco de fruta fruit drink with ice
rehogado lightly fried
relleno stuffed
remolacha beetroot
repollo cabbage
requesón cream cheese similar to cottage cheese
reserva wines of good quality that have been aged, but not as long as *gran reserva*

repollo

revuelto scrambled eggs often cooked with another ingredient
revuelto de champiñones scrambled eggs with mushrooms
revuelto de espárragos scrambled eggs with asparagus tips
revuelto de espinacas scrambled eggs with spinach
revuelto de gambas scrambled eggs with prawns
revuelto de morcilla scrambled eggs with black pudding
riñones al jerez kidneys in sherry sauce
rodaballo turbot
romana, ...a la fried in batter (generally squid – *calamares*)
romero rosemary
romesco sauce made traditionally with olive oil, red pepper and bread. Other ingredients are often added, such as almonds and garlic
  romesco de pescado fish in a sauce of peppers, olive oil and bread with almonds
ron rum
rosco type of doughnut
  roscón de reyes a large bun-like cake in the shape of a ring, similar to Italian panettone and eaten at Epiphany

S

sal salt
salchicha sausage
salchichón salami-type sausage
salmón salmon
  salmón a la parilla grilled salmon
  salmón a la ribereña salmon fried with ham cooked with cider
  salmón ahumado smoked salmon
salmonete red mullet
  salmonete frito fried red mullet
salpicón chopped seafood or meat with onion, tomato, garlic and peppers
salsa sauce
  salsa de tomate tomato sauce
  salsa romesco sauce made of almonds and hazelnuts with mild chilli. Often served with fish and chicken

salsa verde garlic and parsley sauce often served with fish

salteado sautéed

samfaina a dish of peppers, aubergines and tomatoes to which meat is often added

sandía water melon

sándwich toasted sandwich

sangría red wine mixed with lemonade, fruit, sugar and ice, often with cinnamon added

sardinas sardines
  sardinas a la santanderina sardines cooked with tomato, Santander style
  sardinas asadas barbecued sardines
  sardinas frescas/fritas fresh/fried sardines
  sardinas rebozadas sardines cooked in batter

sargo type of bream

seco dry

sepia cuttlefish

sesos brains
  sesos a la romana brains fried in batter
  sesos fritos fried brains

setas wild mushrooms

sidra cider

sifón soda water

sobrasada a paprika-flavoured pork sausage from Mallorca

sofrito basic sauce made with slowly fried onions, garlic and tomato

solomillo sirloin
  solomillo de ternera veal sirloin

sopa soup
  sopa castellana see *sopa de ajo*
  sopa de ajo garlic soup with bread. May contain poached egg or cured ham
  sopa de arroz rice soup
  sopa de cebolla onion soup
  sopa de cocido meat soup
  sopa de fideos noodle soup
  sopa de gallina chicken soup
  sopa de rabo oxtail soup
  sopa mallorquina tomato, onion and pepper soup thickened with breadcrumbs
  sopa de mariscos shellfish soup
  sopa de pescado fish soup

sopa

sopa de pollo chicken soup
sopa de verduras vegetable soup

sorbete sorbet
  sorbetes de frutas fruit sorbets

suquet fish, potato and tomato stew

suspiros meringues
  suspiros de monja meringues served with thick custard

T

tapas appetizers

tarta cake/tart/gâteau
  tarta de manzana apple tart
  tarta de Santiago flat almond cake
  tarta helada ice-cream cake

té tea
  té con leche tea with milk
  té con limón tea with lemon
  té helado iced tea

ternasco young lamb

ternera veal
  ternera con naranja veal cooked with orange
  ternera rellena stuffed veal

tomates

tisana herbal tea

tocinillo sweet made with egg yolk and sugar

tocino bacon

tomates tomatoes
tomates rellenos stuffed tomatos

tomillo thyme

toronja grapefruit

torrija bread dipped in milk and then fried and sprinkled with sugar and cinnamon

tortilla (española) omelette cooked with potatoes. Often sliced and served as a tapa
tortilla de champiñones mushroom omelette
tortilla de chorizo omelette with *chorizo*
tortilla de espárragos asparagus omelette
tortilla de jamón cured ham omelette
tortilla murciana tomato and pepper omelette

trucha trout
trucha a la navarra trout stuffed with cured ham slices
trucha con almendras fried trout with almonds

tumbet layers of peppers, aubergine and tomato cooked with potato in an earthenware dish. Originally from Majorca

turrón nougat
turrón de Alicante hard nougat
turrón de Jijona soft nougat

txangurro spider crab

U

uvas grapes

V

vapor,...al steamed

verduras vegetables
verduras con patatas boiled potatoes with greens

vermú vermouth

vieiras scallops
vieiras de Santiago scallops served in their shell. Cooked in brandy, topped with breadcrumbs and grilled

vinagre vinegar

vinagreta vinaigrette

vino wine
vino blanco white wine
vino clarete rosé wine
vino de jerez sherry wine
vino de mesa table wine
vino rosado rosé wine
vino tinto red wine

Y

yemas small cakes that look like egg yolks

yogur yoghurt

Z

zanahorias carrots

zarzuela de mariscos mixed seafood with wine and saffron
zarzuela de pescado fish stew

zumo juice
zumo de fruta fruit juice
zumo de albaricoque apricot juice
zumo de lima lime juice
zumo de limón lemon juice
zumo de melocotón peach juice
zumo de naranja orange juice
zumo de piña pineapple juice
zumo de tomate tomato juice

zurrukutuna salt cod cooked with green peppers

uvas

DICTIONARY

english–spanish

spanish–english

A

a(n) un(a)
abbey la abadía
able: *to be able* poder
abortion el aborto
about *(concerning)* sobre
  (approximately) más o menos
  about 2 o'clock alrededor de las
  dos
above arriba ; por encima
abroad en el extranjero
abscess el absceso
accelerator el acelerador
accent *(pronunciation)* el acento
to accept aceptar
  do you accept this card? ¿acepta
  esta tarjeta?
access el acceso
  wheelchair access el acceso para
  sillas de ruedas
accident el accidente
accident & emergency department
  Urgencias
accommodation el alojamiento
to accompany acompañar
account *(bank, etc)* la cuenta
account number el número de
  cuenta
to ache doler
  my head aches me duele la cabeza
  it aches duele
acid el ácido
actor/actress el actor/la actriz
adaptor *(electrical)* el adaptador
address la dirección
  what is the address? ¿cuál es la
  dirección?
address book la agenda
admission charge/fee el precio de
  entrada
to admit *(to hospital)* ingresar
adult el/la adulto(a)
  for adults para adultos
advance: *in advance* por adelantado
advertisement el anuncio
to advise aconsejar
A&E Urgencias
aeroplane el avión
aerosol el aerosol
afraid: *to be afraid of...* tener
  miedo de...

after después
afternoon la tarde
  this afternoon esta tarde
  in the afternoon por la tarde
  tomorrow afternoon mañana por
  la tarde
aftershave el aftershave
again otra vez
against contra
age la edad
agency la agencia
ago: *a week ago* hace una semana
to agree estar de acuerdo
agreement el acuerdo
AIDS el sida
airbag *(in car)* el airbag
air bed el colchón inflable
air conditioning el aire
  acondicionado
air freshener el ambientador
airline la linea aérea
air mail: *by airmail* por avión
airplane el avión
airport el aeropuerto
airport bus el autobús del
  aeropuerto
air ticket el billete de avión
aisle el pasillo
alarm la alarma
alarm clock el despertador
alcohol el alcohol
alcohol-free sin alcohol
alcoholic alcohólico(a)
  is it alcoholic? ¿tiene alcohol?
all todo(a)/todos(as)
allergic to alérgico(a) a
  I'm allergic to... soy alérgico(a) a...
allergy la alergia
to allow permitir
  it's not allowed no está
  permitido
all right *(agreed)* de acuerdo
  (OK) vale
  are you all right? ¿está bien?
almost casi
alone solo(a)
alphabet el alfabeto
already ya
also también
altar el altar
always siempre
a.m. de la mañana
am soy/estoy
amber *(traffic light)* amarillo ; ámbar
ambulance la ambulancia

America América del Norte
American norteamericano(a)
amount: *total amount* el total
anaesthetic la anestesia
  local anaesthetic la anestesia local
  general anaesthetic la anestesia general
anchor el ancla
ancient antiguo(a)
and y
angina la angina de pecho
angry enfadado(a)
animal el animal
aniseed el anís
ankle el tobillo
anniversary el aniversario
to announce anunciar
announcement el anuncio
annual anual
another otro(a)
  another beer, please otra cerveza, por favor
answer la respuesta
to answer responder
answerphone el contestador automático
antacid el antiácido
antibiotic el antibiótico
antifreeze el anticongelante
antihistamine el antihistamínico
anti-inflammatory antiinflamatorio(a)
antiques las antigüedades
antique shop el anticuario
antiseptic el antiséptico
any alguno(a)
  have you any pears? ¿tiene peras?
anyone alguien
anything alguna cosa
anywhere en alguna parte
apartment el apartamento
appendicitis la apendicitis
apple la manzana
application form el impreso de solicitud
appointment *(meeting)* la cita
  (dentist, hairdresser) la hora
approximately aproximadamente
April abril
apron el delantal
architect el/la arquitecto(a)
architecture la arquitectura
are son
area code el prefijo
arm el brazo

armbands *(to swim)* los manguitos de nadar
armchair el sillón
to arrange organizar
to arrest detener
arrival la llegada
to arrive llegar
art el arte
art gallery la galería de arte
arthritis la artritis
artificial artificial
artist el/la artista
ashtray el cenicero
to ask *(question)* preguntar
  (to ask for something) pedir
aspirin la aspirina
asthma el asma
  I have asthma tengo asma
at a ; en
  at home en casa
  at 8 o'clock a las ocho
  at once ahora mismo
  at night por la noche
Atlantic Ocean el Océano Atlántico
atmosphere el ambiente
attack *(terrorist)* el atentado
  (medical) el ataque
to attack atacar
attractive atractivo(a)
auction la subasta
audience el público
August agosto
aunt la tía
au pair el/la au pair
Australia Australia
Australian australiano(a)
author el/la autor(a)
automatic automático(a)
automatic car el coche automático
auto-teller el cajero automático
autumn el otoño
available disponible
avalanche la avalancha
avenue la avenida
average medio(a)
to avoid *(issue)* evitar
  (obstacle) esquivar
awake: *to be awake* estar despierto(a)
away: *far away* lejos
awful espantoso(a)
axle *(in car)* el eje

B

baby el bebé
baby food los potitos
baby milk la leche infantil
baby's bottle el biberón
babyseat *(in car)* el asiento del bebé
babysitter el/la canguro
baby wipes las toallitas infantiles
back *(of body)* la espalda
backpack la mochila
bacon el beicon ; el bacon
bad *(weather, news)* mal/malo(a)
  (fruit and vegetables) podrido(a)
badminton el bádminton
bag la bolsa
baggage el equipaje
baggage allowance el equipaje permitido
baggage reclaim la recogida de equipajes
bail bond la fianza
bait *(for fishing)* el cebo
baked al horno
baker's la panadería
balcony el balcón
bald *(person)* calvo(a)
  (tyre) gastado(a)
ball *(large: football, etc)* el balón
  (small: golf, tennis, etc) la pelota
ballet el ballet
balloon el globo
banana el plátano
band *(rock)* el grupo
bandage la venda
bank el banco
  (river) la ribera
bank account la cuenta bancaria
banknote el billete
bar el bar
bar of chocolate la tableta de chocolate
barbecue la barbacoa
  to have a barbecue hacer una barbacoa
barber's la barbería
to bark ladrar
barn el granero
barrel *(wine/beer)* el barril
basement el sótano
basil la albahaca

basket la cesta
basketball el baloncesto
bat *(baseball, cricket)* el bate
  (creature) el murciélago
bath el baño
  to have a bath bañarse
bathing cap el gorro de baño
bathroom el cuarto de baño
  with bathroom con baño
battery *(radio, camera, etc)* la pila
  (in car) la batería
bay *(along coast)* la bahía
Bay of Biscay el golfo de Vizcaya
to be estar; ser
beach la playa
  private beach la playa privada
  sandy beach la playa de arena
  nudist beach la playa nudista
beach hut la caseta de playa
bean la alubia
beard la barba
beautiful hermoso(a)
beauty salon el salón de belleza
because porque
to become hacerse ; convertirse en ; llegar a ser
bed la cama
  double bed la cama de matrimonio
  single bed la cama individual
  sofa bed el sofá-cama
  twin beds las camas gemelas
bed clothes la ropa de cama
bedroom el dormitorio
bee la abeja
beef la ternera
beer la cerveza
before antes de
  before breakfast antes de desayunar
to begin empezar
behind detrás de
  behind the house detrás de la casa
beige beige ; beis
to believe creer
bell *(church)* la campana
  (door bell) el timbre
to belong to *(possess)* pertenecer a
  (club) ser miembro de
below debajo
belt el cinturón
bend *(in road)* la curva
berth *(plane, train, ship)* la litera
beside *(next to)* al lado de
  beside the bank al lado del banco
best el/la mejor
bet la apuesta

to bet on apostar por
better mejor
  better than mejor que
between entre
bib el babero
bicycle la bicicleta
  by bicycle en bicicleta
bicycle repair kit la caja de herramientas
bidet el bidé
big grande
  bigger than mayor que
bike *(pushbike)* la bicicleta
  (motorbike) la moto
bike lock el candado de la bicicleta
bikini el bikini
bill la factura
  (in restaurant) la cuenta
bin el cubo
bin liner la bolsa de la basura
binoculars los prismáticos
bird el pájaro
biro el bolí(grafo)
birth el nacimiento
birth certificate la partida de nacimiento
birthday el cumpleaños
  happy birthday! ¡feliz cumpleaños!
  my birthday is on ... mi cumpleaños es el...
birthday card la tarjeta de cumpleaños
birthday present el regalo de cumpleaños
biscuits las galletas
bit: *a bit of* un poco de
bite *(insect)* la picadura
  (animal) el mordisco
to bite morder
  (insect) picar
bitten *(by animal)* mordido(a)
  (by insect) picado(a)
bitter *(taste)* amargo(a)
black negro(a)
black ice la capa invisible de hielo en la carretera
blanket la manta
bleach *(household)* la lejía
to bleed sangrar
blender *(for food)* la licuadora
blind *(person)* ciego(a)
blind *(for window)* la persiana
  (roman) el estor
blister la ampolla
blocked *(road)* cortado(a)
  (pipe) obstruido(a)

blond *(person)* rubio(a)
blood la sangre
blood group el grupo sanguíneo
blood pressure la presión sanguínea
blood test el análisis de sangre
blouse la blusa
blow-dry el secado a mano
blue azul
  dark blue azul marino
  light blue azul claro
blunt *(knife, blade)* desafilado(a)
boar el jabalí
to board *(train, plane, etc)* subir
boarding card/pass la tarjeta de embarque
boarding house la pensión
boat *(large)* el barco
  (small) la barca
boat trip la excursión en barco
body el cuerpo
to boil hervir
boiled hervido(a)
boiler la caldera
bomb la bomba
bone el hueso
  (fish bone) la espina
bonfire la hoguera
bonnet *(car)* el capó
book el libro
to book reservar
booking la reserva
booking office *(train)* la ventanilla de billetes
bookshop la librería
boot *(car)* el maletero
boots las botas
border *(of country)* la frontera
boring aburrido(a)
born: *I was born in...* nací en...
to borrow pedir prestado
boss el/la jefe(a)
both ambos(as)
bottle la botella
  a bottle of wine una botella de vino
  a half-bottle media botella
bottle opener el abrebotellas
bottom *(of pool, garden)* el fondo
bowl *(for soup, etc)* el tazón ; el bol
bow tie la pajarita
box la caja

box office la taquilla
boxer shorts los calzoncillos
boy el chico
boyfriend el novio
bra el sujetador
bracelet la pulsera
brain el cerebro
brake el freno
to brake frenar
brake fluid el líquido de frenos
brake light la luz de freno
brake pads las pastillas de freno
branch (of tree) la rama
  (of bank, etc) la sucursal
brand (make) la marca
brass el latón
brave valiente
bread el pan
  wholemeal bread el pan integral
  French bread la barra de pan
  sliced bread el pan de molde
bread roll el panecillo
to break romper
breakable frágil
breakdown (car) la avería
  (nervous) la crisis nerviosa
breakdown van la grúa
breakfast el desayuno
breast el pecho
to breast-feed amamantar
to breathe respirar
brick el ladrillo
bride la novia
bridegroom el novio
bridge el puente
briefcase la cartera
Brillo pads® el nanas® ; el estropajo
to bring traer
Britain Gran Bretaña
British británico(a)
broccoli el brócoli
brochure el folleto
broken roto(a)
  my leg is broken me he roto la
  pierna
broken down (car, etc) averiado(a)
bronchitis la bronquitis
bronze el bronce
brooch el broche
broom (brush) la escoba
brother el hermano

brother-in-law el cuñado
brown marrón
bruise el moretón ; el cardenal
brush el cepillo
bubble bath el baño de
  espuma
bucket el cubo
buffet car el coche-comedor
to build construir
building el edificio
bulb (electric) la bombilla
bull el toro
bullfight la corrida de toros
bullfighter el torero
bullring la plaza de toros
bumbag la riñonera
bumper (on car) el parachoques
bunch (of flowers) el ramo
  (grapes) el racimo
bungee jumping el banyi
bureau de change la oficina de
  cambio
burger la hamburguesa
burglar el/la ladrón(a)
burglar alarm la alarma antirrobo
to burn quemar
burnt (food) quemado(a)
bus el autobús
bus pass el bonobús
bus station la estación de autobuses
bus stop la parada de autobús
bus ticket el billete de autobús
business el negocio
  on business de negocios
business card la tarjeta de visita
business class la clase preferente
businessman/woman el hombre/la
  mujer de negocios
business trip el viaje de
  negocios
busy ocupado(a)
but pero
butcher's la carnicería
butter la mantequilla
button el botón
to buy comprar
by (via) por
  (beside) al lado de
  by bus en autobús
  by car en coche
  by train en tren
  by ship en barco
bypass (road) la carretera de
  circunvalación

C

cab *(taxi)* el taxi
cabaret el cabaré
cabin *(on boat)* el camarote
cabin crew la tripulación de cabina
cablecar el teleférico
café el café
  internet café el cibercafé
cafetière la cafetera
cake *(big)* la tarta
  (little) el pastel
cake shop la pastelería
calculator la calculadora
calendar el calendario
call *(telephone)* la llamada
  a long distance call una conferencia
to call *(phone)* llamar por teléfono
calm tranquilo(a)
camcorder la videocámara
camera la cámara
camera case el estuche de la cámara
camera shop la tienda de fotografía
to camp acampar
camping gas el camping gas
camping stove el hornillo de gas
campsite el camping
to can *(to be able)* poder
  I can puedo
  we can podemos
  I cannot no puedo
  we cannot no podemos
can la lata
can opener el abrelatas
Canada (el) Canadá
Canadian canadiense
canal el canal
to cancel anular; cancelar
cancellation la cancelación
cancer el cáncer
candle la vela
canoe la canoa
canoeing: to go canoeing hacer piragüismo
cap *(hat)* la gorra
  (diaphragm) el diafragma
capital *(city)* la capital
car el coche
car alarm la alarma de coche
car ferry el transbordador ; el ferry
car hire el alquiler de coches
car insurance el seguro del coche
car keys las llaves del coche**

car park el aparcamiento
car parts los accesorios para el automóvil
car radio la radio del coche
car seat *(for children)* el asiento para niños
car wash el lavado (automático) de coches
carafe la jarra
caravan la caravana
carburettor el carburador
card *(greetings, business)* la tarjeta
  playing cards las cartas
cardboard el cartón
cardigan la chaqueta de punto
careful cuidadoso(a)
  be careful! ¡ten cuidado!
carpet *(rug)* la alfombra
  (fitted) la moqueta
carriage *(railway)* el vagón
carrot la zanahoria
to carry llevar
carton la caja
  (of cigarettes) el cartón
case *(suitcase)* la maleta
cash el dinero en efectivo
to cash *(cheque)* cobrar
cash desk la caja
cash dispenser el cajero automático
cashier el/la cajero(a)
cashpoint el cajero automático
casino el casino
casserole la cazuela
cassette el casete
cassette player el radiocasete
castanets las castañuelas
castle el castillo
casualty department urgencias
cat el gato
cat food la comida para gatos
catalogue el catálogo
to catch *(bus, train, etc)* coger
cathedral la catedral
Catholic católico(a)
cave la cueva
cavity *(in tooth)* la caries
CD el CD
CD player el lector de CD
ceiling el techo
cellar la bodega
cellphone el teléfono celular

cemetery el cementerio
centimetre el centímetro
central central
central heating la calefacción central
central locking (car) el cierre centralizado
centre el centro
century el siglo
ceramic la cerámica
cereal los cereales
certain (sure) seguro(a)
certificate el certificado
chain la cadena
chair la silla
chairlift el telesilla
chalet el chalet
chambermaid la camarera
Champagne el champán
change el cambio
  (small coins) el suelto
  (money returned) la vuelta
to change cambiar
  (clothes) cambiarse
  (train) hacer transbordo
  to change money cambiar dinero
changing room el probador
chapel la capilla
charcoal el carbón vegetal
charge (fee) el precio
to charge cobrar
  please charge it to my account cárguelo a mi cuenta, por favor
charger (for battery) el cargador
charter flight el vuelo chárter
cheap barato(a)
cheaper más barato(a)
cheap rate la tarifa baja
to check revisar ; comprobar
to check in (at airport) facturar el equipaje
  (at hotel) registrarse
check-in la facturación
cheek la mejilla
cheers! ¡salud!
cheese el queso
chef el chef
chemist's la farmacia
cheque el cheque
cheque book el talonario
cheque card la tarjeta bancaria
chest (of body) el pecho

chewing gum el chicle
chicken el pollo
chickenpox la varicela
child (boy) el niño
  (girl) la niña
children (infants) los niños
  for children para niños
child safety seat (car) el asiento de niños
chilli la guindilla ; el chile
chimney la chimenea
chin la barbilla
china la porcelana
chips las patatas fritas
chocolate el chocolate
chocolates los bombones
choir el coro
to choose escoger
chop (meat) la chuleta
chopping board la tabla de cortar
christening el bautizo
Christian name el nombre de pila
Christmas la Navidad
  merry Christmas! ¡feliz Navidad!
Christmas card la tarjeta de Navidad
Christmas Eve la Nochebuena
church la iglesia
cigar el puro
cigarette el cigarrillo
cigarette lighter el mechero
cigarette paper el papel de fumar
cinema el cine
circle (theatre) el anfiteatro
circuit breaker el cortacircuitos
circus el circo
cistern la cisterna
city la ciudad
city centre el centro de la ciudad
class: first class primera clase
  second class segunda clase
clean limpio(a)
to clean limpiar
cleaner (person) el/la encargado/a de la limpieza
cleanser (for face) el desmaquillador
clear claro(a)
client el/la cliente
cliff (along coast) el acantilado
  (in mountains) el precipicio
to climb (mountains) escalar
climbing boots las botas de escalar
Clingfilm® el rollo de plástico
clinic la clínica

cloakroom el guardarropa
clock el reloj
close by muy cerca
to close cerrar
closed *(shop, etc)* cerrado(a)
cloth *(rag)* el trapo
   (fabric) la tela
clothes la ropa
clothes line el tendedero
clothes peg la pinza
clothes shop la tienda de ropa
cloudy nublado(a)
club el club
clutch *(in car)* el embrague
coach *(bus)* el autocar
coach station la estación de
   autobuses
coach trip la excursión en autocar
coal el carbón
coast la costa
coastguard el/la guardacostas
coat el abrigo
coat hanger la percha
cockroach la cucaracha
cocktail el cóctel
cocoa el cacao
code el código
coffee el café
   black coffee el café solo
   white coffee el café con leche
   cappuccino el capuchino
   decaffeinated coffee el (café)
   descafeinado
coil *(IUD)* el DIU
coin la moneda
Coke® la Coca Cola®
colander el colador
cold frío(a)
   I'm cold tengo frío
   it's cold hace frío
   cold water el agua fría
cold *(illness)* el resfriado
   I have a cold estoy resfriado(a)
cold sore la calentura
collar el cuello
collar bone la clavícula
colleague el/la compañero(a) de
   trabajo
to collect recoger
collection la recogida
colour el color
colour-blind daltónico(a)
colour film *(for camera)* el carrete
   en color
comb el peine

to come venir
   (to arrive) llegar
to come back volver
to come in entrar
   come in! ¡pase!
comedy la comedia
comfortable cómodo(a)
company *(firm)* la empresa
compartment el compartimento
compass la brújula
to complain reclamar
complaint la reclamación ; la queja
complete completo(a)
to complete terminar
compulsory obligatorio(a)
computer el ordenador
computer disk *(floppy)* el disquete
computer game el juego de
   ordenador
computer program el programa de
   ordenador
concert el concierto
concert hall la sala de conciertos
concession el descuento
concussion la conmoción cerebral
conditioner el suavizante
condom el condón
conductor *(on bus)* el/la cobrador(a)
conference el congreso
to confirm confirmar
   please confirm por favor, confirme
confirmation *(flight, booking)* la
   confirmación
congratulations! ¡enhorabuena!
connection *(train, etc)* el enlace
constipated estreñido(a)
consulate el consulado
to consult consultar
to contact ponerse en contacto con
contact lens la lentilla
contact lens cleaner la solución
   limpiadora para lentillas
to continue continuar
contraceptive el anticonceptivo
contract el contrato
convenient: is it convenient? ¿le
   viene bien?
convulsions las convulsiones
to cook cocinar
cooked preparado(a)
cooker la cocina

cookies las galletas
cool fresco(a)
cool-box la nevera portátil
copper el cobre
copy (duplicate) la copia
(of book) el ejemplar
to copy copiar
coral el coral
cork el corcho
corkscrew el sacacorchos
corner la esquina
cornflakes los copos de maíz
corridor el pasillo
cortisone la cortisona
cosmetics los cosméticos
cost (price) el precio
to cost costar
how much does it cost? ¿cuánto
cuesta?
costume (swimming) el bañador
cot la cuna
cottage la casita de campo
cotton el algodón
cotton buds los bastoncillos
cotton wool el algodón hidrófilo
couchette la litera
to cough toser
cough la tos
cough mixture el jarabe para la tos
cough sweets los caramelos para
la tos
counter (in shop) el mostrador
(in bar) la barra
country (not town) el campo
(nation) el país
countryside el campo
couple (2 people) la pareja
a couple of... un par de ...
courgette el calabacín
courier service el servicio de
mensajero
course (of study) el curso
(of meal) el plato
cousin el/la primo(a)
cover charge (in restaurant) el
cubierto
cow la vaca
crafts la artesanía
craftsperson el/la artesano(a)
cramps los calambres
crash (car) el accidente

to crash (car) chocar
crash helmet el casco protector
cream (lotion) la crema
(on milk) la nata
soured cream la nata cortada
whipped cream la nata montada
credit card la tarjeta de crédito
crime el delito
crisps las patatas fritas
cross (crucifix) la cruz
to cross (road) cruzar
cross-channel ferry el transbordador
(que cruza el Canal de la Mancha)
cross country skiing el esquí de
fondo
crossing (sea) la travesía
crossroads el cruce
crossword puzzle el crucigrama
crowd la multitud
crowded concurrido(a)
crown la corona
cruise el crucero
crutches las muletas
to cry (weep) llorar
crystal el cristal
cucumber el pepino
cufflinks los gemelos
cul-de-sac el callejón sin salida
cup la taza
cupboard el armario
currant la pasa
currency la moneda
current (air, water, etc) la corriente
curtain la cortina
cushion el cojín
custom (tradition) la costumbre
customer el/la cliente
customs (control) la aduana
customs declaration la declaración
aduanera
cut el corte
to cut cortar
cutlery los cubiertos
to cycle ir en bicicleta
cycle track el carril bici
cycling el ciclismo
cyst el quiste
cystitis la cistitis

D

daily (each day) cada día; diario
dairy produce los productos lácteos
dam la presa

damage los daños
damp húmedo(a)
dance el baile
to dance bailar
danger el peligro
dangerous peligroso(a)
dark oscuro(a)
  after dark por la noche
date la fecha
date of birth la fecha de nacimiento
daughter la hija
daughter-in-law la cuñada
dawn el amanecer
day el día
  every day todos los días
  per day al día
dead muerto(a)
deaf sordo(a)
dear *(on letter)* querido(a)
  (expensive) caro(a)
debt la deuda
decaffeinated coffee el (café) descafeinado
  have you decaff? ¿tiene (café) descafeinado?
December diciembre
deck chair la tumbona
to declare declarar
  nothing to declare nada que declarar
deep profundo(a)
deep freeze el ultracongelador
deer el ciervo
to defrost descongelar
to de-ice descongelar
delay el retraso
  how long is the delay? ¿cuánto lleva de retraso?
delayed retrasado(a)
delicatessen la charcutería
delicious delicioso(a)
demonstration la manifestación
dental floss el hilo dental
dentist el/la dentista
dentures la dentadura postiza
deodorant el desodorante
department *(gen)* el departamento
  (in shop) la sección
department store los grandes almacenes
departure lounge la sala de embarque
departures las salidas
deposit la fianza
to describe describir

description la descripción
desk *(in hotel, airport)* el mostrador
dessert el postre
details los detalles
  (personal) los datos personales
detergent el detergente
detour el desvío
to develop *(photos)* revelar
diabetes la diabetes
diabetic diabético(a)
  I'm diabetic soy diabético(a)
to dial marcar
dialling code el prefijo
dialling tone el tono de marcar
diamond el diamante
diapers los pañales
diaphragm *(in body, contraception)* el diafragma
diarrhoea la diarrea
diary la agenda
dice los dados
dictionary el diccionario
to die morir
diesel el gasóleo
diet la dieta
  I'm on a diet estoy a dieta
  special diet la dieta especial
different distinto(a)
difficult difícil
to dilute diluir
dinghy el bote
dining room el comedor
dinner *(evening meal)* la cena
  to have dinner cenar
diplomat el/la diplomático(a)
direct *(train, etc)* directo(a)
directions *(instructions)* las instrucciones
  to ask for directions preguntar el camino
directory *(phone)* la guía telefónica
directory enquiries la información telefónica
dirty sucio(a)
disability la discapacidad
disabled minusválido(a)
to disagree no estar de acuerdo
to disappear desaparecer
disaster el desastre
disco la discoteca
discount el descuento

to discover descubrir
disease la enfermedad
dish el plato
dishtowel el paño de cocina
dishwasher el lavavajillas
dishwasher powder el detergente para lavavajillas
disinfectant el desinfectante
disk *(floppy)* el disquete
to dislocate *(joint)* dislocarse
disposable desechable
distant distante ; lejano(a)
distilled water el agua destilada
district el barrio
to disturb molestar
to dive tirarse al agua
diversion el desvío
divorced divorciado(a)
DIY shop la tienda de bricolaje
dizzy mareado(a)
to do hacer
doctor el/la médico(a)
documents los documentos
dog el perro
dog food la comida para perros
dog lead la correa del perro
doll la muñeca
dollar el dólar
domestic *(flight)* nacional
donor card la tarjeta de donante
door la puerta
doorbell el timbre
double doble
double bed la cama de matrimonio
double room la habitación doble
doughnut el donut
down: *to go down* bajar
downstairs abajo
drain el desagüe
draught *(of air)* la corriente
  there's a draught hay corriente
draught lager la cerveza de barril
drawer el cajón
drawing el dibujo
dress el vestido
to dress *(to get dressed)* vestirse
dressing *(for food)* el aliño
  (for wound) el vendaje
dressing gown la bata
drill *(tool)* la taladradora

drink la bebida
to drink beber
drinking water el agua potable
to drive conducir
driver *(of car)* el/la conductor(a)
driving licence el carné de conducir
drought la sequía
to drown ahogarse
drug la droga
  (medicine) la medicina
drunk borracho(a)
dry seco(a)
to dry secar
dry-cleaner's la tintorería ; la limpieza en seco
due: *when is it due?* ¿para cuándo está previsto?
dummy *(for baby)* el chupete
during durante
dust el polvo
duster el trapo del polvo
dustpan and brush el cepillo y recogedor
duty-free libre de impuestos
duvet el edredón
duvet cover la funda de edredón
dye el tinte
dynamo la dinamo

E

each cada
ear *(outside)* la oreja
  (inside) el oído
earache el dolor de oídos
  I have earache me duele el oído
earphones los auriculares
earplugs los tapones para los oídos
earrings los pendientes
earlier antes
early temprano
to earn ganar
earth la tierra
earthquake el terremoto
east el este
Easter la Pascua ; la Semana Santa
easy fácil
to eat comer
egg el huevo
  fried egg el huevo frito
  hard-boiled egg el huevo duro
  scrambled eggs los huevos revueltos
  soft-boiled egg el huevo pasado por agua

either... or... o... o...
elastic band la goma
elastoplast la tirita
elbow el codo
electric eléctrico(a)
electric blanket la manta eléctrica
electric razor la maquinilla de afeitar
electrician el/la electricista
electricity la electricidad
electricity meter el contador de electricidad
electric shock la descarga eléctrica
elevator el ascensor
e-mail el correo electrónico
  to e-mail s.o. mandar un email a alguien
e-mail address la dirección de email ; el email
embassy la embajada
emergency la emergencia
emergency exit la salida de emergencia
empty vacío(a)
end el fin
engaged *(to marry)* prometido(a)
  (toilet, phone) ocupado(a)
engine el motor
England Inglaterra
English inglés (inglesa)
  (language) el inglés
Englishman/-woman el inglés/la inglesa
to enjoy *(to like)* gustar
  I enjoy swimming me gusta nadar
  I enjoy dancing me gusta bailar
  enjoy your meal! ¡que aproveche!
to enjoy oneself divertirse
enough bastante
  that's enough ya basta
enquiry desk la información
to enter entrar en
entertainment el entretenimiento
entrance la entrada
entrance fee el precio de entrada
envelope el sobre
epileptic epiléptico(a)
epileptic fit el ataque epiléptico
equal igual
equipment el equipo
eraser la goma (de borrar)
error el error
escalator la escalera mecánica
to escape escapar
espadrilles las alpargatas

essential imprescindible
estate agent's la agencia inmobiliaria
euro el euro
eurocheque el Eurocheque
Europe la Europa
European el/la europeo(a)
European Union la Unión Europea
evening la tarde
  this evening esta tarde
  tomorrow evening mañana por la tarde
  in the evening por la tarde
evening dress el traje de etiqueta
evening meal la cena
every cada
everyone todo el mundo
everything todo
everywhere en todas partes
examination el examen
example: *for example* por ejemplo
excellent excelente
except excepto
excess baggage el exceso de equipaje
exchange el cambio
to exchange cambiar
exchange rate el tipo de cambio
exciting emocionante
excursion la excursión
excuse: *excuse me!* perdón
exercise *(physical)* el ejercicio
exhaust pipe el tubo de escape
exhibition la exposición
exit la salida
expenses los gastos
expensive caro(a)
expert el/la experto(a)
to expire *(ticket, passport)* caducar
to explain explicar
explosion la explosión
to export exportar
express *(train)* el expreso
express: *to send a letter express* enviar una carta por correo urgente
extension *(electrical)* el alargador
extra *(in addition)* de más
  (more) adicional
eye el ojo
eyebrows las cejas
eye drops el colirio

eyelashes las pestañas
eyeliner el lápiz de ojos

F

fabric la tela
face la cara
face cloth la toallita
facial la limpieza de cutis
facilities las instalaciones
factory la fábrica
to faint desmayarse
fainted desmayado(a)
fair (hair) rubio(a)
  (just) justo(a)
fair (funfair) el parque de atracciones
fake falso(a)
fall (autumn) el otoño
to fall caer ; caerse
  he/she has fallen se ha caído
false teeth la dentadura postiza
family la familia
famous famoso(a)
fan (electric) el ventilador
  (hand-held) el abanico
  (football, etc) el/la hincha
  (jazz, etc) el/la aficionado(a)
fan belt la correa del ventilador
fancy dress el disfraz
far lejos
  is it far? ¿está lejos?
  how far is it? ¿a cuánto está?
farm la granja
farmer el/la granjero(a)
farmhouse la granja
fashionable de moda
fast rápido(a)
  too fast demasiado rápido
to fasten (seatbelt, etc) abrocharse
fat (plump) gordo(a)
  (in food, on person) la grasa
  saturated fats las grasas saturadas
  unsaturated fats las grasas insaturadas
father el padre
father-in-law el suegro
fault (defect) el defecto
  it's not my fault no tengo la culpa
favour el favor
favourite preferido(a)
to fax mandar por fax
fax el fax

by fax por fax
fax number el número de fax
February febrero
to feed dar de comer
to feel sentir
  I don't feel well no me siento bien
  I feel sick estoy mareado(a)
feet los pies
felt-tip pen el rotulador
female mujer
ferry el transbordador
festival el festival
to fetch (to bring) traer
  (to go and get) ir a buscar
fever la fiebre
few pocos(as)
  a few algunos(as)
fiancé(e) el/la novio(a) ; el/la prometido(a)
field el campo
to fight luchar
file (computer) el fichero
  (nail) la lima
to fill llenar
  (form) rellenar
  fill it up, please! (car) lleno, por favor
fillet el filete
filling (in tooth) el empaste
film (at cinema) la película
  (for camera) el carrete
filter el filtro
to find encontrar
fine (to be paid) la multa
finger el dedo
to finish acabar
finished terminado(a)
fire (flames) el fuego
  (blaze) el incendio
  fire! ¡fuego!
fire alarm la alarma de incendios
fire brigade los bomberos
fire engine el coche de bomberos
fire escape la salida de incendios
fire exit la salida de incendios
fire extinguisher el extintor
fireplace la chimenea
fireworks los fuegos artificiales
firm (company) la empresa
first primero(a)
first aid los primeros auxilios
first aid kit el botiquín de primeros auxilios
first class de primera clase
first name el nombre de pila

fish el pescado
to fish pescar
fisherman el pescador
fishing permit la licencia de pesca
fishing rod la caña de pescar
fishmonger's la pescadería
fit *(seizure)* el ataque
to fit *(clothes)* quedar bien
  it doesn't fit no queda bien
to fix arreglar
  can you fix it? ¿puede arreglarlo?
fizzy con gas
flag la bandera
flames las llamas
flash *(for camera)* el flash
flashlight la linterna
flask *(thermos)* el termo
flat *(apartment)* el piso
flat llano(a)
  (battery) descargado(a)
  (beer) sin gas
  it's flat ya no tiene gas
flat tyre la rueda pinchada
flavour el sabor
  which flavour? ¿qué sabor?
flaw el defecto
fleas las pulgas
flesh la carne
flex el cable eléctrico
flight el vuelo
flip flops las chancletas
flippers las aletas
flood la inundación
  flash flood la riada
floor *(of building)* el piso
  (of room) el suelo
  which floor? ¿qué piso?
  on the ground floor en la planta baja
  on the first floor en el primer piso
  on the second floor en el segundo piso
floorcloth el trapo del suelo
florist's shop la floristería
flour la harina
flower la flor
flu la gripe
fly la mosca
to fly volar
fly sheet el toldo impermeable
fog la niebla
foggy: *it's foggy* hay niebla
foil *(tinfoil)* el papel de estaño
to fold doblar
to follow seguir

food la comida
food poisoning la intoxicación por alimentos
foot el pie
  on foot a pie
football el fútbol
football match el partido de fútbol
football pitch el campo de fútbol
football player el/la futbolista
footpath *(in country)* el sendero
for para
  for me para mi
  for you para usted
  for him/her/us para él/ella/nosotros
forbidden prohibido(a)
forehead la frente
foreign extranjero(a)
foreign currency la moneda extranjera
foreigner el/la extranjero(a)
forest el bosque
forever para siempre
to forget olvidar
fork *(for eating)* el tenedor
  (in road) la bifurcación
form *(document)* el impreso
formal dress el traje de etiqueta
fortnight quince días
forward adelante
foul *(football)* la falta
fountain la fuente
four-wheel drive la tracción a cuatro ruedas
fox el zorro
fracture la fractura
fragile frágil
fragrance el perfume
frame *(picture)* el marco
France Francia
free *(not occupied)* libre
  (costing nothing) gratis
freezer el congelador
French francés/francesa
  (language) el francés
French fries las patatas fritas
frequent frecuente
fresh fresco(a)
fresh-water de agua dulce
Friday el viernes
fridge el frigorífico
fried frito(a)

f/g eng-spanish

friend el/la amigo(a)
frisbee® el frisbee®
frog la rana
from de ; desde
  from Scotland de Escocia
  from England de Inglaterra
front la parte delantera
  in front of delante de
front door la puerta de la calle
frost la helada
frozen congelado(a)
fruit la fruta
  dried fruit la fruta seca
fruit juice el zumo (de fruta)
fruit salad la macedonia
to fry freir
frying pan la sartén
fuel *(petrol)* la gasolina
fuel gauge el indicador de la gasolina
fuel tank el depósito de gasolina
fuel pump *(in car)* el surtidor de gasolina
full lleno(a)
  (occupied) ocupado(a)
full board pensión completa
fumes *(of car)* los gases
fun la diversión
funeral el funeral
funfair el parque de atracciones
funny *(amusing)* divertido(a)
fur la piel
furnished amueblado(a)
furniture los muebles
fuse el fusible
fuse box la caja de fusibles
future el futuro

G

gallery la galería
gallon = approx. 4.5 litres
game el juego
  (animal) la caza
garage el garaje
  (for repairs) el taller
  (for petrol) la gasolinera
garden el jardín
garlic el ajo
gas el gas
gas cooker la cocina de gas

gas cylinder la bombona de gas
gastritis la gastritis
gate *(airport)* la puerta
gay *(person)* gay
gear la marcha
  first gear la primera
  second gear la segunda
  third gear la tercera
  fourth gear la cuarta
  neutral el punto muerto
  reverse la marcha atrás
gearbox la caja de cambios
generous generoso(a)
gents *(toilet)* los servicios de caballeros
genuine auténtico(a)
German alemán/alemana
  (language) el alemán
German measles la rubeola
Germany Alemania
to get *(to obtain)* conseguir
  (to receive) recibir
  (to bring) traer
to get in *(vehicle)* subir (al)
to get out *(of vehicle)* bajarse de
gift el regalo
gift shop la tienda de regalos
girl la chica
girlfriend la novia
to give dar
to give back devolver
glacier el glaciar
glass *(for drinking)* el vaso
  (substance) el cristal
  a glass of water un vaso de agua
  a glass of wine un vaso de vino
glasses *(spectacles)* las gafas
glasses case la funda de gafas
gloves los guantes
glue el pegamento
to go ir
  I'm going to ... voy a...
  we're going to ... vamos a...
  to go home irse a casa
to go back volver
to go in entrar (en)
to go out salir
goat la cabra
God Dios
goggles *(for swimming)* las gafas de natación
  (for skiing) las gafas de esquí
gold el oro
golf el golf
golf ball la pelota de golf
golf clubs los palos de golf

golf course el campo de golf
good bueno(a)
  very good muy bueno
good afternoon buenas tardes
goodbye adiós
good day buenos días
good evening buenas tardes
  (later) buenas noches
good morning buenos días
good night buenas noches
goose el ganso
gram(me) el gramo
grandchild el/la nieto(a)
granddaughter la nieta
grandfather el abuelo
grandmother la abuela
grandparents los abuelos
grandson el nieto
grapes las uvas
grass la hierba
grated *(cheese, etc)* rallado(a)
grater *(for cheese, etc)* el rallador
greasy grasiento(a)
great *(big)* grande
  (wonderful) estupendo(a)
Great Britain Gran Bretaña
green verde
green card la carta verde
greengrocer's la frutería
greetings card la tarjeta de
  felicitación
grey gris
grill hacer al grill
  (barbecue) la parrilla
to grill gratinar
  (in barbecue) asar a la parrilla
grilled gratinado(a)
  (in barbecue) a la parrilla
grocer's la tienda de alimentación
ground el suelo
ground floor la planta baja
  on the ground floor en la planta
  baja
groundsheet la tela impermeable
group el grupo
guarantee la garantía
guard *(on train)* el/la jefe(a) de tren
guest el/la invitado(a)
  (in hotel) el/la huésped
guesthouse la pensión
guide *(tour guide)* el/la guía
to guide guiar
guidebook la guía turística
guided tour la visita con guía

guitar la guitarra
gun la pistola
gym el gimnasio
gym shoes las zapatillas de deporte

H

haemorrhoids las hemorroides
hail el granizo
hair el pelo
hairbrush el cepillo del pelo
haircut el corte de pelo
hairdresser el/la peluquero(a)
hairdryer el secador de pelo
hair dye el tinte de pelo
hair gel el gel
hairgrip la horquilla
hair mousse la espuma del pelo
hair spray la laca
half medio(a)
  half an hour media hora
half board media pensión
half fare el billete reducido para
  niños
half-price a mitad de precio
ham el jamón
  (cooked) el jamón de York
  (cured) el jamón serrano
hamburger la hamburguesa
hammer el martillo
hand la mano
handbag el bolso
hand luggage el equipaje de mano
hand-made hecho(a) a mano
handicapped minusválido(a)
handkerchief el pañuelo
handle *(of cup)* el asa
  (of door) el picaporte ; el pomo
handlebars el manillar
hands-free phone el teléfono de
  manos libres
handsome guapo(a)
hanger *(coat hanger)* la percha
hang gliding el vuelo con ala delta
hangover la resaca
to hang up *(phone)* colgar
to happen pasar
  what happened? ¿qué ha pasado?
happy feliz
  happy birthday! ¡feliz cumpleaños!
harbour el puerto

hard duro(a)
  (difficult) difícil
hard disk el disco duro
hardware shop la ferretería
to harm *(person)* hacer daño a
  (crops, etc) dañar
harvest la cosecha
hat el sombrero
to have tener
  I have ... tengo
  I don't have ... no tengo...
  we have ... tenemos...
  we don't have ... no tenemos...
  do you have ...? ¿tiene...?
to have to tener que
hay fever la alergia al polen
he él
head la cabeza
headache el dolor de cabeza
  I have a headache me duele la cabeza
headlights los faros
headphones los auriculares
head waiter el maître
health la salud
health food shop la tienda de dietética
healthy sano(a)
to hear oír
hearing aid el audífono
heart el corazón
heart attack el infarto
heartburn el ardor de estómago
heater el calentador
heating la calefacción
to heat up *(milk, food)* calentar
heavy pesado(a)
heel *(of foot)* el talón
  (of shoe) el tacón
heel bar la tienda de reparación de calzado en el acto
height la altura
helicopter el helicóptero
hello hola
  (on phone) ¿diga?
helmet *(for bike, etc)* el casco
help! ¡socorro!
to help ayudar
  can you help me? ¿puede ayudarme?
hem el dobladillo
hepatitis la hepatitis

her su
herb la hierba
herbal tea la infusión
here aquí
  here is ... aquí tiene...
  here is my passport aquí tiene mi pasaporte
hernia la hernia
hi! ¡hola!
to hide *(something)* esconder
  (oneself) esconderse
high alto(a)
high blood pressure la tensión alta
high chair la silla alta para niños
high tide la marea alta
hill la colina
hill-walking el montañismo
him él
hip la cadera
hip replacement la prótesis de cadera
hire *(bike, boat, etc)* el alquiler
  car hire el alquiler de coches
  bike hire el alquiler de bicicletas
  boat hire el alquiler de barcas
  ski hire el alquiler de esquís
to hire alquilar
hired car el coche de alquiler
his su
historic histórico(a)
history la historia
to hit pegar
to hitchhike hacer autostop
HIV positive seropositivo(a)
hobby el hobby ; el pasatiempo
to hold tener
  (to contain) contener
hold-up *(traffic jam)* el atasco
hole el agujero
holiday las vacaciones
  (public) la fiesta
  on holiday de vacaciones
holiday rep el/la guía turístico(a)
home la casa
  at home en casa
homesick: *to be homesick* tener morriña
  I'm homesick tengo morriña
homosexual homosexual
honest sincero(a)
honey la miel
honeymoon la luna de miel
hood *(jacket)* la capucha
hook *(fishing)* el anzuelo
to hope esperar

I hope so/not espero que sí/no
horn *(car)* el claxon
hors d'oeuvre los entremeses
horse el caballo
horse racing la hípica
horse riding la equitación
hosepipe la manguera
hospital el hospital
hostel el hostal
hot caliente
  I'm hot tengo calor
  it's hot (weather) hace calor
  hot water el agua caliente
hot-water bottle la bolsa de agua caliente
hotel el hotel
hour la hora
  half an hour media hora
house la casa
housewife/husband la/el ama(o) de casa
house wine el vino de la casa
housework las tareas domésticas
how *(in what way)* cómo
  how much? ¿cuánto?
  how many? ¿cuántos?
  how are you? ¿cómo está?
hungry: *to be hungry* tener hambre
to hunt cazar
hunting permit el permiso de caza
hurry: *I'm in a hurry* tengo prisa
to hurt *(injure)* hacer daño
  my back hurts me duele la espalda
  that hurts eso duele
husband el marido
hut *(bathing/beach)* la caseta
  (mountain) el refugio
hydrofoil el hidrodeslizador
hypodermic needle la aguja hipodérmica

I

I yo
ice el hielo
  (cube) el cubito
  with/without ice con/sin hielo
ice box la nevera
icecream el helado
ice lolly el polo
ice rink la pista de patinaje
to ice skate patinar sobre hielo
ice skates los patines de hielo
iced tea el té helado
idea la idea

identity card el carné de identidad
if si
ignition el encendido
ignition key la llave de contacto
ill enfermo(a)
illness la enfermedad
immediately inmediatamente ; en seguida
immersion heater el calentador eléctrico
immigration la inmigración
immunisation la inmunización
to import importar
important importante
impossible imposible
to improve mejorar
in dentro de ; en
  in 10 minutes dentro de diez minutos
  in London en Londres
in front of delante de
inch la pulgada = approx. 2.5 cm
included incluido(a)
inconvenient inoportuno(a)
to increase aumentar
indicator *(in car)* el intermitente
indigestion la indigestión
indigestion tablets las pastillas para la indigestión
indoors dentro
infection la infección
infectious contagioso(a)
information la información
information desk la información
ingredients los ingredientes
inhaler *(for medication)* el inhalador
injection la inyección
to injure herir
injured herido(a)
injury la herida
ink la tinta
inn la pensión
inner tube la cámara
inquiries información
inquiry desk la información
insect el insecto
insect bite la picadura de insecto
insect repellent la loción contra insectos
inside dentro de
instant coffee el café instantáneo

instead of en lugar de
instructor el/la instructor(a)
insulin la insulina
insurance el seguro
insurance certificate el certificado de seguros
to insure asegurar
insured asegurado(a)
to intend to pensar
interesting interesante
international internacional
internet el Internet
  internet café el cibercafé
interpreter el/la intérprete
interval *(theatre, etc)* el descanso; el intermedio
interview la entrevista
into en
  into town al centro
to introduce to presentar a
invitation la invitación
to invite invitar
invoice la factura
Ireland Irlanda
Irish irlandés/irlandesa
iron *(for clothes)* la plancha
  (metal) el hierro
to iron planchar
ironing board la tabla de planchar
ironmonger's la ferretería
is es/está
island la isla
it lo/la
Italian italiano(a)
  (language) el italiano
Italy Italia
itch el picor
to itch picar
  it itches (me) pica
item el artículo
itemized bill la factura detallada

J

jack *(for car)* el gato
jacket la chaqueta
jam *(food)* la mermelada
jammed *(stuck)* atascado(a)
January enero
jar *(honey, jam, etc)* el tarro
jaundice la ictericia

jaw la mandíbula
jealous celoso(a)
jeans los vaqueros
jelly *(dessert)* la gelatina
jellyfish la medusa
jet ski la moto acuática
jetty el embarcadero
Jewish judío(a)
jeweller's la joyería
jewellery las joyas
job el empleo
to jog hacer footing
to join *(club, etc)* hacerse socio de
to join in participar en
joint *(body)* la articulación
to joke bromear
joke la broma
journalist el/la periodista
journey el viaje
judge el/la juez(a)
jug la jarra
juice el zumo
  a carton of juice un brik de zumo
July julio
to jump saltar
jumper el jersey
jump leads *(for car)* los cables de arranque
junction *(road)* la bifurcación
June junio
jungle la jungla
just: *just two* sólo dos
  I've just arrived acabo de llegar

K

to keep *(to retain)* guardar
kennel la caseta
kettle el hervidor (de agua)
key la llave
  card key (ie used in hotel) la llave tarjeta
keyboard el teclado
keyring el llavero
to kick dar una patada a
kid *(child)* el/la crío(a)
kidneys los riñones
to kill matar
kilo(gram) el kilo(gramo)
kilometre el kilómetro
kind *(person)* amable
kind *(sort)* la clase
  what kind? ¿qué clase?
king el rey

kiosk el quiosco
kiss el beso
to kiss besar
kitchen la cocina
kitchen paper el papel de cocina
kite la cometa
knee la rodilla
knee highs las medias cortas
knickers las bragas
knife el cuchillo
to knit hacer punto
to knock (on door) llamar
to knock down (car) atropellar
to knock over (vase, glass) tirar
knot el nudo
to know (have knowledge of) saber
  (person, place) conocer
  I don't know no sé
to know how to saber
  to know how to swim saber nadar
kosher kosher

L

label la etiqueta
lace (fabric) el encaje
laces (for shoes) los cordones
ladder la escalera de mano
ladies (toilet) los servicios de señoras
lady la señora
lager la cerveza
  bottled lager la cerveza de botella
  draught lager la cerveza de barril
lake el lago
lamb el cordero
lamp la lámpara
lamppost la farola
lampshade la pantalla (de lámpara)
land el terreno
to land aterrizar
landlady la dueña (de la casa)
landlord el dueño (de la casa)
landslide el desprendimiento de tierras
lane el carril
language el idioma ; la lengua
language school la escuela de idiomas
laptop el ordenador portátil
large grande
last último(a)
  the last bus el último autobús
  the last train el último tren
  last night anoche
  last week la semana pasada
  last year el año pasado

  last time la última vez
late tarde
  the train is late el tren viene con retraso
  sorry I'm late siento llegar tarde
later más tarde
to laugh reírse
launderette la lavandería automática
laundry service el servicio de lavandería
lavatory (in house) el wáter
  (in public place) los servicios
law la ley
lawn el césped
lawyer el/la abogado(a)
laxative el laxante
layby la zona de descanso
lead (electric) el cable
lead (metal) el plomo
lead-free sin plomo
leaf la hoja
leak (of gas, liquid) la fuga
  (in roof) la gotera
to leak: it's leaking (radiator, etc) está goteando
to learn aprender
lease (rental) el alquiler
leather el cuero
to leave (a place) irse de
  (leave behind) dejar
  when does the train leave? ¿a qué hora sale el tren?
left: on/to the left a la izquierda
left-handed (person) zurdo(a)
left-luggage (office) la consigna
left-luggage locker la consigna automática
leg la pierna
legal legal
leisure centre el polideportivo
lemon el limón
lemonade la gaseosa
to lend prestar
length la longitud
lens (photographic) el objetivo
  (contact lens) la lentilla
lesbian lesbiana
less menos
  less than menos de
lesson la clase
to let (to allow) permitir
  (to hire out) alquilar

letter la carta
   (of alphabet) la letra
letterbox el buzón
lettuce la lechuga
level crossing el paso a nivel
library la biblioteca
licence el permiso
   (driving) el carné de conducir
lid la tapa
lie *(untruth)* la mentira
to lie mentir
to lie down acostarse
lifebelt el salvavidas
lifeboat el bote salvavidas
lifeguard el/la socorrista
life insurance el seguro de vida
life jacket el chaleco salvavidas
life raft la balsa salvavidas
lift *(elevator)* el ascensor
   can you give me a lift? ¿me lleva?
lift pass *(on ski slopes)* el forfait
light *(not heavy)* ligero(a)
light la luz
   have you a light? ¿tiene fuego?
light bulb la bombilla
lighter el encendedor ; el mechero
lighthouse el faro
lightning el relámpago
like *(similar to)* como
to like gustar
   I like coffee me gusta el café
   I don't like... no me gusta...
   I'd like to... me gustaría...
   we'd like to... nos gustaría...
lilo® la colchoneta hinchable
lime *(fruit)* la lima
line *(row, queue)* la fila
   (telephone) la línea
linen el lino
lingerie la lencería
lips los labios
lip-reading la lectura de labios
lip salve el cacao para los labios
lipstick la barra de labios
liqueur el licor
list la lista
to listen to escuchar
litre el litro
litter *(rubbish)* la basura
little pequeño(a)
   a little... un poco...

to live vivir
   I live in Edinburgh vivo en Edimburgo
   he lives in a flat vive en un piso
liver el hígado
living room el cuarto de estar ; el salón
loaf el pan de molde
local de la región ; del país
lock *(on door, box)* la cerradura
   the lock is broken la cerradura está rota
to lock cerrar con llave
locker *(luggage)* la consigna
locksmith el/la cerrajero(a)
log *(for fire)* el leño
log book *(car)* los papeles del coche
lollipop la piruleta
London Londres
   in London en Londres
   to London a Londres
long largo(a)
   for a long time (por) mucho tiempo
long-sighted hipermétrope
to look after cuidar
to look at mirar
to look for buscar
loose suelto(a)
   it's come loose se ha soltado
lorry el camión
to lose perder
lost perdido(a)
   I've lost... he perdido...
   I'm lost me he perdido
lost property office la oficina de objetos perdidos
lot: *a lot of* mucho
lotion la loción
lottery la lotería
loud *(sound, voice)* fuerte
   (volume) alto(a)
lounge el salón
love el amor
to love *(person)* querer
   I love swimming me encanta nadar
   I love you te quiero
lovely precioso(a)
low bajo(a)
low-alcohol con baja graduación
low-fat bajo(a) en calorías
low tide la marea baja
luck la suerte
lucky: to be lucky tener suerte
luggage el equipaje
luggage allowance el equipaje permitido

luggage rack el portaequipajes
luggage tag la etiqueta
luggage trolley el carrito
lump *(swelling)* el bulto
  (on head) el chichón
lunch la comida
lunch break la hora de la comida
lung el pulmón
luxury de lujo

M

machine la máquina
mad loco(a)
magazine la revista
maggot el gusano
magnet el imán
magnifying glass la lupa
maid *(in hotel)* la camarera
maiden name el apellido de soltera
mail el correo
  by mail por correo
main principal
main course *(of meal)* el plato principal
main road carretera principal
Majorca Mallorca
make *(brand)* la marca
to make hacer
make-up el maquillaje
male masculino(a)
mallet el mazo
man el hombre
to manage *(be in charge of)* dirigir
manager el/la gerente
manual *(gear change)* manual
many muchos(as)
map *(of region, country)* el mapa
  (of town) el plano
marble el mármol
March marzo
margarine la margarina
marina el puerto deportivo
mark *(stain)* la mancha
market el mercado
  where is the market? ¿dónde está el mercado?
  when is the market? ¿cuándo hay mercado?
market place la plaza (del mercado)
marmalade la mermelada de naranja
married casado(a)
  I'm married estoy casado(a)
  are you married? ¿está casado(a)?

to marry casarse con
marsh la marisma
mascara el rímel®
masher *(potato)* el pasapurés
mass *(in church)* la misa
mast el mástil
masterpiece la obra maestra
match *(game)* el partido
matches las cerillas
material *(cloth)* la tela
to matter importar
  it doesn't matter no importa
  what's the matter? ¿qué pasa?
mattress el colchón
May mayo
mayonnaise la mayonesa
maximum máximo(a)
meal la comida
to mean querer decir
  what does this mean? ¿qué quiere decir esto?
measles el sarampión
to measure medir
meat la carne
mechanic el/la mecánico(a)
medical insurance el seguro médico
medical treatment el tratamiento médico
medicine la medicina
medieval medieval
Mediterranean el Mediterráneo
medium rare *(meat)* medio(a) hecho(a)
to meet *(by chance)* encontrarse con
  (by arrangement) ver
  I'm meeting her tomorrow he quedado con ella mañana
meeting la reunión
meeting point el punto de reunión
to melt derretir
member *(of club, etc)* el/la socio(a)
membership fee la cuota de socio
memory el recuerdo
men los hombres
to mend arreglar
meningitis la meningitis
menu la carta
  set menu el menú del día
message el mensaje
metal el metal
meter el contador

metre el metro
metro (underground) el metro
metro station la estación de metro
microwave oven el (horno) microondas
midday las doce del mediodía
middle el medio
middle-aged de mediana edad
midge el mosquito enano
midnight la medianoche
 at midnight a medianoche
migraine la jaqueca ; la migraña
 I've a migraine tengo migraña
mile la milla
milk la leche
 fresh milk la leche fresca
 hot milk la leche caliente
 long-life milk la leche de larga duración (UHT)
 powdered milk la leche en polvo
 semi-skimmed milk la leche semidesnatada
 skimmed milk la leche desnatada
 soya milk la leche de soja
 with milk con leche
milkshake el batido
millimetre el milímetro
mince (meat) la carne picada
mind: do you mind if ...? ¿le importa que...?
 I don't mind no me importa
mineral water el agua mineral
minibar el minibar
minimum el mínimo
minister (political) el/la ministro(a)
 (church) el/la pastor(a)
minor road la carretera secundaria
mint (herb) la menta
 (sweet) la pastilla de menta
minute el minuto
mirror el espejo
miscarriage el aborto no provocado
to miss (train, etc) perder
Miss la señorita
missing (lost) perdido(a)
 my son is missing se ha perdido mi hijo
mistake el error
misty: it's misty hay neblina
misunderstanding la equivocación
to mix mezclar
mixer (food processor) el robot
 (hand-held) la batidora

mobile phone el (teléfono) móvil
modem el módem
modern moderno(a)
moisturizer la leche hidratante
mole (on skin) el lunar
moment el momento
 just a moment un momento
monastery el monasterio
Monday el lunes
money el dinero
 I've no money no tengo dinero
moneybelt la riñonera
money order el giro postal
month el mes
 this month este mes
 last month el mes pasado
 next month el mes que viene
monthly mensualmente
monument el monumento
moon la luna
mooring el atracadero
mop la fregona
moped la moto
more más
 more than más que
 more wine más vino
morning la mañana
 in the morning por la mañana
 this morning esta mañana
 tomorrow morning mañana por la mañana
morning-after pill la píldora (anticonceptiva) del día después
mosque la mezquita
mosquito el mosquito
mosquito bite la picadura de mosquito
mosquito net la mosquitera
mosquito repellent el repelente contra mosquitos
most: most of la mayor parte de
moth (clothes) la polilla
mother la madre
mother-in-law la suegra
motor el motor
motorbike la moto
motorboat la lancha motora
motorway la autopista
mountain la montaña
mountain bike la bicicleta de montaña
mountain rescue el rescate de montaña
mountaineering el montañismo
mouse (animal, computer) el ratón

moustache el bigote
mouth la boca
mouthwash el enjuague bucal
to move mover
  it isn't moving no se mueve
movie la película
to mow cortar (el césped)
Mr el señor (Sr.)
Mrs la señora (Sra.)
Ms la señora (Sra.)
much mucho
  too much demasiado
muddy embarrado(a)
mugging el atraco
mumps las paperas
muscle el músculo
museum el museo
mushrooms los champiñones
music la música
musical musical
must *(to have to)* deber
  I must debo
  we must debemos
  I musn't no debo
  we musn't no debemos
mustard la mostaza
my mi

N

nail *(fingernail)* la uña
  (metal) el clavo
nailbrush el cepillo de uñas
nail clippers el cortaúñas
nail file la lima de uñas
nail polish el esmalte de uñas
nail polish remover el quitaesmalte
nail scissors las tijeras de uñas
name el nombre
  my name is... me llamo...
  what's your name? ¿cómo se llama?
nanny la niñera
napkin la servilleta
nappies los pañales
narrow estrecho(a)
national nacional
national park el parque nacional
nationality la nacionalidad
natural natural
nature la naturaleza
nature reserve la reserva natural
navy blue azul marino
near to cerca de
  near to the bank cerca del banco

  is it near? ¿está cerca?
necessary necesario(a)
neck el cuello
necklace el collar
nectarine la nectarina
to need necesitar
  I need... necesito...
  we need... necesitamos...
  I need to go tengo que ir
needle la aguja
  a needle and thread una aguja e hilo
negative *(photo)* el negativo
neighbour el/la vecino(a)
nephew el sobrino
net la red
  the Net la Red
never nunca
  I never drink wine nunca bebo vino
new nuevo(a)
news *(TV, radio, etc)* las noticias
newsagent's la tienda de prensa
newspaper el periódico
newsstand el kiosko de prensa
New Year el Año Nuevo
  happy New Year! ¡feliz Año Nuevo!
New Year's Eve la Nochevieja
New Zealand Nueva Zelanda
next próximo(a)
  next to al lado de
  next week la próxima semana
  the next stop la próxima parada
  the next train el próximo tren
nice *(person)* simpático(a)
  (place, holiday) bonito(a)
niece la sobrina
night la noche
  at night por la noche
  last night anoche
  per night por noche
  tomorrow night mañana por la noche
  tonight esta noche
night club la discoteca
nightdress el camisón
night porter el guarda nocturno
no no
  no entry prohibida la entrada
  no smoking prohibido fumar
  (without) sin
  no sugar sin azúcar
  no ice sin hielo
  no problem ¡por supuesto!

nobody nadie
noise el ruido
  it's very noisy hay mucho ruido
non-alcoholic sin alcohol
none ninguno(a)
non-smoker el/la no fumador(a)
non-smoking no fumador
north el norte
Northern Ireland Irlanda del Norte
nose la nariz
not no
  I am not... no estoy ...; no soy ...
note *(banknote)* el billete
  (written) la nota
note pad el bloc
nothing nada
  nothing else nada más
notice *(sign)* el anuncio
  (warning) el aviso
notice board el tablón de anuncios
novel la novela
November noviembre
now ahora
nowhere en ninguna parte
nuclear nuclear
nudist beach la playa nudista
number el número
numberplate *(car)* la matrícula
nurse la/el enfermera(o)
nursery school la guardería infantil
nursery slope la pista para principiantes
nut *(for bolt)* la tuerca
nuts *(to eat)* los frutos secos

O

oar el remo
oats los copos de avena
to obtain obtener
occupation *(work)* la profesión
ocean el océano
October octubre
odd *(strange)* raro(a)
of de
  a glass of wine un vaso de vino
  made of ... hecho(a) de...
off *(light, etc)* apagado(a)
  (rotten) pasado(a)
office la oficina
often a menudo
  how often? ¿cada cuánto?
oil el aceite
oil filter el filtro de aceite
oil gauge el indicador del aceite
ointment la pomada
OK vale
old viejo(a)
  how old are you? ¿cuántos años tiene?
  I'm ... years old tengo ... años
old age pensioner el/la pensionista de la tercera edad
olive la aceituna
olive oil el aceite de oliva
olive tree el olivo
on *(light, TV, engine)* encendido(a)
on sobre ; encima
  on the table sobre la mesa
  on time a la hora
once una vez
  at once en seguida
one-way dirección única
onion la cebolla
only sólo
open abierto(a)
to open abrir
opera la ópera
operation la operación
operator *(phone)* el/la telefonista
opposite (to) enfrente (de)
  opposite the bank enfrente del banco
  quite the opposite! ¡todo lo contrario!
optician's la óptica
or o
orange *(fruit)* la naranja
  (colour) color naranja
orange juice el zumo de naranja
orchestra la orquesta
order: out of order averiado(a)
to order *(in restaurant)* pedir
  can I order? ¿puedo pedir?
organic biológico(a)
to organize organizar
ornament el adorno
other: the other one el/la otro(a)
  have you any others? ¿tiene otros(as)?
ounce = approx. 30 g
our nuestro(a)
out *(light)* apagado(a)
  he's (gone) out ha salido
outdoor *(pool, etc)* al aire libre
outside: it's outside está fuera

oven el horno
ovenproof dish resistente al horno
over *(on top of)* (por) encima de
to be overbooked tener overbooking
to overcharge cobrar demasiado
overdone *(food)* demasiado hecho(a)
overdose la sobredosis
to overheat recalentar
to overload sobrecargar
to oversleep quedarse dormido(a)
to overtake *(in car)* adelantar
to owe deber
I owe you... le debo...
you owe me... me debe...
owner el/la propietario(a)
oxygen el oxígeno

P

pace el ritmo
pacemaker el marcapasos
to pack *(luggage)* hacer las maletas
package el paquete
package tour el viaje organizado
packet el paquete
padded envelope el sobre acolchado
paddling pool la piscina hinchable
padlock el candado
page la página
paid pagado(a)
I've paid he pagado
pain el dolor
painful doloroso(a)
painkiller el analgésico ; el calmante
to paint pintar
paintbrush el pincel
painting *(picture)* el cuadro
pair el par
palace el palacio
pale pálido(a)
pan *(saucepan)* la cazuela
(frying) la sartén
pancake el crep(e)
panniers *(for bike)* las alforjas
panties las bragas
pants *(men's underwear)* los calzoncillos
panty liner el salvaslips
paper el papel
paper hankies los pañuelos de papel ; los kleenex®
paper napkins las servilletas de

papel
papoose *(for carrying baby)* la mochila portabebés
paragliding el parapente
paralysed paralizado(a)
parcel el paquete
pardon? ¿cómo?
I beg your pardon! ¿perdón?
parents los padres
park el parque
to park aparcar
parking disk el tique de aparcamiento
parking meter el parquímetro
parking ticket *(fine)* la multa por aparcamiento indebido
partner *(business)* el/la socio(a)
(boy/girlfriend) el/la compañero(a)
party *(group)* el grupo
(celebration) la fiesta
(political) el partido
pass *(mountain)* el puerto
(train) el abono
(bus) el bonobús
passenger el/la pasajero(a)
passport el pasaporte
passport control el control de pasaportes
pasta la pasta
pastry *(dough)* la masa
(cake) el pastel
path el camino
patient *(in hospital)* el/la paciente
pavement la acera
to pay pagar
I'd like to pay quisiera pagar
where do I pay ¿dónde se paga?
payment el pago
payphone el teléfono público
peace la paz
peach el melocotón
peak rate la tarifa máxima
pear la pera
pearls las perlas
peas los guisantes
pedal el pedal
pedalo el hidropedal
pedestrian el peatón
pedestrian crossing el paso de peatones
to pee hacer pipí
to peel *(fruit)* pelar

peg *(for clothes)* la pinza
  (for tent) la clavija
pen el bolígrafo
pencil el lápiz
penfriend el/la amigo(a) por correspondencia
penicillin la penicilina
penis el pene
penknife la navaja
pensioner el/la jubilado(a)
people la gente
pepper *(spice)* la pimienta
  (vegetable) el pimiento
per por
  per day al día
  per hour por hora
  per week a la semana
  per person por persona
  50 km per hour 50 km por hora
perfect perfecto(a)
performance la función
perfume el perfume
perhaps quizás
period *(menstruation)* la regla
perm la permanente
permit el permiso
person la persona
personal organizer la agenda
personal stereo el walkman®
pet el animal doméstico
pet food la comida para animales
pet shop la pajarería
petrol la gasolina
  4-star petrol la gasolina súper
  unleaded petrol la gasolina sin plomo
petrol cap el tapón del depósito
petrol pump el surtidor
petrol station la gasolinera
petrol tank el depósito
pharmacy la farmacia
phone el teléfono
  by phone por teléfono
to phone llamar por teléfono
phonebook la guía (telefónica)
phonebox la cabina (telefónica)
phone call la llamada (telefónica)
phonecard la tarjeta telefónica
photocopy la fotocopia
to photocopy fotocopiar
photograph la fotografía
  to take a photograph hacer una

fotografía
phrase book la guía de conversación
piano el piano
to pick *(choose)* elegir
  (pluck) coger
pickled en vinagre
pickpocket el/la carterista
picnic el picnic
  to have a picnic ir de picnic
picnic area el merendero
picnic hamper el cesto de la merienda
picnic rug la mantita
picture *(painting)* el cuadro
  (photo) la foto
pie *(fruit)* la tarta
  (meat) el pastel de carne
  (and/or vegetable) la empanada
piece el trozo
pier el embarcadero ; el muelle
pig el cerdo
pill la píldora
  to be on the pill tomar la píldora
pillow la almohada
pillowcase la funda
pilot el/la piloto
pin el alfiler
pink rosa
pint = approx. 0.5 litre
pipe *(smoker's)* la pipa
  (drain, etc) la tubería
pity: what a pity ¡qué pena!
pizza la pizza
place el lugar
place of birth el lugar de nacimiento
plain *(yoghurt)* natural
plait la trenza
plan *(of town)* el plano
plane *(airplane)* el avión
plant la planta
plaster *(sticking)* la tirita®
  (for broken limb) la escayola
plastic *(made of)* de plástico
plastic bag la bolsa de plástico
plate el plato
platform el andén
  which platform? ¿qué andén?
play *(theatre)* la obra
to play *(games)* jugar
play area la zona recreativa
play park el parque infantil
playroom el cuarto de juegos
pleasant agradable
please por favor

pleased contento(a)
pleased to meet you encantado(a)
de conocerle
pliers los alicates
plug *(electrical)* el enchufe
(for sink) el tapón
to plug in enchufar
plum la ciruela
plumber el/la fontanero(a)
plumbing *(pipes)* las cañerías
(craft) la fontanería
plunger *(for sink)* el desatascador
p.m. de la tarde
poached *(egg, fish)* escalfado(a)
pocket el bolsillo
point el punto
points *(in car)* los platinos
poison el veneno
poisonous venenoso(a)
police *(force)* la policía
policeman/woman el/la policía
police station la comisaría
polish *(for shoes)* el betún
(for furniture) el limpiamuebles
pollen el polen
polluted contaminado(a)
pony el poni
pony-trekking la excursión a caballo
pool la piscina
pool attendant el/la encargado(a)
de la piscina
poor pobre
pop socks los calcetines cortos
popular popular
pork el cerdo
port *(seaport)* el puerto
(wine) el oporto
porter *(hotel)* el portero
(at station) el mozo
portion la porción ; la ración
Portugal Portugal
Portuguese portugués/portuguesa
(language) el portugués
possible posible
post: *by post* por correo
to post echar
postbox el buzón
postcard la postal
postcode el código postal
poster el póster
postman/woman el/la cartero(a)
post office (la oficina de) Correos
to postpone aplazar
pot *(for cooking)* la olla

potato la patata
baked potato la patata asada
boiled potatoes las patatas
hervidas
fried potatoes las patatas fritas
mashed potatoes el puré de
patatas
roast potatoes las patatas asadas
sautéed potatoes las patatas
salteadas
potato masher el pasapurés
potato peeler el pelador
potato salad la ensalada de patatas
pothole el bache
pottery la cerámica
pound *(weight)* = approx. 0.5 kilo
(money) la libra
to pour echar ; servir
powder el polvo
in powder form en polvo
powdered milk la leche en polvo
power*(electicity)* la electricidad
power cut el apagón
pram el cochecito (del bebé)
to pray rezar
to prefer preferir
pregnant embarazada
I'm pregnant estoy embarazada
to prepare preparar
to prescribe prescribir
prescription la receta médica
present *(gift)* el regalo
preservative el conservante
president el/la presidente(a)
pressure la presión
pretty bonito(a)
price el precio
price list la lista de precios
priest el sacerdote
print *(photo)* la copia
printer la impresora
prison la cárcel
private privado(a)
prize el premio
probably probablemente
problem el problema
professor el/la catedrático(a)
programme *(TV, radio)* el programa
prohibited prohibido(a)
promise la promesa
to promise prometer
to pronounce pronunciar

how's it pronounced? ¿cómo se pronuncia?
Protestant protestante
to provide proporcionar
public público(a)
public holiday la fiesta
pudding el postre
to pull tirar
 I've pulled a muscle me ha dado un tirón en el músculo
to pull over *(car)* hacerse a un lado
pullover el jersey
pump *(bike, etc)* la bomba
 (petrol) el surtidor
puncture el pinchazo
puncture repair kit el kit para reparar pinchazos
puppet la marioneta
puppet show el espectáculo de marionetas
purple morado(a)
purpose el propósito
 on purpose a propósito
purse el monedero
to push empujar
pushchair la silla de paseo
to put *(place)* poner
pyjamas el pijama
Pyrenees los Pirineos

Q

quality la calidad
quantity la cantidad
quarantine la cuarentena
to quarrel discutir ; pelearse
quarter el cuarto
quay el muelle
queen la reina
query la pregunta
question la pregunta
queue la cola
to queue hacer cola
quick rápido(a)
quickly de prisa
quiet *(place)* tranquilo(a)
quilt el edredón
quite bastante
 it's quite good es bastante bueno
 quite expensive bastante caro
quiz el concurso

R

rabbit el conejo
rabies la rabia
race *(sport)* la carrera
race course *(horses)* el hipódromo
racket *(tennis, etc)* la raqueta
radiator *(car, heater)* el radiador
radio la radio
railcard el carné para obtener descuento en el tren
railway el ferrocarril
railway station la estación de tren
rain la lluvia
to rain: *it's raining* está lloviendo
raincoat el impermeable
rake el rastrillo
rape la violación
to rape violar
rare *(unique)* excepcional
 (steak) poco hecho(a)
rash *(skin)* el sarpullido
rat la rata
rate *(price)* la tarifa
rate of exchange el tipo de cambio
raw crudo(a)
razor la maquinilla de afeitar
razor blades las hojas de afeitar
to read leer
ready listo(a)
 to get ready prepararse
real verdadero(a)
to realize darse cuenta de
rearview mirror el (espejo) retrovisor
receipt el recibo
receiver *(phone)* el auricular
reception desk la recepción
receptionist el/la recepcionista
to recharge *(battery, etc)* recargar
recipe la receta
to recognize reconocer
to recommend recomendar
to record *(on tape, etc)* grabar
 (facts) registrar
to recover *(from illness)* recuperarse
to recycle reciclar
red rojo(a)
to reduce reducir
reduction el descuento
to refer to referirse a
refill el recambio
refund el reembolso

to refuse negarse
regarding con respecto a
region la región
register el registro
to register *(at hotel)* registrarse
registered *(letter)* certificado(a)
registration form la hoja de registro
to reimburse reembolsar
relation *(family)* el/la pariente
relationship la relación
to remain *(stay)* quedarse
to remember acordarse (de)
  I don't remember no me acuerdo
remote control el mando a distancia
removal firm la empresa de mudanzas
to remove quitar
rent el alquiler
to rent alquilar
rental el alquiler
repair la reparación
to repair reparar
to repeat repetir
to reply contestar
report el informe
to report informar
request la solicitud
to request solicitar
to require necesitar
to rescue rescatar
reservation la reserva
to reserve reservar
reserved reservado(a)
resident el/la residente
resort el centro turístico
rest *(repose)* el descanso
  (remainder) el resto
to rest descansar
restaurant el restaurante
restaurant car el cocherestaurante
retired jubilado(a)
to return *(to go back)* volver
  (to give back something) devolver
return *(ticket)* de ida y vuelta
to reverse dar marcha atrás
to reverse the charges llamar a cobro revertido
reverse charge call la llamada a cobro revertido
reverse gear la marcha atrás
rheumatism el reumatismo
rib la costilla
rice el arroz
rich *(person)* rico(a)

  (food) pesado(a)
to ride a horse montar a caballo
right *(correct)* correcto(a)
  to be right tener razón
right: on/to the right a la derecha
right of way el derecho de paso
to ring *(bell, to phone)* llamar
  it's ringing está sonando
ring el anillo
ring road la carretera de circunvalación
ripe maduro(a)
river el río
road la carretera
road sign la señal de tráfico
roadworks las obras
roast asado(a)
roll *(bread)* el panecillo
rollerblades los patines (en línea)
romantic romántico(a)
roof el tejado
roof-rack la baca
room *(in house, hotel)* la habitación
  (space) sitio
  double room la habitación doble
  single room la habitación individual
  family room la habitación familiar
room number el número de habitación
room service el servicio de habitaciones
root la raíz
rope la cuerda
rose la rosa
rosé wine el rosado
rotten *(fruit, etc)* podrido(a)
rough *(sea)* picado(a)
round *(shape)* redondo(a)
roundabout *(traffic)* la rotonda
row *(line, theatre)* la fila
to row *(boat)* remar
rowing *(sport)* el remo
rowing boat el bote de remos
royal real
rubber *(material)* la goma
  (eraser) la goma de borrar
rubber band la goma
rubber gloves los guantes de goma
rubbish la basura
rubella la rubeola
rucksack la mochila

rug la alfombra
ruins las ruinas
ruler *(for measuring)* la regla
to run correr
rush hour la hora punta
rusty oxidado(a)
rye el centeno

S

sad triste
saddle *(bike)* el sillín
  (horse) la silla de montar
safe seguro(a)
  is it safe? ¿es seguro(a)?
safe *(for valuables)* la caja fuerte
safety belt el cinturón de seguridad
safety pin el imperdible
to sail *(sport, leisure)* navegar
sailboard la tabla de windsurf
sailing *(sport)* la vela
sailing boat el velero
saint el/la santo(a)
salad la ensalada
  green salad la ensalada verde
  mixed salad la ensalada mixta
  potato salad la ensalada de patatas
  tomato salad la ensalada de tomate
salad dressing el aliño
salami el salchichón ; el salami
salary el sueldo
sale(s) las rebajas
salesman/woman el/la vendedor(a)
sales rep el/la representante
salt la sal
salt water el agua salada
salty salado(a)
same mismo(a)
sample la muestra
sand la arena
sandals las sandalias
sandwich el bocadillo
  toasted sandwich el sándwich
sanitary towels las compresas
satellite dish la antena parabólica
satellite TV la televisión por satélite
Saturday el sábado
sauce la salsa
  tomato sauce la salsa de tomate

saucepan la cazuela
saucer el platillo
sauna la sauna
sausage la salchicha
to save *(life)* salvar
  (money) ahorrar
savoury salado(a)
saw la sierra
to say decir
scales *(weighing)* el peso
scarf *(woollen)* la bufanda
  (headscarf) el pañuelo
scenery el paisaje
schedule el programa
school la escuela
  primary school la escuela primaria
  secondary school el instituto de enseñanza secundaria
scissors las tijeras
score *(of match)* la puntuación
to score a goal marcar un gol
Scot el escocés/la escocesa
Scotland Escocia
Scottish escocés/escocesa
scouring pad el estropajo
screen *(computer, TV)* la pantalla
screenwash el limpiacristales
screw el tornillo
screwdriver el destornillador
  phillips screwdriver® el destornillador de estrella
scuba diving el submarinismo
sculpture la escultura
sea el mar
seafood los mariscos
seam *(of dress)* la costura
to search buscar
seasick mareado(a)
seaside la playa
  at the seaside en la playa
season *(of year)* la estación
  (holiday) la temporada
  in season del tiempo
seasonal estacional
season ticket el abono
seasoning el condimento
seat *(chair)* la silla
  (in bus, train) el asiento
seatbelt el cinturón de seguridad
seaweed las algas
second segundo(a)
second *(time)* el segundo
second class de segunda clase
second-hand de segunda mano
secretary el/la secretario(a)

security guard el/la guarda jurado
sedative el sedante
to see ver
self-catering sin servicio de comidas
self-employed autónomo(a)
self-service el autoservicio
to sell vender
  do you sell...? ¿tiene...?
sell-by date la fecha de limite de venta
Sellotape® el celo
to send enviar
senior citizen el/la jubilado(a)
sensible sensato(a)
separated *(couple)* separado(a)
separately: *to pay separately* pagar por separado
September septiembre
septic tank el pozo séptico
serious *(accident, etc)* grave
to serve servir
service *(in church)* la misa
  (in restaurant) el servicio
  is service included? ¿está incluido el servicio?
service charge el servicio
service station la estación de servicio
serviette la servilleta
set menu el menú del día
settee el sofá
several varios(as)
to sew coser
sex el sexo
shade la sombra
  into the shade a la sombra
to shake *(bottle)* agitar
shallow poco profundo(a)
shampoo el champú
shampoo and set lavar y marcar
to share repartir
sharp *(razor, knife)* afilado(a)
to shave afeitarse
shaving cream la crema de afeitar
shawl el chal
she ella
sheep la oveja
sheet *(bed)* la sábana
shelf la balda ; el estante
shell *(seashell)* la concha
  (egg, nut) la cáscara
sheltered protegido(a)
shepherd el/la pastor(a)
sherry el jerez

to shine brillar
shingles *(illness)* la culebrilla
ship el barco
shirt la camisa
shock el susto
  (electric) la descarga
shock absorber el amortiguador
shoe el zapato
shoelaces los cordones (de los zapatos)
shoe polish el betún
shoe shop la zapatería
shop la tienda
to shop hacer las compras ; comprar
shop assistant el/la dependiente(a)
shopping las compras
  to go shopping ir de compras
shopping centre el centro comercial
shore la orilla
short corto(a)
shortage la escasez
short circuit el cortocircuito
short cut el atajo
shorts los pantalones cortos
short-sighted miope
shoulder el hombro
to shout gritar
show *(theatrical)* el espectáculo
to show enseñar
shower *(bath)* la ducha
  (rain) el chubasco
  to take a shower ducharse
shower cap el gorro de ducha
shower gel el gel de ducha
to shrink encoger
shut *(closed)* cerrado(a)
to shut cerrar
shutters *(outside)* las persianas
shuttle service el servicio regular de enlace
sick *(ill)* enfermo(a)
  I feel sick tengo ganas de vomitar
side el lado
side dish la guarnición
sidelight la luz de posición
sidewalk la acera
sieve *(for liquids)* el colador
  (for flour, etc) el tamiz
sightseeing: *to go sightseeing* hacer turismo

sightseeing tour el recorrido turístico

sign la señal

to sign firmar

signature la firma

signpost la señal

silk la seda

silver la plata

similar to parecido(a) a

since desde ; puesto que
since 1974 desde 1974
since you're not Spanish puesto que no es español(a)

to sing cantar

single *(unmarried)* soltero(a)
(bed, room) individual

single ticket el billete de ida

sink *(in kitchen)* el fregadero

sir señor

sister la hermana

sister-in-law la cuñada

to sit sentarse
sit down, please siéntate, por favor

size *(clothes)* la talla
(shoes) el número

to skate patinar

skateboard el monopatín

skates los patines

skating rink la pista de patinaje

ski el esquí

to ski esquiar

ski boots las botas de esquí

skiing el esquí

ski instructor el/la monitor(a) de esquí

ski jump el salto de esquí

ski lift el telesquí

ski pants los pantalones de esquí

ski pass el forfait

ski pole/stick el bastón de esquí

ski run/piste la pista de esquí

ski suit el traje de esquí

skin la piel

skirt la falda

sky el cielo

sledge el trineo

to sleep dormir
to sleep in quedarse dormido(a)

sleeper *(on train)* la litera

sleeping bag el saco de dormir

sleeping car el cochecama

sleeping pill el somnífero

slice *(of bread)* la rebanada
(of ham) la loncha

sliced bread el pan de molde

slide *(photograph)* la diapositiva

to slip resbalarse

slippers las zapatillas

slow lento(a)

to slow down reducir la velocidad

slowly despacio

small pequeño(a)

smaller than más pequeño(a) que

smell el olor
a bad smell un mal olor
a nice smell un buen olor

smile la sonrisa

to smile sonreír

to smoke fumar
I don't smoke no fumo
can I smoke? ¿puedo fumar?

smoke el humo

smoke alarm la alarma contra incendios

smoked ahumado(a)

smokers *(sign)* fumadores

smooth liso(a)

snack el tentempié
to have a snack tomar algo

snack bar la cafetería

snake la serpiente

snake bite la mordedura de serpiente

to sneeze estornudar

to snore roncar

snorkel el esnórquel

snow la nieve

to snow nevar
it's snowing está nevando

snow board el snowboard

snowboarding: *to go snowboarding* ir a hacer snowboard

snow chains las cadenas (para la nieve)

snow tyres los neumáticos antideslizantes

snowed up aislado(a) por la nieve

soap el jabón

soap powder el detergente

sober sobrio(a)

socket *(for plug)* el enchufe

socks los calcetines

soda water la soda

sofa el sofá

sofa bed el sofá-cama

soft blando
soft drink el refresco
software el software
soldier el soldado
sole *(of foot, shoe)* la suela
soluble soluble
some algunos(as)
someone alguien
something algo
sometimes a veces
son el hijo
son-in-law el yerno
song la canción
soon pronto
  as soon as possible lo antes posible
sore throat el dolor de garganta
sorry: *sorry!* ¡perdón!
  I'm sorry! ¡lo siento!
sort el tipo
  what sort? ¿qué tipo?
soup la sopa
sour amargo(a)
soured cream la nata agria
south el sur
souvenir el recuerdo ; el souvenir
spa el balneario
space el espacio
spade la pala
Spain España
Spaniard el/la español(a)
Spanish español(a)
spanner la llave inglesa
spare parts los repuestos
spare room el cuarto de invitados
spare tyre la rueda de repuesto
spare wheel la rueda de repuesto
sparkling espumoso(a)
  sparkling water el agua con gas
  sparkling wine el vino espumoso
spark plug la bujía
to speak hablar
  do you speak English? ¿habla inglés?
special especial
specialist el/la especialista
speciality la especialidad
speed la velocidad
speedboat la lancha motora
speeding el exceso de velocidad
speeding ticket la multa por exceso de velocidad
speed limit la velocidad máxima
  to exceed the speed limit exceder la velocidad máxima

speedometer el velocímetro
spell: *how is it spelt?* ¿cómo se escribe?
to spend *(money)* gastar
spice la especia
spicy picante
spider la araña
to spill derramar
spine la columna vertebral
spin-dryer la secadora-centrifugadora
spirits el alcohol
splinter la astilla
spoke *(wheel)* el radio
sponge la esponja
spoon la cuchara
sport el deporte
sports centre el polideportivo
sports shop la tienda de deportes
spot *(pimple)* la espinilla
sprain el esguince
spring *(season)* la primavera
  (metal) el muelle
square *(in town)* la plaza
squash *(game)* el squash
to squeeze apretar
  (lemon) exprimir
squid el calamar
stadium el estadio
stage el escenario
stain la mancha
stained glass la vidriera
stairs las escaleras
stale *(bread)* duro(a)
stalls *(theatre)* las butacas (de patio)
stamp *(postage)* el sello
to stand estar de pie
star la estrella
to start *(car)* poner en marcha
starter *(in meal)* entrante
  (in car) la puesta en marcha
station la estación
stationer's la papelería
statue la estatua
stay la estancia
  enjoy your stay! ¡que lo pase bien!
to stay *(remain)* quedarse
  I'm staying at the hotel... estoy alojado(a) en el hotel...
steak el filete
to steal robar

steamed al vapor
steel el acero
steep: *is it steep?* ¿hay mucha subida?
steeple la aguja
steering wheel el volante
step el peldaño
stepdaughter la hijastra
stepfather el padrastro
stepmother la madrastra
stepson el hijastro
stereo el estéreo
sterling *(pounds)* las libras esterlinas
steward *(on plane)* el auxiliar de vuelo
stewardess *(on plane)* la azafata
to stick *(with glue)* pegar
sticking plaster la tirita®
still *(not fizzy)* sin gas
sting la picadura
to sting picar
stitches *(surgical)* los puntos
stockings las medias
stomach el estómago
stomach upset el trastorno estomacal
stone la piedra
to stop parar
store *(shop)* la tienda
storey el piso
storm la tormenta
  (at sea) el temporal
story la historia
straightaway inmediatamente
straight on todo recto
strange extraño(a)
straw *(for drinking)* la pajita
strawberries las fresas
stream el arroyo
street la calle
street map el plano de la ciudad
strength la fuerza
stress el estrés
strike *(of workers)* la huelga
string la cuerda
striped a rayas
stroke *(medical)* la trombosis
strong fuerte
stuck: *it's stuck* está atascado(a)
student el/la estudiante

student discount el decuento para estudiantes
stuffed relleno(a)
stung picado(a)
stupid tonto(a)
subscription la suscripción
subtitles los subtítulos
subway *(train)* el metro
  (passage) el paso subterráneo
suddenly de repente
suede el ante
sugar el azúcar
sugar-free sin azúcar
to suggest sugerir
suit *(men's and women's)* el traje
suitcase la maleta
sum la suma
summer el verano
summer holidays las vacaciones de verano
summit la cumbre
sun el sol
to sunbathe tomar el sol
sunblock la protección solar total
sunburn la quemadura del sol
Sunday el domingo
sunglasses las gafas de sol
sunny: *it's sunny* hace sol
sunrise la salida del sol
sunroof el techo solar
sunscreen el filtro solar
sunset la puesta de sol
sunshade la sombrilla
sunstroke la insolación
suntan el bronceado
suntan lotion el bronceador
supermarket el supermercado
supper la cena
supplement *(to pay)* el suplemento
to supply suministrar
to surf hacer surf
  to surf the Net navegar por Internet
surfboard la tabla de surf
surgery *(operation)* la operación
surname el apellido
surprise la sorpresa
surrounded by rodeado(a) de
to survive sobrevivir
to swallow tragar
to sweat sudar
sweater el jersey
sweatshirt la sudadera
sweet *(not savoury)* dulce

sweet (dessert) el dulce
sweetener el edulcorante ; la sacarina®
sweets los caramelos
to swell (injury, etc) hincharse
to swim nadar
swimming pool la piscina
swimsuit el traje de baño ; el bañador
swing (for children) el columpio
Swiss suizo(a)
switch el interruptor
to switch off apagar
to switch on encender
Switzerland Suiza
swollen hinchado(a)
synagogue la sinagoga
syringe la jeringuilla

T

table la mesa
tablecloth el mantel
tablespoon la cuchara de servir
table tennis el ping-pong
tablet (pill) la pastilla
tailor's la sastrería
to take (medicine, etc) tomar
  how long does it take? ¿cuánto tiempo se tarda?
take-away (food) para llevar
to take off despegar
to take out (of bag, etc) sacar
talc los polvos de talco
to talk to hablar con
tall alto(a)
tampons los tampones
tangerine la mandarina
tank (petrol) el depósito
  (fish) la pecera
tap el grifo
tap water el agua corriente
tape (video) la cinta
tape measure el metro
tape recorder el casete ; la grabadora
tart la tarta
taste el sabor
to taste probar
  can I taste it? ¿puedo probarlo?
tax el impuesto
taxi el taxi
taxi driver el/la taxista
taxi rank la parada de taxis
tea el té
  herbal tea la infusión

  lemon tea el té con limón
  strong tea el té cargado
teabag la bolsita de té
teapot la tetera
teaspoon la cucharilla
tea towel el paño de cocina
to teach enseñar
teacher el/la profesor(a)
team el equipo
tear (in material) el rasgón
teat (on baby's bottle) la tetina
teenager el/la adolescente
teeth los dientes
telegram el telegrama
telephone el teléfono
to telephone llamar por teléfono
telephone box la cabina telefónica
telephone call la llamada telefónica
telephone card la tarjeta telefónica
telephone directory la guía telefónica
telephone number el número de teléfono
television la televisión
to tell decir
temperature la temperatura
  to have a temperature tener fiebre
temporary provisional
tenant el/la inquilino(a)
tendon el tendón
tennis el tenis
tennis ball la pelota de tenis
tennis court la pista de tenis
tennis racket la raqueta de tenis
tent la tienda de campaña
tent peg la clavija
terminal (airport) la terminal
terrace la terraza
to test (try out) probar
testicles los testículos
tetanus el tétano(s)
than que
  more than you más que tú
  more than five más de cinco
to thank agradecer
thank you gracias
  thank you very much muchas gracias
that ese/esa
  (more remote) aquel/aquella
  that one ése/ésa
  (more remote) aquél/aquélla

the el/la/los/las
theatre el teatro
theft el robo
their su/sus
them ellos/ellas
  (direct) los/las
there *(over there)* allí
there is/there are hay
thermometer el termómetro
these estos/estas
  these ones éstos/éstas
they ellos/ellas
thick *(not thin)* grueso(a)
thief el ladrón/la ladrona
thigh el muslo
thin *(person)* delgado(a)
thing la cosa
  my things mis cosas
to think pensar
  (to be of opinion) creer
thirsty: *I'm thirsty* tengo sed
this este/esta
  this one éste/ésta
thorn la espina
those esos/esas
  (more remote) aquellos/aquellas
  those ones ésos/ésas
  (more remote) aquéllos/aquéllas
thread el hilo
throat la garganta
throat lozenges las pastillas para
  la garganta
through por
thumb el pulgar
thunder el trueno
thunderstorm la tormenta
Thursday el jueves
thyme el tomillo
ticket *(bus, train, etc)* el billete
  (entrance fee) la entrada
  a single ticket un billete de ida
  a return ticket un billete de ida y
  vuelta
  a tourist ticket un billete turístico
  a book of tickets un abono
ticket collector el/la revisor(a)
ticket office el despacho de billetes
tide *(sea)* la marea
  low tide la marea baja
  high tide la marea alta
tidy arraglado(a)
to tidy up ordenar

tie la corbata
tight *(fitting)* ajustado(a)
tights las medias
tile *(roof)* la teja
  (floor) la baldosa
till *(cash desk)* la caja
till *(until)* hasta
  till 2 o'clock hasta las 2
time el tiempo
  (clock) la hora
  what time is it? ¿qué hora es?
timer *(on cooker)* el temporizador
timetable el horario
tin *(can)* la lata
tinfoil el papel de estaño
tin-opener el abrelatas
tip la propina
to tip dar propina
tipped *(cigarette)* con filtro
tired cansado(a)
tissues los kleenex®
to a
  to London a Londres
  to the airport al aeropuerto
toadstool el hongo venenoso
toast *(to eat)* la tostada
  (raising glass) el brindis
tobacco el tabaco
tobacconist's el estanco
today hoy
toddler el/la niño(a) pequeño(a)
toe el dedo del pie
together juntos(as)
toilet los aseos ; los servicios
  toilet for disabled los servicios
  para minusválidos
toilet brush la escobilla del wáter
toilet paper el papel higiénico
toiletries los artículos de baño
token *(for bus)* el vale
toll *(motorway)* el peaje
tomato el tomate
  tinned tomatoes los tomates en
  lata
tomato juice el zumo de tomate
tomato soup la sopa de tomate
tomorrow mañana
  tomorrow morning mañana por la
  mañana
  tomorrow afternoon mañana por
  la tarde
  tomorrow evening mañana por la
  tarde/noche
tongue la lengua
tonic water la tónica
tonight esta noche

tonsillitis la amigdalitis
too (also) también
  too big demasiado grande
  too small demasiado pequeño(a)
  too hot (food) demasiado caliente
  too noisy demasiado ruidoso(a)
tool la herramienta
toolkit el juego de herramientas
tooth el diente
toothache el dolor de muelas
toothbrush el cepillo de dientes
toothpaste la pasta de dientes
toothpick el palillo
top: *the top floor* el último piso
top (of hill) la cima
  (shirt) el top
  (t-shirt) la camiseta
  on top of... sobre...
topless: *to go topless* hacer topless
torch (flashlight) la linterna
torn rasgado(a)
total (amount) el total
to touch tocar
tough (meat) duro(a)
tour (trip) la vuelta
  (of museum, etc) la visita
  guided tour la visita con guía
tour guide el/la guía turístico(a)
tour operator el/la touroperador(a)
tourist el/la turista
tourist office la oficina de turismo
tourist route la ruta turística
tourist ticket el billete turístico
to tow remolcar
towbar la barra de remolque
tow rope el cable de remolque
towel la toalla
tower la torre
town la ciudad
town centre el centro de la ciudad
town hall el ayuntamiento
town plan el plano de la ciudad
toxic tóxico(a)
toy el juguete
toy shop la juguetería
tracksuit el chándal
traditional tradicional
traffic el tráfico
traffic jam el atasco
traffic lights el semáforo
traffic warden el/la guardia de
  tráfico
trailer el remolque
train el tren
  by train en tren

  the next train el próximo tren
  the first train el primer tren
  the last train el último tren
trainers las zapatillas de deporte
tram el tranvía
tranquillizer el tranquilizante
to translate traducir
translation la traducción
to travel viajar
travel agent's la agencia de viajes
travel guide la guía de viajes
travel insurance el seguro de viaje
travel sickness el mareo
traveller's cheque el cheque de
  viaje
tray la bandeja
tree el árbol
trip la excursión
trolley (luggage, shopping) el carrito
trouble el apuro
  to be in trouble estar en un apuro
trousers los pantalones
truck el camión
true verdadero(a)
trunk (luggage) el baúl
trunks (swimming) el bañador
to try (attempt) probar
to try on (clothes) probarse
t-shirt la camiseta
Tuesday el martes
tumble-dryer la secadora
tunnel el túnel
to turn girar
to turn around girar
to turn off (light, etc) apagar
  (tap) cerrar
to turn on (light, etc) encender
  (tap) abrir
turquoise (colour) turquesa
tweezers las pinzas
twice dos veces
twin-bedded room la habitación con
  dos camas
twins los/las mellizos(as)
  identical twins los/las gemelos(as)
to type escribir a máquina
typical típico(a)
tyre el neumático
tyre pressure la presión de los
  neumáticos

U

ugly feo(a)
ulcer la úlcera
umbrella el paraguas
  (sunshade) la sombrilla
uncle el tío
uncomfortable incómodo(a)
unconscious inconsciente
under debajo de
undercooked medio crudo
underground *(metro)* el metro
underpants los calzoncillos
underpass el paso subterráneo
to understand entender
  I don't understand no entiendo
  do you understand? ¿entiende?
underwear la ropa interior
underwater debajo del agua
to undress desvestirse
unemployed desempleado(a)
United Kingdom el Reino Unido
United States Estados Unidos
university la universidad
unleaded petrol la gasolina sin
  plomo
unlikely poco probable
to unlock abrir (con llave)
to unpack *(suitcases)* deshacer las
  maletas
unpleasant desagradable
to unplug desenchufar
to unscrew destornillar
up: to get up levantarse
upstairs arriba
urgent urgente
urine la orina
us nosotros(as)
USA EE. UU.
to use usar
useful útil
usual habitual
usually por lo general
U-turn el cambio de sentido

V

vacancy *(in hotel)* la habitación libre
vacant libre
vacation las vacaciones

vaccination la vacuna
vacuum cleaner la aspiradora
vagina la vagina
valid válido(a)
valley el valle
valuable de valor
valuables los objetos de valor
value el valor
valve la válvula
van la furgoneta
vase el florero
VAT el IVA
vegan vegetariano(a) estricto(a)
  I'm vegan soy vegetariano(a)
  estricto(a)
vegetables las verduras
vegetarian vegetariano(a)
  I'm vegetarian soy vegetariano(a)
vehicle el vehículo
vein la vena
velvet el terciopelo
vending machine el distribuidor
  automático
venereal disease la enfermedad
  venérea
ventilator el ventilador
very muy
vest la camiseta
vet el/la veterinario(a)
via por
to video *(from TV)* grabar (en
  vídeo)
video el vídeo
video camera la videocámara
video cassette la cinta de vídeo
video game el videojuego
video recorder el vídeo
video tape la cinta de vídeo
view la vista
village el pueblo
vinegar el vinagre
vineyard la viña
viper la víbora
virus el virus
visa el visado
visit la visita
to visit visitar
visiting hours *(hospital)* las horas de
  visita
visitor el/la visitante
vitamin la vitamina
voice la voz
volcano el volcán
volleyball el voleibol**

voltage el voltaje
to vomit vomitar
voucher el vale

W

wage el sueldo
waist la cintura
waistcoat el chaleco
to wait for esperar
waiter/waitress el/la camarero(a)
waiting room la sala de espera
to wake up despertarse
Wales Gales
walk un paseo
to go for a walk dar un paseo
to walk andar
walking boots las botas de montaña
walking stick el bastón
wall *(inside)* la pared
(outside) el muro
wallet la cartera
to want querer
I want quiero
we want queremos
war la guerra
ward *(hospital)* la sala
wardrobe el ropero
warehouse el almacén
warm caliente
it's warm (weather) hace calor
to warm up *(milk, etc)* calentar
warning triangle el triángulo
señalizador
to wash (oneself) lavar(se)
wash and blow dry lavado y secado
a mano
washbasin el lavabo
washing machine la lavadora
washing powder el detergente
washing-up bowl el barreño
washing-up liquid el líquido
lavavajillas
wasp la avispa
wasp sting la picadura de avispa
waste bin el cubo de la basura
to watch *(look at)* mirar
watch el reloj
watchstrap la correa de reloj
water el agua
bottled water el agua mineral
cold water el agua fría
drinking water el agua potable
hot/cold water el agua caliente/fría
mineral water el agua mineral

sparkling water el agua con gas
still water el agua sin gas
waterfall la cascada
water heater el calentador de agua
watermelon la sandía
waterproof impermeable
(watch) sumergible
to waterski hacer esquí acuático
watersports los deportes acuáticos
waterwings los manguitos
waves *(on sea)* las olas
waxing *(hair removal)* la depilación
(con cera)
way *(manner)* la manera
(route) el camino
way in *(entrance)* la entrada
way out *(exit)* la salida
we nosotros(as)
weak *(coffee, tea)* flojo(a)
to wear llevar
weather el tiempo
weather forecast el pronóstico del
tiempo
web *(internet)* el Internet
website la página web
wedding la boda
wedding anniversary el aniversario
de boda
wedding present el regalo de boda
Wednesday el miércoles
week la semana
last week la semana pasada
next week la semana que viene
per week por semana
this week esta semana
during the week durante la
semana
weekday el día laborable
weekend el fin de semana
next weekend el próximo fin de
semana
this weekend este fin de semana
weekly semanal
weekly ticket el billete semanal
to weigh pesar
weight el peso
welcome! ¡bienvenido(a)!
well *(water)* el pozo
well bien
he's not well no se encuentra bien
well done *(steak)* muy hecho(a)
wellington boots las botas de agua

Welsh galés/galesa
(language) el galés
west el oeste
wet mojado(a)
(weather) lluvioso(a)
wetsuit el traje de bucear
what? ¿qué?
wheel la rueda
wheelchair la silla de ruedas
wheel clamp el cepo
when? ¿cuándo?
where? ¿dónde?
which? ¿cuál?
which one? ¿cuál?
which ones? ¿cuáles?
while: *in a while* dentro de un rato
white blanco(a)
who? ¿quién?
whole entero(a)
wholemeal bread el pan integral
whose? ¿de quién?
why? ¿por qué?
wide ancho(a)
widow la viuda
widower el viudo
width el ancho
wife la mujer
wig la peluca
to win ganar
wind el viento
windbreak el cortavientos
windmill el molino de viento
window la ventana
(shop) el escaparate
(in car, train) la ventanilla
windscreen el parabrisas
windscreen wipers los limpia-parabrisas
to windsurf hacer windsurf
windy: *it's windy* hace viento
wine el vino
red wine el vino tinto
white wine el vino blanco
dry wine el vino seco
rosé wine el vino rosado
sparkling wine el vino espumoso
house wine el vino de la casa
wine list la carta de vinos
wing el ala
wing mirror el retrovisor exterior
winter el invierno
with con

with ice con hielo
with milk con leche
with sugar con azúcar
without sin
without ice sin hielo
without milk sin leche
without sugar sin azúcar
woman la mujer
wonderful maravilloso(a)
wood *(material)* la madera
(forest) el bosque
wooden de madera
wool la lana
word la palabra
work el trabajo
to work *(person)* trabajar
(machine, car) funcionar
it doesn't work no funciona
work permit el permiso de trabajo
world el mundo
world-wide mundial
worried preocupado(a)
worse peor
worth: *it's worth...* vale...
to wrap *(parcel)* envolver
wrapping paper el papel de envolver
wrinkles las arrugas
wrist la muñeca
to write escribir
please write it down escríbalo, por favor
writing paper el papel de escribir
wrong: *what's wrong* ¿qué pasa?
wrought iron el hierro forjado

X

X-ray la radiografía
to x-ray hacer una radiografía

Y

yacht el yate
year el año
this year este año
next year el año que viene
last year el año pasado
yearly anual
yellow amarillo(a)
Yellow Pages las Páginas amarillas
yes sí
yesterday ayer
yet: *not yet* todavía no

yoghurt el yogur
  plain yoghurt el yogur natural
yolk la yema
you *(polite singular* usted
  (polite plural) ustedes
  (singular with friends) tú
  (plural with friends) vosotros
young joven
your *(polite)* su/sus
  (familiar) tu/tus
youth hostel el albergue juvenil

Z

zebra crossing el paso de peatones
zero el cero
zip la cremallera
zone la zona
zoo el zoo
zoom lens el zoom

A

a to ; at
  a la estación to the station
  a las 4 at 4 o'clock
  a 30 kilómetros 30 km away
abadejo *m* haddock
abadía *f* abbey
abajo below ; downstairs
abanico *m* fan *(hand-held)*
abeja *f* bee
abierto(a) open
abogado(a) *m/f* lawyer
abonado(a) *m/f* season-ticket holder
abonar to pay ; to credit
abono *m* season ticket
aborto *m* abortion
  aborto no provocado miscarriage
abrebotellas *m* bottle opener
abrelatas *m* tin-opener
abrigo *m* coat
abril *m* April
abrir to open ; to turn on *(tap)*
abrocharse to fasten *(seatbelt, etc)*
absceso *m* abscess
abuela *f* grandmother
abuelo *m* grandfather
aburrido(a) boring
acá here
acabar to finish
acampar to camp
acceso *m* access
  acceso andenes to the platforms
  acceso prohibido no access
  acceso vías to the platforms
accidente *m* accident
aceite *m* oil
  aceite bronceador suntan oil
  aceite de oliva olive oil
  aceite de girasol sunflower oil
aceituna *f* olive
  aceitunas aliñadas marinated olives
acelerador *m* accelerator
acento *m* accent
aceptar to accept
acera *f* pavement ; sidewalk
acero *m* steel
ácido *m* acid
acompañar to accompany
aconsejar to advise
acto *m* act
  en el acto while you wait *(repairs)*
actor *m* actor

actriz *f* actress
acuerdo *m* agreement
  ¡de acuerdo! OK ; alright
adaptador *m* adaptor *(electrical)*
adelantar to overtake *(in car)*
adelante forward
adicional extra ; additional
adiós goodbye
administración *f* management
admitir to accept ; to permit
  no se admiten... ...not permitted
adolescente *m/f* teenager
aduana *f* customs
adulto(a) *m/f* adult
advertir to warn
aerodeslizador *m* hovercraft
aerolínea *f* airline
aeropuerto *m* airport
aerosol *m* aerosol
afeitarse to shave
aficionado(a) *m/f* fan *(cinema, jazz, etc)*
afilado(a) sharp *(razor, knife)*
agencia *f* agency
  agencia de seguros insurance company
  agencia de viajes travel agency
agenda *f* diary ; personal organizer
agente *m/f* agent
  agente de policía policeman/ woman
agitar to shake *(bottle)*
agosto *m* August
agotado(a) sold out ; out of stock
agradable pleasant
agradecer to thank
agridulce sweet and sour
agua *f* water
  agua caliente/fría hot/cold water
  agua destilada distilled water
  agua dulce fresh water
  agua mineral mineral water
  agua potable drinking water
  agua salada salt water
agudo(a) sharp ; pointed
águila *m* eagle
aguja *f* needle ; hand *(on watch)*
  aguja hipodérmica hypodermic needle
agujero *m* hole
ahogarse to drown
ahora now

ahorrar to save *(money)*

ahumado(a) smoked

aire *m* air
 al aire libre open-air ; outdoor
 aire acondicionado air-conditioning

ajo *m* garlic

ala *f* wing

alargador *m* extension *(electrical)*

alarma *f* alarm

albahaca *f* basil

albarán *m* delivery note

albaricoque *m* apricot

albergue *m* hostel
 albergue juvenil youth hostel

alcanzar to reach ; to get

alcohol *m* alcohol ; spirits

alcohólico(a) alcoholic

alemán/alemana German

Alemania *f* Germany

alergia *f* allergy
 alergia al polen hay fever

alérgico(a) a allergic to

aletas *fpl* flippers

alfarería *f* pottery

alfiler *m* pin

alfombra *f* carpet ; rug

alforjas *fpl* panniers *(for bike)*

algas *fpl* seaweed

algo something

algodón *m* cotton
 algodón hidrófilo cotton wool

alguien someone

alguno(a) any

algunos(as) some ; a few

alicates *mpl* pliers

alimentación *f* grocer's ; food

alimento *m* food

aliño *m* dressing *(for food)*

allí there *(over there)*

almacén *m* store ; warehouse
 grandes almacenes department stores

almendra *f* almond

almohada *f* pillow

almuerzo *m* lunch

alojamiento *m* accommodation
 alojamiento y desayuno bed and breakfast

alpargatas *fpl* espadrilles

alquilar to rent ; to hire
 se alquila for hire

alquiler *m* rent ; rental
 alquiler de coches car hire

alrededor about ; around

alto(a) high ; tall
 alta tensión high voltage

altura *f* altitude ; height

alubia *f* bean
 alubias blancas butter beans
 alubias pintas red kidney beans

amable pleasant ; kind

amapola *f* poppy

amargo(a) bitter ; sour

amarillo(a) yellow ; amber *(traffic light)*

ambientador *m* air freshener

ambos(as) both

ambulancia *f* ambulance

ambulatorio *m* health centre

América del Norte *f* America

amigo(a) *m/f* friend
 amigo(a) por correspondencia penfriend

amor *m* love

amortiguador *m* shock absorber

ampolla *f* blister

analgésico *m* painkiller

análisis *m* analysis
 análisis de sangre blood test

ananá(s) *m* pineapple

ancho *m* width

ancho(a) wide

anchoa *f* anchovy *(salted)*

anchura *f* width

ancla *f* anchor

andaluz(a) Andalusian

andar to walk

andén *m* platform

añejo(a) mature ; vintage

anestesia *f* anaesthetic
 anestesia local local anaesthetic
 anestesia general general anaesthetic

anfiteatro *m* circle *(theatre)*

angina de pecho *f* angina

anillo *m* ring

animal *m* animal
 animal doméstico pet

anís *m* aniseed liqueur ; aniseed

aniversario *m* anniversary
 aniversario de boda wedding anniversary

año *m* year

3 **Año Nuevo** New Year's Day
ante m suede
antena f aerial
  antena parabólica satellite dish
anteojos mpl binoculars
antes (de) before
antiácido m antacid
antibiótico m antibiotic
anticonceptivo m contraceptive
anticongelante m antifreeze
anticuario m antique shop
antigüedades fpl antiques
antiguo(a) old ; ancient
antihistamínico m antihistamine
antiséptico m antiseptic
anual annual
anular to cancel
anunciar to announce ; to advertise
anuncio m advertisement ; notice
anzuelo m hook (fishing)
apagado(a) off (light, etc)
apagar to switch off ; to turn off
aparato m appliance
aparcamiento m car park
aparcar to park
apartado de Correos m PO Box
apartamento m flat (apartment)
apellido m surname
  apellido de soltera maiden name
apendicitis f appendicitis
aperitivo m apéritif ; appetizer
apertura f opening
apio m celery
aplazar to postpone
apostar por to bet on
aprender to learn
apretar to squeeze
apto(a) suitable
aquí here
  aquí tiene... here is...
araña f spider
árbitro m referee
árbol m tree
arco iris m rainbow
ardor de estómago m heartburn
arena f sand
armario m wardrobe ; cupboard
arquitecto(a) m/f architect
arquitectura f architecture
arrancar to start
arreglar to fix ; to mend
arriba upstairs ; above

  hacia arriba upward(s)
arroyo m stream
arroz m rice
arruga f wrinkle
arte m art
artesanía f crafts
artesano(a) m/f craftsman/woman
articulación f joint (body)
artículo m article
  artículos de ocasión bargains
  artículos de tocador toiletries
artista m/f artist
artritis f arthritis
asado(a) roast
asar a la parrilla to barbecue
ascensor m lift
asegurado(a) insured
asegurar to insure
aseos mpl toilets
asiento m seat
  asiento de niños child safety seat
asistencia f help ; assistance
  asistencia técnica repairs
asma m asthma
aspirador m vacuum cleaner
aspirina f aspirin
astilla f splinter
atacar to attack
atajo m short cut
ataque m fit (seizure)
  ataque epiléptico epileptic fit
atascado(a) jammed (stuck)
atasco m hold-up (traffic jam)
atención f attention
  atención al cliente customer service
aterrizar to land
ático m attic
atracadero m mooring
atraco m mugging
atrás behind
atropellar to knock down (car)
ATS m/f nurse
atún m tuna fish
audífono m hearing aid
aumentar to increase
auricular m receiver (phone)
auriculares mpl headphones
auténtico(a) genuine ; real

autostop *m* hitch-hiking
autobús *m* bus
autocar *m* coach *(bus)*
automático(a) automatic
autónomo(a) self-employed
autopista *f* motorway
autor(a) *m/f* author
autoservicio *m* self-service
auxiliar de vuelo *m/f* air steward/
  stewardess
Av./Avda. *abbrev. for* **avenida**
avalancha *f* avalanche
ave *f* bird
  aves de corral poultry
avellana *f* hazelnut
avena *f* oats
avenida *f* avenue
avería *f* breakdown *(car)*
averiado(a) out of order ; broken
  down
avión *m* airplane ; aeroplane
aviso *m* notice ; warning
avispa *f* wasp
ayer yesterday
ayudar to help
ayuntamiento *m* town hall
azafata *f* air hostess
azafrán *m* saffron
azúcar *m* sugar
  azúcar glasé icing sugar
azul blue
  azul claro light blue
  azul marino dark/navy blue
  día azul cheap day for train travel
  zona azul controlled parking area

B

babero *m* baby's bib
baca *f* roof rack
bahía *f* bay *(along coast)*
bailar to dance
baile *m* dance
bajar to go down(stairs) ; to drop
  (temperature)
bajarse (del) to get off *(bus, etc)*
bajo(a) low ; short ; soft *(sound)*
  bajo en calorías low-fat
  más bajo lower
balcón *m* balcony

balneario *m* spa
balón *m* ball
baloncesto *m* basketball
balsa salvavidas *f* life raft
bañador *m* swimming costume/
  trunks
banana *f* banana
bañarse to go swimming ; to bathe ;
  to have a bath
banca *f* banking ; bank
banco *m* bank ; bench
banda *f* band *(musical)*
bandeja *f* tray
bandera *f* flag
bañista *m/f* bather
baño *m* bath ; bathroom
  con baño with bath
bar *m* bar
barato(a) cheap
barba *f* beard
barbacoa *f* barbecue
barbería *f* barber's
barbillla *f* chin
barca *f* small boat
barco *m* ship ; boat
  barco de vela sailing boat
barra *f* bar ; counter ; bread stick
  barra de labios lipstick
  barra de pan French bread
barreño (de plástico) *m* washing-up
  bowl
barrera *f* barrier ; crash barrier
barrio *m* district ; suburb
  barrio chino red light district
barro *m* mud
bastante enough ; quite
bastón *m* walking stick
  bastón de esquí ski pole/stick
basura *f* rubbish ; litter
bata *f* dressing gown
bate *m* bat *(baseball, cricket)*
batería *f* battery *(in car)*
batido *m* milkshake
batidora *f* blender *(hand-held)*
baúl *m* trunk *(luggage)*
bautizo *m* christening
to be ser ; estar
bebé *m* baby
beber to drink
bebida *f* drink
  bebida sin alcohol soft drink
beicon *m* bacon
béisbol *m* baseball

berenjena f aubergine
berro m watercress
berza f cabbage
besar to kiss
beso m kiss
betún m shoe polish
biberón m baby's bottle
biblioteca f library
bici f bicycle
bicicleta f bicycle
  bicicleta de montaña mountain bike
bien well
bienvenido(a) welcome
bifurcación f fork (in road)
bigote m moustache
billete m ticket
  billete de ida y vuelta return ticket
  billete turístico tourist ticket
billetera f wallet
bistec m steak
bisutería f costume jewellery
blanco(a) white
  dejar en blanco leave blank (on form)
blando(a) soft
bloc m note pad
blusa f blouse
boca f mouth
bocadillo m sandwich (made with French bread)
boda f wedding
bodega f wine cellar ; restaurant
boite f night club
bolígrafo m biro ; pen
bollo m roll ; bun
bolsa f bag ; stock exchange
bolsillo m pocket
bolsita de té f teabag
bolso m handbag
bomba f pump (bike, etc) ; bomb
bombero m fireman
bomberos mpl fire brigade
bombilla f light bulb
bombona de gas f gas cylinder
bombonería f confectioner's
bombones mpl chocolates
bonito(a) pretty ; nice-looking
bono m voucher
bonobús m bus pass
borracho(a) drunk
bosque m forest ; wood

bota f boot
bote m boat ; tin ; can
  bote neumático rubber dinghy
  bote salvavidas lifeboat
botella f bottle
botón m button
bragas fpl knickers
brazo m arm
brécol m broccoli
bricolaje m do-it-yourself
brillar to shine
brindis m toast (raising glass)
británico(a) British
broma f joke
bromear to joke
bronceado m suntan
bronceado(a) sun-tanned
bronceador m suntan lotion
broncearse to tan
bronquitis f bronchitis
brújula f compass
bucear to dive
bueno(a) good ; fine
  ¡buenos días! good morning!
  ¡buenas tardes! good afternoon/evening!
  ¡buenas noches! good evening/night!
bufanda f scarf (woollen)
bufé m buffet
búho m owl
bujía f spark plug
bulto m lump (swelling)
buñuelo m fritter ; doughnut
bunyi m bungee jumping
buscar to look for
butacas fpl stalls (theatre)
butano m Calor gas®
butifarra f Catalan sausage
buzón m postbox ; letterbox

C

caballeros mpl gents
caballo m horse
  montar a caballo to go riding
cabello m hair
cabeza f head
cabina f cabin
  cabina telefónica phone box

cable *m* wire ; cable
  cables de arranque jump leads
  cable de remolque tow rope
cabra *f* goat
cacahuete *m* peanut
cacao *m* cocoa
  cacao para los labios lip salve
cacerola *f* saucepan
cachemira *f* cashmere
cada every ; each
  cada día daily (each day)
  cada uno each (one)
cadera *f* hip
caducado(a) out-of-date
caducar to expire (ticket, passport)
caer(se) to fall
café *m* café ; coffee
  café cortado espresso with dash of milk
  corto de café milky coffee
  café descafeinado decaff coffee
  café exprés espresso coffee
  café en grano coffee beans
  café con hielo iced coffee
  café con leche white coffee
  café instantáneo instant coffee
  café molido ground coffee
  café solo black coffee
cafetera *f* cafetière
cafetería *f* snack bar ; café
caja *f* cashdesk ; box
  caja de ahorros savings bank
  caja de cambios gearbox
  caja de fusibles fuse box
  caja fuerte safe
cajero(a) *m/f* teller ; cashier
  cajero automático cash dispenser ; auto-teller
cajón *m* drawer
calabacín *m* courgette
calabaza *f* pumpkin
calamares *mpl* squid
calambre *m* cramp
calcetines *mpl* socks
calculadora *f* calculator
caldereta *f* stew (fish, lamb)
caldo *m* stock ; consommé
calefacción *f* heating
calendario *m* calendar
calentador *m* heater
  calentador de agua water heater
calentar to heat up (milk, food)

calentura *f* cold sore
calidad *f* quality
caliente hot
calle *f* street ; fairway (golf)
callejón sin salida *m* cul-de-sac
calmante *m* painkiller
calvo(a) bald
calzada *f* roadway
  calzada deteriorada uneven road surface
calzado *m* footwear
  calzados shoe shop
calzoncillos *mpl* underpants
cama *f* bed
  dos camas twin beds
  cama individual single bed
  cama de matrimonio double bed
cámara *f* camera ; inner tube
camarera *f* waitress ; chambermaid
camarero *m* barman ; waiter
camarote *m* cabin
cambiar to change ; to exchange
  cambiarse to get changed
cambio *m* change ; exchange ; gear
caminar to walk
camino *m* path ; road ; route
  camino particular private road
camión *m* lorry
camisa *f* shirt
camisería *f* shirt shop
camiseta *f* t-shirt ; vest
camisón *m* nightdress
campana *f* bell
camping *m* campsite
campo *m* countryside ; field ; pitch
  campo de fútbol football pitch
  campo de golf golf course
caña *f* cane ; rod
  caña (de cerveza) glass of beer
  caña de pescar fishing rod
Canadá *m* Canada
canadiense Canadian
Canal de la Mancha *m* English Channel
canasto *m* basket
cancelación *f* cancellation
cancelar to cancel
cáncer *m* cancer
cancha de tenis *f* tennis court
canción *f* song
candado *m* padlock
  candado de bicicleta bike lock
candela *f* candle ; fire
candidiasis *f* thrush

canela *f* cinnamon
canguro *m* kangaroo
canguro *m/f* babysitter
canoa *f* canoe
cansado(a) tired
cantante *m/f* singer
cantar to sing
cantidad *f* quantity
capilla *f* chapel
capital *f* capital (city)
capitán *m* captain
capó *m* bonnet ; hood (of car)
capucha *f* hood (jacket)
cara *f* face
caramelo *m* sweet ; caramel
caravana *f* caravan
carbón *m* coal
  carbón vegetal charcoal
carburador *m* carburettor
carburante *m* fuel
cárcel *f* prison
cargar to load
  cargar en cuenta to charge to account
cargo *m* charge
  a cargo del cliente at the customer's expense
Caribe *m* Caribbean
carnaval *m* carnival
carne *f* meat
  carne asada roast meat
  carne picada mince (meat)
carné de conducir *m* driving licence
carné de identidad *m* identity card
carnicería *f* butcher's
caro(a) dear ; expensive
carpintería *f* carpenter's shop
carrera *f* career ; race (sport)
carrete *m* film (for camera) ; fishing reel
carretera *f* road
  carretera de circunvalación ring road
carril *m* lane (on road)
carrito *m* trolley
carta *f* letter ; playing card ; menu
  carta aérea air mail letter
  carta certificada registered letter
  carta verde green card
  carta de vinos wine list
cartel *m* poster
cartelera *f* entertainments guide
cartera *f* wallet ; briefcase
carterista *m/f* pickpocket

cartero(a) *m/f* postman/woman
cartón *m* cardboard
casa *f* home ; house ; household
  casa de socorro first-aid post
casado(a) married
casarse (con) to marry
cascada *f* waterfall
cáscara *f* shell (egg, nut)
casco *m* helmet
casero(a) home-made
  comida casera home cooking
caseta *f* beach hut ; kennel
casete *m* cassette ; tape recorder
casi almost
caso: en caso de in case of
caspa *f* dandruff
castaña *f* chestnut
castañuelas *fpl* castanets
castellano(a) Spanish ; Castilian
castillo *m* castle
catalán(lana) Catalonian
catálogo *m* catalogue
catedral *f* cathedral
católico(a) Catholic
causa *f* cause
  a causa de because of
causar to cause
cava *m* sparkling white wine
caza *f* hunting ; game
cazar to hunt
cebo *m* bait (for fishing)
cebolla *f* onion
ceder to give way
  ceda el paso give way
celeste light blue
celo *m* Sellotape®
celoso(a) jealous
cementerio *m* cemetery
cena *f* dinner ; supper
cenar to have dinner
cenicero *m* ashtray
centímetro *m* centimetre
centralita *f* switchboard
centro *m* centre
Centroamérica *f* Central America
cepillo *m* brush
  cepillo de dientes toothbrush
  cepillo de uñas nailbrush
  cepillo del pelo hairbrush

cera f wax
cerámica f ceramics ; pottery
cerca (de) near ; close to
cercanías fpl outskirts ; proximity
  tren de cercanías suburban train
cerdo m pig ; pork
cereza f cherry
cerillas fpl matches
cero m zero
cerrado(a) closed
  cerrado por reforma closed for repairs
cerradura f lock
cerrar con llave to lock
cerro m hill
certificado m certificate
  certificado de seguros insurance certificate
certificado(a) registered
certificar to register
cervecería f pub
cerveza f beer ; lager
cesta f basket
cestería f basketwork (shop)
chalé m villa
chaleco m waistcoat ; tanktop
  chaleco salvavidas life jacket
champán m champagne
champiñón m mushroom
champú m shampoo
chancletas fpl flip flops
chaqueta f jacket
charcutería f delicatessen
cheque m cheque
  cheque de viaje traveller's cheque
chica f girl
chichón m lump (on head)
chico m boy
chico(a) small
chile m chilli
chimenea f fireplace ; chimney
chiringuito m bar ; stall
chocar to crash (car)
chocolate m chocolate ; hot chocolate
  chocolate puro plain chocolate
chocolatería f café serving hot chocolate
chófer m chauffeur ; driver
chorizo m hard pork sausage

chubasco m shower (rain)
chuleta f cutlet ; chop
chupete m dummy (for baby)
churrería f fritter shop or stand
churro m fritter
ciclista m/f cyclist
ciego(a) blind
cielo m sky ; heaven
cien hundred
CIF m tax number (for business)
cifra f number ; figure
cigarra f cicada
cigarrillo m cigarette
cigarro m cigar ; cigarette
cima f top ; peak
cine m cinema
cinta f tape ; ribbon
  cinta de vídeo video cassette
  cinta virgen blank tape
cintura f waist
cinturón m belt
  cinturón de seguridad safety belt
circulación f traffic
circular to drive ; to circulate
  circule por la derecha keep right (road sign)
ciruela f plum
  ciruela pasa prune
cirujano(a) m/f surgeon
cisterna f cistern
cistitis f cystitis
cita f appointment
ciudad f city ; town
ciudadano(a) m/f citizen
clarete m light red wine
claro(a) light (colour) ; clear
clase f class ; type ; lesson
  clase preferente club/business class
  clase turista economy class
clavícula f collar bone
clavija f tent peg
clavo m nail (metal) ; clove (spice)
cliente m/f customer ; client
climatizado(a) air-conditioned
clínica f clinic ; private hospital
club nocturno m night club
cobrador m conductor (train)
cobrar to charge ; to cash
  cobrar demasiado to overcharge
cobro m payment
cocer to cook ; to boil
coche m car ; coach (on train)

cochecama m sleeping car
cochecomedor m dining car
cocherestaurante m restaurant car
cochecito (del bebé) m pram
cocido m thick stew
cocido(a) cooked ; boiled
cocina f kitchen ; cooker ; cuisine
cocinar to cook
coco m coconut
código m code
　código de barras barcode
　código postal post-code
codo m elbow
coger to catch ; to get ; to pick up *(phone)*
cola f glue ; queue ; tail
colador m strainer ; colander
colchón m mattress
colega m/f colleague
colegio m school
colgar to hang up
coliflor f cauliflower
colina f hill
colisionar to crash
collar m necklace
color m colour
columna vertebral f spine
columpio m swing *(for children)*
comedor m dining room
comenzar to begin
comer to eat
comercio m trade ; business
comestibles mpl groceries
comida f food ; meal
　se sirven comidas meals served
　comidas caseras home cooking
comisaría f police station
¿cómo? how? ; pardon?
como as ; like ; since
cómodo(a) comfortable
compañero/a m/f colleague ; partner
compañía f company
compartimento m compartment
completo(a) full ; no vacancies *(sign)*
comportarse to behave
compositor(a) m/f composer
compra f purchase
　compras shopping
comprar to buy
comprender to understand
compresa f sanitary towel
comprobar to check

con with
concha f sea-shell
concierto m concert
concurrido(a) busy ; crowded
concurso m competition ; quiz
condón m condom
conducir to drive
conductor(a) m/f driver
conectar to connect ; to plug in
conejo m rabbit
conferencia f conference
confirmación f confirmation
confirmar to confirm
confitería f cake shop
confitura f jam
congelado(a) frozen
congelador m freezer
conjunto m group *(music)*
conmoción cerebral f concussion
conocer to know ; to be acquainted with
conseguir to obtain
conserje m caretaker
conservar to keep
conservas fpl tinned foods
consigna f left-luggage office
construir to build
consulado m consulate
consultorio m doctor's surgery
consumición f consumption ; drink
consumir to eat ; to use
　consumir antes de... best before...
contacto m contact ; ignition *(car)*
contador m meter
contagioso(a) infectious
contaminado(a) polluted
contener to hold *(to contain)*
contenido m contents
contento(a) pleased
contestador automático m answer-phone
contestar to answer ; to reply
continuación f sequel *(film, etc)*
continuar to continue
contra against
contrato m contract
control m inspection ; check
convento m convent ; monastery
copa f glass ; goblet

copa de helado mixed ice cream
tomar una copa to have a drink
copia f copy ; print *(photo)*
copiar to copy
corazón m heart
corbata f tie
corcho m cork
cordero m lamb ; mutton
cordillera f mountain range
coro m choir
correa f strap ; belt
correa de reloj watchstrap
correcto(a) right *(correct)*
correo m mail
correo electrónico e-mail
Correos m post office
correr to run
corrida de toros f bullfight
corriente f power ; current
(electric, water) ; draught *(of air)*
cortacircuitos m circuit breaker
cortado m espresso with dash of
milk
cortado(a) blocked *(road)*
cortar to cut
corte m cut
cortina f curtain
corto(a) short
cosa f thing
cosecha f harvest ; vintage *(wine)*
coser to sew
costa f coast
costar to cost
costero(a) coastal
costumbre f custom *(tradition)*
coto m reserve
coto de caza hunting by licence
coto de pesca fishing by licence
crédito m credit
a crédito on credit
creer to think ; to believe
crema f cream
crema de afeitar shaving cream
crema bronceadora suntan lotion
cremallera f zip
crisis nerviosa f nervous breakdown
cruce m junction ; crossroads
crucero m cruise
crucigrama m crossword puzzle
crudo(a) raw

cruzar to cross
c/u (cada uno) each (one)
cuaderno m exercise book
cuadro m picture ; painting
a cuadros checked *(pattern)*
cuajada f curd
¿cuál? which?
¿cuándo? when?
¿cuánto? how much?
¿cuántos? how many?
cuarentena f quarantine
Cuaresma f Lent
cuarto m room
cuarto de baño bathroom
cuarto de estar living room
cubierto m cover charge *(in
restaurant)* ; menu
cubierto(a) covered ; indoor
cubiertos mpl cutlery
cubo m bucket ; pail ; bin
cubrir to cover
cucaracha f cockroach
cuchara f spoon ; tablespoon
cucharilla f teaspoon
cuchillo m knife
cuenta f bill ; account *(at bank, etc)*
cuerda f string ; rope
cuero m leather
cuerpo m body
cuidado m care
¡cuidado! look out!
ten cuidado be careful!
cuidadoso(a) careful
cultivar to grow ; to farm
cumpleaños m birthday
¡feliz cumpleaños! happy
birthday!
cuna f cradle ; cot
cuñado(a) m/f brother/sister-in-law
curva f bend ; curve
curvas peligrosas dangerous bends

D

dados mpl dice
daltónico(a) colour-blind
damas fpl ladies
daños mpl damage
dar to give
dar de comer to feed
dar marcha atrás to reverse
dar propina to tip *(waiter, etc)*
dar un paseo to go for a walk

dátil m date (fruit)
datos mpl data ; information
DCHA. abbrev. for **derecha**
de of ; from
de acuerdo all right (agreed)
debajo (de) under ; underneath
deber to owe ; to have to
debido(a) due
decir to tell ; to say
declarar to declare
dedo m finger
   dedo del pie toe
defecto m fault ; defect
degustación f tasting (wine, etc)
dejar to let ; to leave
   dejar libre la salida keep clear
delante de in front of
delegación f regional office (government)
delgado(a) thin ; slim
delicioso(a) delicious
delito m crime
demasiado too much
   demasiado hecho(a) overdone
demora f delay
denominación de origen f guarantee of quality of wine
dentadura postiza f dentures
dentífrico m toothpaste
dentista m/f dentist
dentro (de) inside
departamento m compartment ; department
dependiente(a) m/f sales assistant
deporte m sport
depósito de gasolina m petrol tank
derecha f right(-hand side)
   a la derecha on/to the right
derecho m right ; law
   derechos de aduana customs duty
derecho(a) right ; straight
derramar to spill
derretir to melt
desabrochar to unfasten
desafilado(a) blunt (knife, blade)
desaparecer to disappear
desarrollar to develop
desatascador m plunger (for sink)
desayuno m breakfast
descafeinado(a) decaffeinated
descansar to rest
descanso m rest ; interval
descarga electrica f electric shock

descargado(a) flat (battery)
descolgar to take down ; to pick up (phone)
descongelar to defrost ; to de-ice
describir to describe
descubrir to discover
descuento m discount ; reduction
desde since ; from
desear to want
desembarcadero m quay
desempleado(a) unemployed
desenchufado(a) off ; disconnected
deseo m wish ; desire
desfile m parade
deshacer to undo ; to unpack
desinfectante m disinfectant
desmaquillador m make-up remover
desmayado(a) fainted
desnatado(a) skimmed
desodorante m deodorant
despacho m office
despacio slowly ; quietly
despegar to take-off
despertador m alarm (clock)
despertarse to wake up
después after ; afterward(s)
desteñir: *no destiñe* colourfast
destino m destination
destornillador m screwdriver
   destornillador de estrella phillips screwdriver
destornillar to unscrew
desvestirse to get undressed
desvío m detour ; diversion
detalle m detail ; nice gesture
   al detalle retail (commercial)
detener to arrest
detergente m detergent ; washing powder
detrás (de) behind
deuda f debt
devolver to give/put back
día m day
   todo el día all day
   día festivo public holiday
   día laborable working day ; weekday
diabético(a) m/f diabetic
diamante m diamond
diario(a) daily

diarrea f diarrhoea
dibujo m drawing
diccionario m dictionary
diciembre m December
diente m tooth
dieta f diet
 estar a dieta to be on a diet
difícil difficult
¿diga? hello *(on phone)*
dinero m money
 dinero en efectivo cash
Dios m God
diplomático(a) m/f diplomat
dirección f direction ; address
 dirección de correo electrónico e-mail address
 dirección particular home address
 dirección prohibida no entry
 dirección única one-way
directo(a) direct *(train, etc)*
director(a) m/f director ; manager
dirigir to manage *(be in charge of)*
disco m record ; disk
 disco duro hard disk
discoteca f disco ; nightclub
discrecional optional
disculpar to pardon ; to forgive
discutir to quarrel ; to argue
diseño m design ; drawing
disquete m computer disk *(floppy)*
disponible available
distancia f distance
distinto(a) different
distribuidor automático m vending machine
distrito m district
DIU m coil *(IUD)*
diversión f fun
divertido(a) funny *(amusing)*
divertirse to enjoy oneself
divisa f foreign currency
divorciado(a) divorced
doblado(a) folded ; dubbed *(film)*
doblar to fold
doble double
docena f dozen
documentos mpl documents
dólar m dollar
dolor m ache ; pain
 dolor de cabeza headache
 dolor de garganta sore throat
 dolor de muelas toothache
 dolor de oídos earache
doloroso(a) painful
domicilio m home address
domingo m Sunday
dominó m dominoes
¿dónde? where?
dormir to sleep
dormitorio m bedroom
dorso m back
 véase al dorso please turn over
dosis f dose ; dosage
droga f drug
ducha f shower
ducharse to take a shower
dueño(a) m/f owner
dulce sweet
 el agua dulce fresh water
dulce m dessert
durante during
duro(a) hard ; tough

E

echar to pour ; to throw ; to post
ecológico(a) organic ; environmentally friendly
edad f age *(of person)*
 edad mínima age limit
edificio m building
edredón m duvet ; quilt
edulcorante m sweetener
EE. UU. USA
efecto m effect
 efectos personales belongings
eje m axle *(car)*
ejemplar m copy *(of book)*
el the
él he ; him
electricidad f electricity
electricista m/f electrician
eléctrico(a) electric(al)
elegir to choose
ella she ; her
ello it
ellos(as) they ; them
embajada f embassy
embalse m reservoir
embarazada pregnant
embarcadero m jetty ; pier
embarcarse to board

3 **embarque** m boarding
embrague m clutch (in car)
emisión f broadcasting (radio, TV)
emitido por issued by
emocionante exciting
empachado(a) upset (stomach)
empezar to begin
empleo m employment ; use
empresa f firm ; company
empujar to push
  empuje push
en in ; into ; on
encaje m lace (fabric)
encantado(a) pleased to meet you!
encargado(a) m/f person in charge
encargar to order in advance
encendedor m cigarette lighter
encender to switch on ; to light
  encender las luces switch on
  headlights
encendido(a) on (light, TV, engine)
enchufar to plug in
enchufe m plug ; point ; socket
encima de onto ; on top of
encontrar to find
encontrarse con to meet (by chance)
enero m January
enfadado(a) angry
enfermedad f disease
enfermera(o) f/m nurse
enfermería f infirmary ; first-aid post
enfermo(a) ill
enfrente (de) opposite
¡enhorabuena! congratulations!
enjuagar to rinse
enjuague bucal m mouthwash
enlace m connection (train, etc)
ensalada f salad
enseñar to show ; to teach
entender to understand
entero(a) whole
entierro m funeral
entrada f entrance ; admission
  entrada libre admission free
  entrada por delante enter at
  the front
entrar to go in ; to get in ;
  to enter
entre among ; between
entreacto m interval
entregar to deliver
entremeses mpl hors d'œuvres

entrevista f interview
envase m container ; packaging
enviar to send
envío m shipment
envolver to wrap
epiléptico(a) epileptic
equipaje m luggage ; baggage
  equipaje de mano hand-luggage
equipo m team ; equipment
equitación f horseriding
equivocación f mistake ;
  misunderstanding
error m mistake
es he/she/it is
escala f stopover
escalar to climb (mountains)
escalera f stairs ; ladder
  escalera de incendios fire escape
  escalera de mano ladder
  escalera mecánica escalator
escalón m step (stair)
escapar to escape
escaparate m shop window
escenario m stage (theatre)
escoba f broom (brush)
escocés/escocesa Scottish
Escocia f Scotland
escoger to choose
esconder to hide
escribir to write
escrito: *por escrito* in writing
escuchar to listen to
escuela f school
escultura f sculpture
escurrir to wring
ese/esa this
esguince m sprain
esmalte m varnish
esos/esas those
espacio m space
espalda f back (of body)
España f Spain
español(a) Spanish
espantoso(a) awful
esparadrapo m sticking plaster
especia f spice
especialidad f speciality
especialista m/f specialist
espectáculo m entertainment ; show

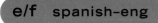

espectáculo de marionetas puppet show

espejo *m* mirror
 espejo retrovisor rear-view mirror

esperar to wait (for) ; to hope
 espere su turno please wait your turn

espina *f* fish bone ; thorn
 espina dorsal spine

espinacas *fpl* spinach

espinilla *f* spot *(pimple)*

esponja *f* sponge

esposa *f* wife

esposo *m* husband

espuma *f* foam ; mousse *(for hair)*
 espuma de afeitar shaving foam

espumoso(a) frothy ; sparkling

esq. *abbrev. for* **esquina**

esquí *m* skiing ; ski
 esquí acuático water-skiing
 esquí de fondo cross-country skiing

esquiar to ski

esquina *f* street corner

está you/he/she/it is

estación *f* railway station ; season
 estación de autobuses bus/coach station
 estación de servicio petrol/service station

estacionamiento *m* parking space

estacionar to park

estadio *m* stadium

Estados Unidos *mpl* United States

estanco *m* tobacconist's

estante *m* shelf

estar to be

estatua *f* statue

este *m* east

este/esta this

estéreo *m* stereo

estómago *m* stomach

estornudar to sneeze

estos/estas these

estragón *m* tarragon

estrecho(a) narrow

estrella *f* star

estreñimiento *m* constipation

estreno *m* première ; new release

estropeado(a) out of order

estudiante *m/f* student

etiqueta *f* label ; ticket ; tag
 de etiqueta formal dress

euro *m* Euro

Eurocheque *m* Eurocheque

Europa *f* Europe

evidente obvious

evitar to avoid

examen *m* examination

excelente excellent

excepcional rare *(unique)*

excepto except

exceso *m* excess

excursión *f* tour ; excursion

éxito *m* success

expedido(a) issued

experto(a) expert

explicar to explain

exportación *f* export

exportar to export

exposición *f* exhibition

expreso *m* express train

exprimir to squeeze

extintor *m* fire extinguisher

extranjero(a) *m/f* foreigner
 en el extranjero abroad

F

f.c. *abbrev. for* **ferrocarril**

fabada *f* pork and bean stew

fábrica *f* factory

fácil easy

factura *f* receipt ; bill ; account
 factura detallada itemized bill

facturación *f* check-in

falda *f* skirt

falso(a) fake

falta *f* foul *(football)* ; lack

familia *f* family

famoso(a) famous

farmacia *f* chemist's ; pharmacy
 farmacia de guardia duty chemist

faro *m* headlamp ; lighthouse
 faro antiniebla fog-lamp

farola *f* lamppost

faros *mpl* headlights

favor *m* favour
 por favor please

favorito(a) favourite

fax *m* fax

febrero *m* February

5 **fecha** f date
  fecha de adquisición date of purchase
  fecha de caducidad expiry date
  fecha de expedición date of issue
  fecha de nacimiento date of birth

feliz happy
  ¡feliz Año Nuevo! happy New Year!

femenino(a) feminine

feo(a) ugly

feria f trade fair ; funfair

ferrocarril m railway

festivos mpl public holidays

fiambre m cold meat

fianza f bail bond ; deposit

fibra sintética f man-made fibre

ficha f token ; counter

fichero m file *(computer)*

fiebre f fever

fiesta f party ; public holiday

fila f row ; line *(row, queue)*

filete m fillet ; steak

filial f branch

filtro m filter
  filtro de aceite oil filter
  filtro solar sunscreen

fin m end
  fin de semana weekend

finalizar to end ; to finish

finca f farm ; property

fino fine ; thin

fino m light, dry, very pale sherry

firma f signature

firmar to sign
  firme aquí sign here

flan m crème caramel

flojo(a) weak *(coffee, tea)*

flor f flower

florero m vase

floristería f florist's shop

foca f seal

foco m spotlight ; headlamp

folleto m leaflet ; brochure

fonda f inn ; small restaurant

fondo m bottom *(of pool, etc)*

fontanero m plumber

forfait m lift pass *(skiing)*

formulario m form

fósforo m match

foto f picture ; photo

fotocopia f photocopy

fotocopiar to photocopy

fotografía f photograph

fotógrafo(a) m/f photographer

fractura f fracture

frágil fragile ; handle with care

francés(esa) French

Francia f France

frecuente frequent

fregadero m sink *(in kitchen)*

fregona f mop *(for floor)*

freír to fry

frenar to brake

freno m brake

frente a opposite

frente f forehead

fresa f strawberry

fresco(a) fresh ; crisp ; cool

frigorífico m fridge

frío(a) cold

frito(a) fried

frontera f border ; frontier

frotar to rub

fruta f fruit
  fruta del tiempo fruit in season

frutería f fruit shop

frutos secos mpl nuts *(to eat)*

fuego m fire

fuente f fountain

fuera outdoors ; out

fuerte strong ; loud

fuga f leak *(of gas, liquid)*

fumadores mpl smokers

fumar to smoke
  prohibido fumar no smoking

función f show

funcionar to work *(machine, car)*
  no funciona out of order

funcionario(a) m/f civil servant

funda f case ; crown *(for tooth)* ; pillowcase
  funda de gafas glasses case

funda nórdica f duvet cover

fusible m fuse

fútbol m football

futbolista m/f football player

G

gafas fpl glasses
  gafas de sol sunglasses

galería f gallery

galería de arte art gallery
galés/galesa Welsh
gallego(a) Galician
galleta f biscuit
ganar to earn ; to win *(sports, etc)*
garaje m garage
garantía f guarantee
garganta f throat
gas m gas
  gas butano Calor gas®
  con gas fizzy
  sin gas non-fizzy ; still
gasa f gauze ; nappy
gaseosa f lemonade
gasoil m diesel fuel
gasóleo m diesel oil
gasolina f petrol
  gasolina sin plomo unleaded petrol
  gasolina súper 4-star petrol
gasolinera f petrol station
gastado(a) worn
gastar to spend *(money)*
gastos mpl expenses
gastritis f gastritis
gato m cat ; jack *(for car)*
gaviota f seagull
gemelo(a) m/f identical twin
género m type ; material
generoso(a) generous
gente f people
gerente m/f manager/manageress
ginebra f gin
girar to turn around
globo m balloon
glorieta f roundabout
golfo de Vizcaya m Bay of Biscay
goma f rubber ; eraser
gomita f rubber band
gordo(a) fat
gorra f cap *(hat)*
gorro m hat
gotera f hole
Gótico(a) Gothic
grabar en vídeo to video *(from TV)*
gracias thank you
grada f tier
gramo m gram(me)
Gran Bretaña f Great Britain

grande large ; big ; tall
grandes almacenes mpl department store
granja f farm
granjero(a) m/f farmer
grasiento(a) greasy
gratinado(a) au gratin ; grilled
gratinar to grill
gratis free *(costing nothing)*
grave serious *(accident, etc)*
grifo m tap
gripe f flu
gris grey
gritar to shout
grosella negra f blackcurrant
grosella roja f redcurrant
grúa f crane ; breakdown van
grueso(a) thick *(not thin)*
grupo m group ; band *(rock)*
  grupo sanguíneo blood group
guacamole m avocado dip
guantes mpl gloves
  guantes de goma rubber gloves
guapo(a) handsome ; attractive
guardacostas m/f coastguard
guardar to put away ; to keep
guardarropa m cloakroom
guardería f nursery
guardería infantil f nursery school
guardia f guard
  Guardia Civil Civil Guard
  Guardia Nacional National Guard
  de guardia on duty
guarnición f garnish
guerra f war
guía m/f courier ; guide
Guía del ocio f What's on
guía telefónica f phone directory
guiar to guide
guindilla f chilli pepper
guiso m stew ; casserole
guitarra f guitar
gusano m maggot ; worm
gustar to like ; to enjoy

H

haba f broad bean
habano m Havana cigar
habitación f room
  habitación doble double room
  habitación individual single room

hablar (con) to speak/talk (to)
  se habla inglés English spoken
hacer to do ; to make
  hacer autostop to hitchhike
  hacer cola to queue
  hacer daño to hurt ; to damage
  hacer footing to jog
  hacer las maletas to pack *(case)*
  hacer punto to knit
  hacer surf to surf
  hacer topless to go topless
  hacer transbordo de to change *(bus/train)*
  hacer turismo to sightsee
hacia toward(s)
  hacia adelante forwards
  hacia atrás backwards
hamburguesa f hamburger
harina f flour
hasta until ; till
hay there is/there are
hecho(a) finished ; done
  hecho a mano handmade
  hecho(a) de... made of...
helada f frost
heladería f ice-cream parlour
helado m ice cream
helicóptero m helicopter
hemorragia f haemorrhage
hemorroides fpl haemorrhoids
hepatitis f hepatitis
herida f wound ; injury
herido(a) injured
herir to hurt
hermana f sister
hermano m brother
hermoso(a) beautiful
hernia f hernia
herramienta f tool
hervido(a) boiled
hervidor (de agua) m kettle
hervir to boil
hidrofoil m hydrofoil
hidropedal m pedal boat/pedalo
hielo m ice
  con hielo with ice
hierba f grass ; herb
hierbabuena f mint
hierro m iron
  hierro forjado wrought iron
hígado m liver
higo m fig
  higos chumbos prickly pears
hija f daughter

hijo m son
hilo m thread
hincha m/f fan *(football, etc)*
hinchado(a) swollen
hipermercado m hypermarket
hipermétrope long sighted
hípica f showjumping
hipódromo m racecourse *(horses)*
histórico(a) historic
hogar m home ; household
hoja f sheet ; leaf
  hoja de registro registration form
  hoja de afeitar razor blade
hola hello ; hi!
hombre m man
hombro m shoulder
hora f hour ; appointment
  hora punta rush hour
  horas de visita visiting hours
horario m timetable
horchata de chufa f refreshing tiger nut drink
hormiga f ant
horno m oven
  (horno) microondas microwave
  al horno baked ; roasted
horquilla f hairgrip
hospital m hospital
hostal m small hotel ; hostel
hotel m hotel
hoy today
huelga f strike *(of workers)*
hueso m bone
huésped(a) m/f guest
huevo m egg
  huevos de corral free-range eggs
  huevo de Pascua Easter egg
  huevos duros hard-boiled eggs
  huevos escalfados poached eggs
  huevos al plato baked eggs
  huevos revueltos scrambled eggs
humo m smoke

I

ida f outward journey
  de ida y vuelta return *(ticket)*
idioma m language
iglesia f church
igual equal

imán m magnet
impar odd (number)
imperdible m safety pin
impermeable m raincoat ; waterproof
importante important
importar to matter ; to import
importe total m total (amount)
imprescindible essential
impreso m form
  impreso de solicitud application form
  impresos printed matter
impuesto m tax
incendio m fire
incluido(a) included
incómodo(a) uncomfortable
inconsciente unconscious
indicaciones fpl directions
índice m index
indigestión f indigestion
individual individual ; single
infarto m heart attack
infección f infection
inferior inferior ; lower
inflamación f inflammation
información f information
informe m report (medical, police)
infracción f offence
  infracción de tráfico traffic offence
ingeniero(a) m/f engineer
Inglaterra f England ; Britain
inglés/inglesa English
ingredientes mpl ingredients
inhalador m inhaler (for medication)
inmediatamente immediately
inmunización f immunisation
inquilino(a) m/f tenant
insecto m insect
insolación f sunstroke
instituto m institute ; secondary school
instrucciones fpl directions ; instructions
instructor(a) m/f instructor
instrumento m tool
insulina f insulin
interesante interesting
interior inside

intermitente m indicator (in car)
internacional international
Internet m internet
intérprete m/f interpreter
interruptor m switch
intoxicación por alimentos f food poisoning
introducir to introduce ; to insert
  introduzca monedas insert coins
inundación f flood
invierno m winter
invitación f invitation
invitado(a) m/f guest
invitar to invite
inyección f injection
ir to go
  ir a buscar to fetch
  ir de compras to go shopping
  ir en bicicleta to cycle
  irse a casa to go home
  irse de to leave (a place)
Irlanda f Ireland
Irlanda del Norte f Northern Ireland
irlandés/irlandesa Irish
isla f island
Italia f Italy
italiano(a) Italian
itinerario m route ; schedule
IVA m VAT
IZQ. / IZQDA. abbrev. for **izquierda**
izquierda f left
izquierdo(a) left

J

jabón m soap
jamás never
jamón m ham
  jamón serrano cured ham
  jamón de York cooked ham
Japón m Japan
japonés/japonesa m/f Japanese
jaqueca f migraine
jardín m garden
jarra f jug ; mug ; carafe
jefe(a) m/f chief ; head ; boss
jerez m sherry
jerga f slang
jeringuilla f syringe
joven young
joya f jewel
  joyas jewellery
joyería f jeweller's

9 **jubilado(a)** *m/f* retired person
jubilarse to retire
judías *fpl* beans
judío(a) Jew
juego *m* game
jueves *m* Thursday
juez(a) *m/f* judge
jugador(a) *m/f* player
jugar to play ; to gamble
julio *m* July
jugo *m* juice
juguete *m* toy
juguetería *f* toy shop
junio *m* June
junto(a) together
  junto a next to
juventud *f* youth

K

kilo *m* kilo(gram)
kilometraje *m* mileage
  kilometraje ilimitado unlimited mileage
kilómetro *m* kilometre
kiosko (de prensa) *m* newsstand
kiwi *m* kiwi fruit

L

la the ; her ; it ; you *(formal)*
labio *m* lip
laborable working *(day)*
  laborables weekdays
laca *f* hair spray
lado *m* side
  al lado de beside
ladrar to bark
ladrillo *m* brick
ladrón(ona) *m/f* thief
lago *m* lake
lámpara *f* lamp
lana *f* wool
lancha *f* launch
  lancha motora motor launch
lápiz *m* pencil
  lápiz de ojos eyeliner
largo(a) long
  largo recorrido long-distance *(train, etc)*
lata *f* can *(container)* ; tin
latón *m* brass

lavable washable
lavabo *m* lavatory ; washbasin
lavado de coches *m* car wash
lavado(a) washed
  lavado en seco dry-cleaning
  lavado y marcado shampoo and set
lavadora *f* washing machine
lavanda *f* lavender
lavandería *f* laundry ; launderette
lavavajillas *m* dishwasher
lavar to wash
  lavarse to wash oneself
laxante *m* laxative
leche *f* milk
  leche de soja soya milk
  leche de vaca cow's milk
  leche desnatada skimmed milk
  leche entera whole milk
  leche hidratante moisturizer
  leche semidesnatada semi-skimmed milk
lechuga *f* lettuce
lector de CD *m* CD player
lectura de labios *f* lip-reading
leer to read
legumbres *fpl* pulses
lejía *f* bleach
lejos far
lencería *f* lingerie ; linen ; draper's
lengua *f* language ; tongue
lente *f* lens
  lentes de contacto contact lenses
lentejas *fpl* lentils
lentillas *fpl* contact lenses
lento(a) slow
león *m* lion
lesbiana *f* lesbian
letra *f* letter *(of alphabet)*
levantar to lift
levantarse to get up ; to rise
ley *f* law
libra *f* pound *(currency, weight)*
  libra esterlina pound sterling
libre free/vacant
  libre de impuestos tax-free
  dejen el paso libre keep clear
librería *f* bookshop
libro *m* book
licencia *f* permit ; licence
licenciarse to graduate

licor *m* liqueur
  licores spirits
lidia *f* bullfight
ligero(a) light *(not heavy)*
lima *f* file *(for nails)* ; lime
límite *m* limit ; boundary
  límite de velocidad speed limit
limón *m* lemon
limonada *f* lemonade
limpiar to clean
limpieza en seco *f* dry-cleaning
limpio(a) clean
línea *f* line
lino *m* linen
linterna *f* torch ; flashlight
liquidación *f* sales
líquido *m* liquid
  líquido de frenos brake fluid
liso(a) plain ; smooth
lista *f* list
  lista de correos poste restante
  lista de precios price list
  listo(a) para comer ready-cooked
listo(a) ready
litera *f* berth ; couchette ; sleeper
litoral *m* coast
litro *m* litre
llaga *f* ulcer *(mouth)*
llamada *f* call
  llamada a cobro revertido reverse
  charge call
llamar to call ; to ring ; to knock *(on
  door)*
llano(a) flat
llanta *f* tyre
llave *f* key ; tap ; spanner
  llave de contacto ignition key
  llaves del coche car keys
  llave inglesa spanner
  llave tarjeta card key
llavero *m* keyring
Lleg. *abbrev. for* **llegadas**
llegada *f* arrival
  llegadas (Lleg.) arrivals
llegar to arrive ; to come
llenar to fill ; to fill in
lleno(a) full (up)
  lleno, por favor fill it up, please
llevar to bring ; to wear ; to carry
  para llevar to take away
llorar to cry *(weep)*

lluvia *f* rain
lobo *m* wolf
local *m* premises ; bar
localidad *f* place
  localidades tickets *(theatre)*
loción *f* lotion
loncha *f* slice *(ham, etc)*
Londres *m* London
longitud *f* length
lotería *f* lottery
luces *fpl* lights
luchar to fight
lugar *m* place
  lugar de nacimiento place of birth
  lugar de expedición issued in
  lugar fresco cool place
lujo *m* luxury
luna *f* moon
  luna de miel honeymoon
lunes *m* Monday
lupa *f* magnifying glass
luz *f* light
  luz de freno brake light
  luz de posición sidelight

M

macedonia *f* fruit salad
madera *f* wood
madrastra *f* stepmother
madre *f* mother
maduro(a) ripe ; mature
mago *m* magician ; wizard
maíz *m* maize ; corn
mal/malo(a) bad *(weather, news)*
maleta *f* case ; suitcase
maletero *m* boot *(car)*
Mallorca *f* Majorca
malo(a) bad
mañana tomorrow
mañana *f* morning
mancha *f* stain ; mark
mandar to send
  mandar por fax to fax
mandíbula *f* jaw
mando a distancia *m* remote
  control
manera *f* way ; manner
manga *f* sleeve
manguera *f* hosepipe
manillar *m* handlebars
mano *f* hand
  de segunda mano secondhand

manopla f mitten
  manopla de horno oven glove
manso(a) tame *(animal)*
manta f blanket
mantel m tablecloth
mantener to maintain ; to keep
mantequería f dairy products
mantequilla f butter
  mantequilla de cacahuete peanut
  butter
mantita f picnic rug
manzana f apple ; block *(of houses)*
manzanilla f camomile tea ; dry
  sherry
mapa m map
  mapa de carreteras road map
maquillaje m make-up
máquina f machine
  máquina de afeitar razor
  máquina de fotos camera
mar m sea
marca f brand ; make
marcapasos m pacemaker
marcar to dial
  marcar un gol to score a goal
marcha f gear
  marcha atrás reverse gear
marco m picture frame
marea f tide
  marea alta/baja high/low tide
mareado(a) sick *(car, sea etc)* ; dizzy
margarina f margarine
marido m husband
marioneta f puppet
mariposa f butterfly
mariscos mpl seafood ; shellfish
marisquería f seafood restaurant
mármol m marble
marrón brown
marroquí Moroccan
marroquinería f leather goods
martes m Tuesday
martillo m hammer
marzo m March
más more ; plus
  más que more than
  más tarde later
masa f pastry *(dough)*
masculino(a) male
matar to kill
matrícula f car number plate
matrimonio m marriage
máximo m maximum

mayo m May
mayonesa f mayonnaise
mayor bigger ; biggest
  mayor parte de most of
  mayor que bigger than
  mayores de 18 años over-18s
mayúscula f capital letter
mazapán m marzipan
mazo m mallet
mecánico m mechanic
mechero m lighter
medianoche f midnight
medias fpl tights ; stockings
medicina f medicine ; drug
médico(a) m/f doctor
medida f measurement ; size
medio m the middle
medio(a) half
medio(a) half
  media hora half an hour
  media pensión half board
  medio hecho(a) medium rare
mediodía :*las doce del
  mediodía* midday ; noon
medir to measure
Mediterráneo m Mediterranean
medusa f jellyfish
mejicano(a) m/f Mexican
Méjico m Mexico
mejilla f cheek
mejor best ; better
  mejor que better than
mejorana f marjoram
melocotón m peach
melón m melon
menaje m kitchen utensils
  menaje de hogar household goods
mendigo(a) m/f beggar
menestra f vegetable stew
meningitis f meningitis
menor smaller/smallest ; least
Menorca f Minorca
menos minus ; less ; except
  menos que less than
mensaje m message
mensual monthly
menta f mint ; peppermint
mentira f lie *(untruth)*
menú m menu
  menú del día set menu

m/n spanish–eng

mercado *m* market
mercancías *fpl* goods
mercería *f* haberdasher's
merendero *m* open-air snack bar ; picnic area
merienda *f* afternoon snack ; picnic
mermelada *f* jam
  mermelada de naranja orange marmalade
mes *m* month
mesa *f* table
mesón *m* traditional restaurant
metal *m* metal
metro *m* metre ; underground ; tape measure
México *m* Mexico
mezclar to mix
mi my
mí me
miel *f* honey
mientras while
miércoles *m* Wednesday
miga *f* crumb
migraña *f* migraine
mil thousand
mil millones billion
milímetro *m* millimetre
millón *m* million
mínimo *m* minimum
minusválido(a) *m/f* disabled person
minuto *m* minute
miope short-sighted
mirar to look at ; to watch
misa *f* mass *(in church)*
mismo(a) same
mitad *f* half
mixto(a) mixed
mochila *f* backpack ; rucksack
  mochila portabebés baby sling
moda *f* fashion
moderno(a) modern
modo *m* way ; manner
  modo de empleo how to use
mojado(a) wet
mole *m* black chilli sauce
molestar to disturb
molestia *f* nuisance ; discomfort
molido(a) ground *(coffee beans, etc)*
molino *m* mill

molino de viento windmill
monasterio *m* monastery
moneda *f* currency ; coin
  introduzca monedas insert coins
monedero *m* purse
monitor(a) de esquí *m/f* ski instructor
montaña *f* mountain
montañismo *m* mountaineering
montar to ride
  montar a caballo to horse ride
montilla *m* a sherry-type wine
monumento *m* monument
moqueta *f* fitted carpet
mora *f* mulberry ; blackberry
morado(a) purple
mordedura *f* bite
morder to bite
moretón (moratón) *m* bruise
morir to die
mosca *f* fly
mosquitera *f* mosquito net
mostrador *m* counter ; desk
mostrar to show
moto *f* (motor)bike ; moped
  moto acuática jet ski
motocicleta *f* motorbike
motor *m* engine ; motor
mozo *m* luggage porter
mucho a lot
mucho(a) a lot (of) ; much
muchos(as) many
muela *f* tooth
muelle *m* quay ; pier
muerto(a) dead
muestra *f* exhibition ; sample
mujer *f* woman ; wife
multa *f* fine *(to be paid)*
mundo *m* world
muñeca *f* wrist ; doll
muro *m* wall
músculo *m* muscle
museo *m* museum ; art gallery
música *f* music
muy very
  muy hecho(a) well done *(steak)*

N

nacer to be born
nacimiento *m* birth
nación *f* nation

3 nacional national ; domestic *(flight)*
nacionalidad *f* nationality
nada nothing
  de nada don't mention it
  nada más nothing else
nadador(a) *m/f* swimmer
nadar to swim
nadie nobody
naipes *mpl* playing cards
naranja *f* orange
naranjada *f* orangeade
nariz *f* nose
nata *f* cream
  nata agria soured cream
  nata batida whipped cream
  nata montada whipped cream
natación *f* swimming
natural natural ; fresh ; plain
naturista *m/f* naturist
navaja *f* pocketknife ; penknife
Navidad *f* Christmas
neblina *f* mist
necesario(a) necessary
necesitar to need ; to require
nectarina *f* nectarine
negarse to refuse
negativo *m* negative *(photo)*
negocios *mpl* business
negro(a) black
neumático *m* tyre
  neumáticos antideslizantes
  snow tyres
nevar to snow
nevera *f* refrigerator
  nevera portátil cool-box
nido *m* nest
niebla *f* fog
nieto(a) *m/f* grandson/daughter
nieve *f* snow
NIF *m* tax number *(of company)*
niña *f* girl ; baby girl
niñera *f* nanny
ningún/ninguno(a) none
niño *m* boy ; baby ; child
  niños children *(infants)*
nivel *m* level ; standard
N° *abbrev. for* **número**
noche *f* night
  esta noche tonight
Nochebuena *f* Christmas Eve
Nochevieja *f* New Year's Eve
nocivo(a) harmful
nombre *m* name

  nombre de pila first name
norte *m* north
Norteamérica *f* America ; USA
norteamericano(a) American
nosotros(as) we
notaría *f* solicitor's office
notario(a) *m/f* notary ; solicitor
noticias *fpl* news
novela *f* novel
novia *f* girlfriend ; fiancée ; bride
noviembre *m* November
novio *m* boyfriend ; fiancé ; bridegroom
nube *f* cloud
nublado(a) cloudy
nudo *m* knot
nuestro(a) our ; ours
Nueva Zelanda *f* New Zealand
nuevo(a) new
nuez *f* walnut
número *m* number ; size ; issue
  número par even *(number)*
nunca never

O

o or
  o... o... either... or...
obispo *m* bishop
objetivo *m* lens *(on camera)*
objeto *m* object
  objetos de valor valuables
  objetos de regalo gifts
obligatorio(a) compulsory
obra *f* work ; play *(theatre)*
  obra maestra masterpiece
  obras road works
observar to watch
obstruido(a) blocked *(pipe)*
obtener to get *(to obtain)*
océano *m* ocean
ocio *m* spare time
octubre *m* October
ocupado engaged
oeste *m* west
oferta *f* special offer
oficina *f* office
  Oficina de Correos Post Office
oficio *m* church service ;
profession

ofrecer to offer
oído *m* ear
oír to hear
ojo *m* eye
  ¡ojo! look out!
ola *f* wave *(on sea)*
olivo *m* olive tree
olor *m* smell
oloroso *m* cream sherry
olvidar to forget
onda *f* wave
ópera *f* opera
operación *f* operation
operador(a) *m/f* operator
oportunidades *fpl* bargains
orden *f* command
orden *m* order
ordenador *m* computer
  ordenador portátil laptop
oreja *f* ear
organizar to arrange ; to organize
orilla *f* shore
orina *f* urine
oro *m* gold
oscuro(a) dark ; dim
oso *m* bear *(animal)*
ostra *f* oyster
otoño *m* autumn ; fall
otro(a) other ; another
  otra vez again
oxígeno *m* oxygen

P

paciente *m/f* patient *(in hospital)*
padrastro *m* stepfather
padre *m* father
  padres parents
paella *f* paella *(rice dish)*
pagado(a) paid
pagar to pay for ; to pay
  pagar al contado to pay cash
  pagar por separado to pay separately
pagaré *m* IOU
página *f* page
  página web website
  Páginas Amarillas Yellow Pages
pago *m* payment
  pago por adelantado payment in advance

pague en caja please pay at cash desk
país *m* country
paisaje *m* landscape ; countryside
pájaro *m* bird
pajita *f* straw *(for drinking)*
palabra *f* word
palacio *m* palace
palco *m* box *(in theatre)*
pálido(a) pale
palillo *m* toothpick
palo *m* stick ; mast
  palo de golf golf club
paloma *f* pigeon ; dove
pan *m* bread ; loaf of bread
  pan de centeno rye bread
  pan integral wholemeal bread
  pan de molde sliced bread
  pan tostado toast
panadería *f* bakery
pañal *m* nappy
panecillo *m* bread roll
paño *m* flannel ; cloth
pantalla *f* screen
pantalones *mpl* trousers
  pantalones cortos shorts
pantys *mpl* tights
pañuelo *m* handkerchief ; scarf
  pañuelo de papel tissue
papa *m* pope
papel *m* paper
  papel higiénico toilet paper
  papeles del coche log book *(car)*
papelería *f* stationer's
paquete *m* packet ; parcel
par even (number)
par *m* pair
para for; towards
parabrisas *m* windscreen
parachoques *m* bumper *(on car)*
parada *f* stop
parado(a) unemployed
parador *m* state-run hotel
parafina *f* paraffin
paraguas *m* umbrella
parar to stop
parecido(a) a similar to
pared *f* wall *(inside)*
pareja *f* couple *(2 people)*
parque *m* park
  parque de atracciones funfair
  parque nacional national park*

5 **parquímetro** *m* parking meter
parrilla *f* grill ; barbecue
  a la parrilla grilled
particular private
partida *f* game ; departure
  partida de nacimiento birth
  certificate
partido *m* match *(sport)* ; party
  (political)
partir to depart
pasa *f* raisin ; currant
pasado(a) stale *(bread)* ; rotten
pasaje *m* ticket ; fare ; alleyway
pasajero(a) *m/f* passenger
pasaporte *m* passport
pasar to happen
pasatiempo *m* hobby ; pastime
Pascua *f* Easter
  Pascua de Navidad Christmas
  ¡felices Pascuas! merry Christmas!
paseo *m* walk ; avenue ;
  promenade
  Paseo Colón Columbus Avenue
pasillo *m* corridor ; aisle
paso *m* step ; pace
  paso de ganado cattle crossing
  paso inferior subway
  paso a nivel level crossing
  paso de peatones pedestrian
  crossing
  paso subterráneo subway
pasta *f* pastry ; pasta
  pasta de dientes toothpaste
pastel *m* cake ; pie
  pasteles pastries
pastelería *f* cakes and pastries ;
  cake shop
pastilla *f* tablet *(medicine)* ; pill
  pastilla de jabón bar of soap
pastor(a) *m/f* shepherd ; minister
patata *f* potato
  patatas fritas french fries ; crisps
patinaje *m* skating
patinar to skate
patines *mpl* skates
  patines en línea rollerblades
pato *m* duck
pavo *m* turkey
paz *f* peace
p. ej. *abbrev. for* **por ejemplo**
peaje *m* toll
peatón *m/f* pedestrian
peces *mpl* fish
pecho *m* chest ; breast

pechuga *f* breast *(poultry)*
pedir to ask for ; to order
  pedir prestado to borrow
pegamento *m* gum ; glue
pegar to stick (on) ; to hit
peine *m* comb
pelar to peel *(fruit)*
película *f* film
peligro *m* danger
  peligro de incendio danger of fire
peligroso(a) dangerous
pelo *m* hair
pelota *f* ball ; Basque ball game
  pelota de golf golf ball
  pelota de tenis tennis ball
peluca *f* wig
peluquería *f* hairdresser's
pendientes *mpl* earrings
pene *m* penis
penicilina *f* penicillin
pensar to think
pensión *f* guesthouse
  pensión completa full board
  media pensión half board
pensionista *m/f* senior citizen
peor worse ; worst
pequeño(a) little ; small ; tiny
pera *f* pear
percha *f* coat hanger
perder to lose ; to miss *(train, etc)*
perdido(a) missing *(lost)*
perdiz *f* partridge
perdón *m* pardon ; sorry
perdonar to forgive
perejil *m* parsley
perezoso(a) lazy
perfecto(a) perfect
perforar: *no perforar* do not pierce
perfumería *f* perfume shop
periódico *m* newspaper
periodista *m/f* journalist
perla *f* pearl
permiso *m* permission ; pass ;
  permit ; licence
  permiso de caza hunting permit
  permiso de residencia residence
  permit
  permiso de trabajo work permit
permitido(a) permitted ; allowed
permitir to allow ; to let

pero but
perro m dog
persiana f blind *(for window)*
persona f person
personal m staff
pesado(a) heavy ; boring
pesar to weigh
pesca f fishing
pescadería f fishmonger's
pescado m fish
pescador(a) m/f fisherman/woman
pescar to fish
peso m weight ; scales
petirrojo m robin
pez m fish
picado(a) chopped ; minced ; rough
(sea) ; stung *(by insect)*
picadura f insect bite ; sting
picante peppery ; hot ; spicy
picar to itch ; to sting
pie m foot
piedra f stone
piel f fur ; skin ; leather
pierna f leg
pieza f part ; room
piezas del coche car parts
pijama m pyjamas
pila f battery *(radio, etc)*
píldora f pill
pileta f sink
pimienta f pepper *(spice)*
a la pimienta au poivre
pimiento m pepper *(vegetable)*
piña f pineapple
pinacoteca f art gallery
pinchar to have a puncture
pinchazo m puncture
pinchos mpl savoury titbits
pinchos morunos kebabs
pintar to paint
pintura f paint ; painting
pinza f clothes peg
pinzas tweezers
pipa f pipe *(smoker's)*
pipirrana f tomato/cucumber salad
Pirineos mpl Pyrenees
piruleta f lollipop
pisar to step on ; to tread on
no pisar el césped keep off grass

piscina f swimming pool
piso m floor ; storey ; flat
piso deslizante slippery road
pista f track ; court
pistacho m pistachio
pisto m sautéed vegetables
pistola f gun
placa f licence plate
plancha f iron *(for clothes)*
a la plancha grilled
planchar to iron
plano m plan ; town map
planta f plant ; floor ; sole *(of foot)*
planta baja ground floor
plata f silver ; money
plátano m banana ; plane tree
platea f stalls *(theatre)*
platería f jeweller's
platillo m saucer
platinos mpl points *(in car)*
plato m plate ; dish *(food)* ; course
plato del día dish of the day
plato principal main course
playa f beach ; seaside
plaza f square *(in town)*
plaza de toros bull ring
plazas libres vacancies
plazo m period ; expiry date
plomo m lead *(metal)*
pluma f feather
pobre poor
poco(a) little
poco hecho(a) rare *(steak)*
un poco de a bit of
pocos(as) (a) few
poder to be able
podólogo(a) m/f chiropodist
podrido(a) rotten *(fruit, etc)*
policía f police
Policía Municipal traffic police
policía m/f policeman/woman
polideportivo m leisure centre
póliza f policy ; certificate
póliza de seguros insurance policy
pollería f poultry shop
pollo m chicken
polo m ice lolly
poltrona f armchair
polvo m powder ; dust
polvos de talco talcum powder
pomada f ointment
pomelo m grapefruit
ponche m punch

7 **poner** to put
  poner en marcha to start *(car)*
  ponerse en contacto to contact
por by ; per ; through ; about
  por adelantado in advance
  por correo by mail
  por ejemplo for example
  por favor please
porción f portion
porque because
portaequipajes m luggage rack
portero m caretaker ; doorman
portugués(guesa) Portuguese
posible possible
posología f dosage
postal f postcard
postigos mpl shutters
postre m dessert ; sweet
potable drinkable
potaje m stew ; thick soup
pote m stew
potito m baby food
pozo m well *(water)*
  pozo séptico septic tank
prado m meadow
precio m price ; cost
precioso(a) lovely
precipicio m cliff ; precipice
preciso(a) precise ; necessary
preferir to prefer
prefijo m dialling code
pregunta f question
preguntar to ask
premio m prize
prensa f press
preocupado(a) worried
preparado(a) cooked
preparar to prepare ; to cook
presa f dam
prescribir to prescribe
presentar to introduce
preservativo m condom
presión f pressure
  presión arterial blood pressure
prestar to lend
primavera f spring *(season)*
primer/o(a) first
  primeros auxilios first aid
primo(a) m/f cousin
princesa f princess
principal main
príncipe m prince
principiante m/f beginner

prioridad (de paso) f right of way
prismáticos mpl binoculars
privado(a) private
probadores mpl changing rooms
probar to try ; to taste
probarse to try on *(clothes)*
problema m problem
procedente de... coming from...
productos mpl produce ; products
  productos lácteos dairy products
profesión f profession ; job
profesor(a) m/f teacher
profundo(a) deep
programa m programme
  programa de ordenador computer
  program
prohibido(a) prohibited/no...
  prohibido bañarse no bathing
  prohibido el paso no entry
prometer to promise
prometido(a) engaged *(to be married)*
pronóstico m forecast
  pronóstico del tiempo weather
  forecast
pronto soon
pronunciar to pronounce
propiedad f property
propietario(a) m/f owner
propina f tip
propio(a) own
protegido(a) sheltered
provisional temporary
próximo(a) next
público m audience
público(a) public
puchero m cooking pot ; stew
pueblo m village ; country
puente m bridge
puerro m leek
puerta f door ; gate
  cierren la puerta close the door
  puerta de embarque boarding
  gate
  puerta principal front door
puerto m port ; pass *(mountain)*
puesta de sol f sunset
puesta en marcha f starter *(of car)*
puesto que since
pulgada f = approx. 2.5 cm inch

p/q/r spanish–eng

pulgar m thumb
pulgas fpl fleas
pulmón m lung
pulpo m octopus
pulsera f bracelet
punto m stitch
  punto muerto neutral (car)
puntuación f score (of match)
puré m purée
puro m cigar
puro(a) pure

Q

que than ; that
¿qué? what? ; which?
  ¿qué tal? how are you?
quedar to remain ; to be left
  quedar bien to fit (clothes)
queja f complaint
quemado(a) burnt
quemadura f burn
  quemadura del sol sunburn
quemar to burn
querer to want ; to love
  querer decir to mean
querido(a) dear (on letter)
queroseno m paraffin
queso m cheese
¿quién? who?
quincena f fortnight
quinientos(as) five hundred
quiosco m kiosk
quiste m cyst
quitaesmalte m nail polish remover
quitamanchas m stain remover
quitar to remove
quizá(s) perhaps

R

rabia f rabies
ración f portion
  raciones snacks
radiador m radiator
radio f radio
radio m spoke (wheel)
radiocasete m cassette player
radiografía f X-ray

rallador m cheese grater
rama f branch (of tree)
ramo m bunch (of flowers)
rápido m express train
rápido(a) quick ; fast
raqueta f racket
rasgar to tear ; to rip
rastrillo m rake
rastro m flea market
rata f rat
ratero m pickpocket
rato m a while
ratón m mouse
razón f reason
real royal
rebajas fpl sale
recalentar to overheat
recambio m spare ; refill
recargar to recharge (battery, etc)
recepción f reception
recepcionista m/f receptionist
receta f prescription ; recipe
recibir to receive
recibo m receipt
recientemente recently
reclamación f claim ; complaint
reclamar to claim
recoger to collect
recogida f collection
  recogida de equipajes baggage reclaim
recomendar to recommend
reconocer to recognize
recordar to remember
recorrido m journey ; route
  de largo recorrido long-distance
recuerdo m souvenir
recuperarse to recover (from illness)
red f net
redondo(a) round (shape)
reducción f reduction
reducir to reduce
reembolsar to reimburse ; to refund
reembolso m refund
refresco m refreshment ; drink
refugio m shelter ; moutain hut
regadera f watering can
regalo m gift ; present
régimen m diet
región f district ; area ; region
registrarse to register (at hotel)
regla f period (menstruation) ; ruler (for measuring)

reina f queen
Reino Unido m United Kingdom
reintegro m withdrawal *(from bank account)*
reírse to laugh
rejilla f rack *(luggage)*
relámpago m lightning
rellenar to fill in
reloj m clock ; watch
remar to row *(boat)*
remitente m/f sender
remolcar to tow
remolque m tow rope ; trailer
RENFE f Spanish National Railways
reparación f repair
reparar to repair
repetir to repeat
repollo m cabbage
representante m/f sales rep
repuestos mpl spare parts
resaca f hangover
resbaladizo(a) slippery
resbalarse to slip
rescatar to rescue
reserva f booking(s) ; reservation
reservado(a) reserved
reservar to reserve ; to book
resfriado m cold *(illness)*
residente m/f resident
resistente a resistant to
  resistente al agua waterproof
  resistente al horno ovenproof
respirar to breathe
responder to answer ; to reply
responsabilidad f responsibility
respuesta f answer
restaurante m restaurant
resto m the rest
retrasado(a) delayed
retraso m delay
  sin retraso on schedule
retrato m portrait
retrovisor exterior m wing mirror
reumatismo m rheumatism
reunión f meeting
revelar to develop *(photos)*
revisar to check
revisión f car service ; inspection
revisor(a) m/f ticket collector
revista f magazine
rey m king
rezar to pray

riada f flash flood
rico(a) rich *(person)*
rincón m corner
riñón m kidney
riñonera f bumbag
río m river
robar to steal
robo m robbery ; theft
robot m food processor
rodaballo m turbot
rodeado(a) de surrounded by
rodilla f knee
rodillo m rolling pin
rojo(a) red
románico(a) Romanesque
romántico(a) romantic
romería f pilgrimage
romper to break ; to tear
ron m rum
roncar to snore
ropa f clothes
  ropa interior underwear
  ropa de cama bed clothes
ropero m wardrobe
rosa f rose
rosa pink
rosado m rosé
roto(a) broken
rotonda f roundabout *(traffic)*
rotulador m felt-tip pen
rubeola f rubella ; German measles
rubio(a) blond ; fair haired
rueda f wheel
  rueda de repuesto spare tyre
  rueda pinchada flat tyre
ruido m noise
ruinas fpl ruins
ruta f route
  ruta turística tourist route

S

SA abbrev. for **Sociedad Anónima**
sábado m Saturday
sábana f sheet *(bed)*
saber to know *(facts)* ; to know how
sabor m taste ; flavour
sacacorchos m corkscrew

sacar to take out *(of bag, etc)*

sacarina f saccharin

saco m sack
  saco de dormir sleeping bag

sagrado(a) holy

sal f salt
  sin sal unsalted

sala f hall ; hospital ward
  sala de conciertos concert hall
  sala de embarque departure lounge
  sala de espera waiting room

salado(a) savoury ; salty

salario m wage

salchicha f sausage

saldo m balance of account

saldos mpl sales

salida f exit/departure
  salida de incendios fire escape
  salida del sol sunrise

salir to go out ; to come out

salmón m salmon
  salmón ahumado smoked salmon

salsa f gravy ; sauce ; dressing

saltar to jump

salteado(a) sauté, sautéed

salud f health
  ¡salud! cheers!

salvar to save *(life)*

salvaslips m panty liner

salvavidas m lifebelt

salvia f sage *(herb)*

sandalias fpl sandals

sandía f watermelon

sangrar to bleed

sangría f red wine and fruit punch

santo(a) saint ; holy

sarampión m measles

sarpullido m skin rash

sartén f frying pan

sastrería f tailor's

secado a mano m blow-dry

secador (de pelo) m hairdryer

secadora f dryer *(spin, tumble)*

secar to dry

seco(a) dry ; dried *(fruit, beans)*

secretario(a) m/f secretary

seda f silk
  seda dental dental floss

seguida: en seguida straight away

seguido(a) continuous
  todo seguido straight on

seguir to continue ; to follow

según according to

segundo m second *(time)*

segundo(a) second
  de segunda mano secondhand

seguramente probably

seguridad f reliability ; safety ; security

seguro m insurance
  seguro de vida life insurance
  seguro del coche car insurance
  seguro médico medical insurance

seguro(a) safe ; certain

sello m stamp *(postage)*

semáforo m traffic lights

semana f week
  Semana Santa Holy Week ; Easter

semanal weekly

semilla f seed ; pip

señal f sign ; signal ; road sign

sencillo(a) simple ; single *(ticket)*

señor m gentleman
  Señor (Sr.) Mr. ; sir

señora f lady
  Señora (Sra.) Mrs. ; Ms ; Madam

señorita f Miss
  Señorita (Srta.)... Miss...

sentarse to sit

sentir to feel

separado(a) separated *(couple)*

septentrional northern

septiembre m September

sequía f drought

ser to be

seropositivo(a) HIV positive

serpiente f snake

servicio m service ; service charge
  servicio incluido service included
  área de servicios service area
  servicios toilets
  servicios de urgencia emergency services

servilleta f serviette ; napkin

servir to serve

sesión f performance ; screening
  sesión de noche late night performance
  sesión numerada seats bookable in advance
  sesión de tarde eve performance

sesos mpl brains

seta f mushroom

sexo m sex ; gender
sí yes
sida m AIDS
sidra f cider
siempre always
siento: lo siento I'm sorry
sierra f mountain range ; saw
siga follow
  siga adelante carry on
  siga recto keep straight on
siglo m century
siguiente following ; next
silencio m silence
silla f chair ; seat
  silla de paseo pushchair
  silla de ruedas wheelchair
sillón m armchair
simpático(a) nice ; kind
sin without
  sin plomo unleaded
síntoma m symptom
sírvase vd. mismo serve yourself
sistema m system
sitio m place ; space ; position
slip m pants ; briefs
sobre on ; upon ; about ; on top of
sobre m envelope
  sobre acolchado padded
  envelope
sobrecarga f surcharge
sobrecargar to overload
sobredosis f overdose
sobrino(a) m/f nephew/niece
sobrio(a) sober
sociedad f society
  Sociedad Anónima Ltd. ; plc
socio(a) m/f member ; partner
socorrista m/f lifeguard
¡socorro! help!
soja f soya
sol m sun ; sunshine
solamente only
soldado m/f soldier
solicitar to request
solitario m patience (cardgame)
solo(a) lone ; lonely ; only
sólo only
solomillo m sirloin
soltero(a) m/f bachelor ; single woman
soltero(a) single (unmarried)
sombra f shade ; shadow
  sombra de ojos eye shadow
sombrero m hat

sombrilla f sunshade ; parasol
somnífero m sleeping pill
sonido m sound
sonreír to smile
sonrisa f smile
sopa f soup
sordo(a) deaf
sorpresa f surprise
sótano m basement
soya (soja) f soya
Sr. abbrev. for **señor**
Sra. abbrev. for **señora**
Srta. abbrev. for **señorita**
stop m stop (sign)
su his/her/their/your
suavizante m hair conditioner ; fabric softener
submarinismo m scuba diving
subterráneo(a) underground
subtítulo m subtitle
sucio(a) dirty
sucursal f branch (of bank, etc)
sudadera f sweatshirt
sudar to sweat
suegro(a) m/f mother/father-in-law
suela f sole (of foot, shoe)
sueldo m wage
suelo m soil ; ground ; floor
suelto m loose change (money)
sueño m dream
suerte f luck
  ¡(buena) suerte! good luck!
Suiza f Switzerland
suizo(a) Swiss
sujetador m bra
superior higher
supermercado m supermarket
supositorio m suppository
sur m south
surf(ing) m surfing
surtidor m petrol pump
sus his/her/their/your

T

tabaco m tobacco ; cigarettes
tabla f board
  tabla de cortar chopping board

tabla de planchar ironing board
tabla de surf surf board
tablao flamenco m Flamenco show
tableta f tablet ; bar *(chocolate)*
taco m stuffed tortilla
tacón m heel *(shoe)*
taladradora f drill *(tool)*
talco m talc
TALGO m Intercity express train
talla f size
tallarines mpl noodles ; tagliatelle
taller m garage *(for repairs)*
talón m heel ; counterfoil ; stub
talón bancario cheque
talonario m cheque book
también as well ; also ; too
tampoco neither
tampones mpl tampons
tapa f lid
tapas fpl appetizers
tapón m cap *(of bottle etc)*
taquilla f ticket office
tarde f evening ; afternoon
de la tarde pm
tarde late
tarifa f price ; rate
tarifa baja cheap rate
tarifa máxima peak rate
tarjeta f card
tarjeta bancaria bank card
tarjeta de crédito credit card
tarjeta de donante donor card
tarjeta de embarque boarding pass
tarjeta de visita business card
tarjeta telefónica phonecard
tarjeta verde green card
tarro m jar ; pot
tarta f cake ; tart
tasca f bar ; cheap restaurant
taxista m/f taxi driver
taza f cup
tazón m bowl *(for soup, etc)*
té m tea
teatro m theatre
techo m ceiling
techo solar sunroof
tejado m roof
tela f material ; fabric
tela impermeable groundsheet
telaraña f web *(spider)*

teleférico m cablecar
telefonear to phone
telefonista m/f telephonist
teléfono m phone
teléfono móvil mobile phone
teléfono público payphone
telegrama m telegram
telesilla m ski lift ; chairlift
telesquí m ski lift
televisión f television
televisor m television set
télex m telex
temperatura f temperature
templo m temple
temporada f season
temporada alta high season
temporal m storm
temporizador m timer *(on cooker)*
temprano(a) early
tendedero m clothes line
tenedor m fork *(for eating)*
tener to have
tener miedo de to be afraid of
tener morriña to be homesick
tener que to have to
tener razón to be right
tener suerte to be lucky
tener fiebre to have a temperature
tentempié m snack
tequila f tequila
tercero(a) third
terciopelo m velvet
termo m flask *(thermos)*
termómetro m thermometer
ternera f veal
terraza f terrace
terremoto m earthquake
terreno m land
terrorista m/f terrorist
testículos mpl testicles
tetera f teapot
tetina f teat *(on baby's bottle)*
ti you *(sing. with friends)*
tía f aunt
tiempo m time ; weather
tienda f store ; shop ; tent
tienda de modas clothes shop
tierra f earth
tijeras fpl scissors
tijeras de uñas nail scissors
timbre m doorbell ; official stamp
tímido(a) shy

timón m rudder

tinta f ink

tinte f dye
 tinte de pelo hair dye

tinto m red wine

tintorería f dry-cleaner's

tío m uncle

típico(a) typical

tipo m sort
 tipo de cambio exchange rate

tique m ticket

tirador m handle

tirar to throw (away) ; to pull
 para tirar disposable

tirita® f elastoplast

toalla f towel

tobillo m ankle

tocar to touch ; to play (instrument)
 no tocar do not touch

tocino m bacon

todo(a) all
 todo everything
 todo el mundo everyone
 todo incluido all inclusive

tomar to take ; to have (food/drink)
 tomar el sol to sunbathe

tomate m tomato

tomillo m thyme

tónica f tonic water

tono m tone
 tono de marcar dialling tone

tonto(a) stupid

toquen: *no toquen* do not touch

torcedura f sprain

torero m bullfighter

tormenta f thunderstorm

tornillo m screw

toro m bull

torre f tower

torta f cake

tortilla f omelette

tos f cough

toser to cough

tostada f toast

trabajar to work (person)

trabajo m work

tradicional traditional

traducción f translation

traducir to translate

traer to fetch ; to bring

tráfico m traffic

tragar to swallow

traje m suit ; outfit
 traje de baño swimsuit
 traje de bucear wetsuit
 traje de etiqueta evening
 dress (man's)
 traje de noche evening
 dress (woman's)

trampolín m diving board

tranquilo(a) calm ; quiet

tranquilizante m tranquilliser

transbordador m car ferry

transbordo m transfer

tranvía m tram ; short-distance train

trapo m cloth (for cleaning, etc)

tras after ; behind

trastorno estomacal m stomach
 upset

tratar con cuidado handle with care

travesía f crossing

tren m train

triángulo señalizador m warning
 triangle

triste sad

trozo m piece

trucha f trout

trueno m thunder

trufa f truffle

tú you (sing. with friends)

tu your (sing. with friends)

tubería f pipe (drain, etc)

tubo de escape m exhaust pipe

tumbarse to lie down

tumbona f deckchair

túnel m tunnel

turista m/f tourist

turístico(a) tourist

turno m turn
 espere su turno wait your turn

turrón m nougat

TVE abbrev. for Televisión Española

U

úlcera f ulcer (stomach)

últimamente lately

último(a) last

ultracongelador m deep freeze

ultramarinos m grocery shop

un(a) a/an

uña f nail (finger, toe)

u/v spanish–eng

ungüento m ointment
únicamente only
unidad f unit
Unión Europea f European Union
universidad f university
unos(as) some
urgencias fpl casualty department
urgente urgent ; express
usar to use
uso m use ; custom
  uso externo/tópico for external
  use only
usted you (polite sing.)
ustedes you (polite plural)
útil useful
utilizar to use
uva f grape
  uvas verdes/negras green/black
  grapes
UVI/UCI f intensive care unit

V

vaca f cow
vacaciones fpl holiday
  vacaciones de verano summer
  holidays
vacío(a) empty
vacuna f vaccination
vagina f vagina
vagón m railway carriage
vale OK
vale... it's worth...
vale m token ; voucher
válido(a) valid (ticket, licence, etc)
valle m valley
valor m value
válvula f valve
vapor m steam
  al vapor steamed
vaqueros mpl jeans
variado(a) assorted ; mixed
varios(as) several
vasco(a) Basque
vaso m glass (for drinking)
Vd(s). abbrev. for **usted(es)**
veces fpl times
vecino(a) m/f neighbour
vegetariano(a) m/f vegetarian

vehículo m vehicle
vela f candle ; sail ; sailing
velocidad f speed
  velocidad limitada speed limit
  velocidad máxima speed limit
velocímetro m speedometer
vena f vein
venda f bandage
vendedor(a) m/f salesman/woman
vender to sell
  se vende for sale
veneno m poison
venenoso(a) poisonous
venir to come
venta f sale; country inn
ventana f window
ventanilla f window (in car, train)
ventilador m fan (electric)
ver to see ; to watch
verano m summer
verdad f truth
  ¿de verdad? really?
verdadero(a) true ; genuine
verde green
verdulería f greengrocer's
verduras fpl vegetables
vereda f footpath (in the country)
verificar to check
versión f version
  versión original original version
vespa f motor scooter
vestido m dress
vestirse to get dressed
veterinario(a) m/f vet
vez f time
vía f track ; rails ; platform
  por vía oral/bucal orally
viajar to travel
viaje m journey ; trip
  viaje de negocios business trip
  viaje organizado package tour
viajero m traveller
víbora f adder ; viper
vida f life
vídeo m video ; video recorder
vídeocámara f camcorder
videojuego m video game
vidriera f stained-glass window
vidrio m glass (substance)
vieira f scallop
viejo(a) old
viento m wind

viernes *m* Friday
  Viernes Santo Good Friday
viña *f* vineyard
vinagre *m* vinegar
vinagreta *f* vinaigrette *(dressing)*
vino *m* wine
  vino blanco white wine
  vino rosado rosé wine
  vino seco dry wine
  vino tinto red wine
violación *f* rape
violar to rape
violeta *f* violet *(flower)*
virus *m* virus
  virus del sida HIV
visa *f* visa
visita *f* visit
visitar to visit
víspera *f* eve
vista *f* view
viudo(a) *m/f* widow/widower
vivir to live
V.O. (versión original) undubbed version (of film)
volante *m* steering wheel
volar to fly
volcán *m* volcano
voleibol *m* volleyball
voltaje *m* voltage
volumen *m* volume
volver to come/go back ; to return
vomitar to vomit
vosotros you *(plural with friends)*
voz *f* voice
vuelo *m* flight
vuelta *f* turn ; return ; change *(money)*
vuestro(a) your *(plural with friends)*

W

wáter *m* lavatory ; toilet

Y

y and
yate *m* yacht
yerno *m* son-in-law
yo I ; me
yogur *m* yoghurt
  yogur natural plain yoghurt

Z

zanahoria *f* carrot
zapatería *f* shoe shop
zapatillas *fpl* slippers
  zapatillas de deporte trainers
zapato *m* shoe
zarzuela *f* Spanish light opera; casserole
zona *f* zone
  zona azul controlled parking area
  zona de descanso layby
  zona restringida restricted area
zorro *m* fox
zumo *m* juice

HOW SPANISH WORKS

NOUNS

*A **noun** is a word such as **car**, **horse** or **Mary** which is used to refer to a person or thing.*

Unlike English, Spanish nouns have a gender: they are either *masculine* (**el**) or *feminine* (**la**). Therefore words for *the* and *a(n)* must agree with the noun they accompany – whether *masculine*, *feminine* or *plural*:

	masc.	*fem.*	*plural*
the	**el gato**	**la plaza**	**los gatos, las plazas**
a, an	**un gato**	**una plaza**	**unos gatos, unas plazas**

The ending of the noun will usually indicate whether it is *masculine* or *feminine*:

-o or **-or** are generally *masculine*

-a, **-dad**, **-ión**, **-tud**, **-umbre** are generally *feminine*

NOTE: *feminine* nouns beginning with a stressed **a-** or **ha-** take the *masculine* article **el**, though the noun is still *feminine*.

FORMATION OF PLURALS

The articles **el** and **la** become **los** and **las** in the plural. Nouns ending with a vowel become plural by adding -**s**:

> **el gato → los gatos**
>
> **la plaza → las plazas**
>
> **la calle → las calles**

Where the noun ends in a consonant, -**es** is added:

> **el color → los colores**
>
> **la ciudad → las ciudades**

Nouns ending in -**z** change their ending to -**ces** in the plural:

> **el lápiz → los lápices**
>
> **la voz → las voces**

ADJECTIVES

*An **adjective** is a word such as **small**, **pretty** or **practical** that describes a person or thing, or gives extra information about them.*

Adjectives normally follow the noun they describe in Spanish, e.g. **la manzana roja** (the red apple)

Some common exceptions which go before the noun are:

buen good	**gran** great
ningún no, not any	**mucho** much, many
poco little, few	**primer** first
tanto so much, so many	**último** last

e.g. **el último tren** (the last train)

Spanish adjectives also reflect the gender of the noun they describe. To make an adjective *feminine*, the *masculine* -**o** ending is changed to -**a** ; and the endings -**án**, -**ón**, -**or**, -**és** change to -**ana**, -**ona**, -**ora**, -**esa**:

masc. **el libro rojo**	*fem.*	**la manzana roja**
(the red book)		(the red apple)
masc. **el hombre hablador**	*fem.*	**la mujer habladora**
(the talkative man)		(the talkative woman)

To make an adjective plural an -**s** is added to the singular form if it ends in a vowel. If the adjective ends in a consonant, -**es** is added:

masc. **los libros rojos**	*fem.*	**las manzanas rojas**
(the red books)		(the red apples)
masc. **los hombres habladores**	*fem*	**las mujeres habladoras**
(the talkative men)		(the talkative women)

MY, YOUR, HIS, HER...

These words also depend on the gender and number of the noun they accompany and not on the sex of the 'owner'.

	with masc. sing. noun	*with fem. sing. noun*	*with plural nouns*
my	**mi**	**mi**	**mis**
your *(familiar sing.)*	**tu**	**tu**	**tus**
your *(polite sing.)*	**su**	**su**	**sus**
his/her/its	**su**	**su**	**sus**
our	**nuestro**	**nuestra**	**nuestros/nuestras**
your *(familiar pl.)*	**vuestro**	**vuestra**	**vuestros/vuestras**
their	**su**	**su**	**sus**
your *(polite pl.)*	**su**	**su**	**sus**

There is no distinction between **his** and **her** in Spanish: **su billete** can mean either **his** or **her ticket**.

PRONOUNS

*A **pronoun** is a word that you use to refer to someone or something when you do not need to use a noun, often because the person or thing has been mentioned earlier. Examples are it, she, **something** and **myself**.*

subject		*object*	
I	**yo**	me	**me**
you *(familiar sing.)*	**tú**	you	**te**
you *(polite sing.)*	**usted (Vd.)**	you	**le**
he/it	**él**	him/it	**le, lo**
she/it	**ella**	her/it	**le, la**
we	**nosotros**	us	**nos**
you *(familiar pl.)*	**vosotros**	you	**os**
you *(polite pl.)*	**ustedes (Vds.)**	you	**les**
they *(masc.)*	**ellos**	them	**les, los**
they *(fem.)*	**ellas**	them	**les, las**

Subject pronouns (**I**, **you**, **he**, etc.) are generally omitted in Spanish, since the verb ending distinguishes the subject:

habl<u>o</u>	<u>I</u> speak
habl<u>amos</u>	<u>we</u> speak

However, they are used for emphasis or to avoid confusion:

<u>yo</u> voy a Mallorca y <u>él</u> va a Alicante
<u>I</u> am going to Mallorca and <u>he</u> is going to Alicante

Object pronouns are placed before the verb in Spanish:

<u>la</u> veo	I see <u>her</u>
<u>los</u> conocemos	we know <u>them</u>

However, in commands or requests they follow the verb:

¡ayúda<u>me</u>!	help <u>me</u>!
¡escúcha<u>le</u>!	listen to <u>him</u>

except when they are expressed in the negative:

¡no <u>me</u> ayudes!	don't help <u>me</u>
¡no <u>le</u> escuches!	don't listen to <u>him</u>

The object pronouns shown above can be used to mean to me, to us, etc., but to him/to her is **le** and to them is **les**. If **le** and **les** occur in combinations with **lo/la/las/los** then **le/les** change to **se**, e.g. **se lo doy** (I give it to him).

VERBS

*A **verb** is a word such as **sing**, **walk** or **cry** which is used with a subject to say what someone or something does or what happens to them. **Regular verbs** follow the same pattern of endings. **Irregular verbs** do not follow a regular pattern so you need to learn the different endings.*

There are three main patterns of endings for Spanish verbs – those ending -**ar**, -**er** and -**ir** in the dictionary.

	CANT<u>AR</u>	**TO SING**
	canto	I sing
	cantas	you sing
(usted)	**canta**	(s)he sings/you sing
	cantamos	we sing
	cantáis	you sing
(ustedes)	**cantan**	they sing/you sing
	VIV<u>IR</u>	**TO LIVE**
	vivo	I live
	vives	you live
(usted)	**vive**	(s)he lives/you live
	vivimos	we live
	vivís	you live
(ustedes)	**viven**	they live/you live

	COMER	**TO EAT**
	como	I eat
	comes	you eat
(usted)	**come**	(s)he eats/you eat
	comemos	we eat
	coméis	you eat
(ustedes)	**comen**	they eat/you eat

Like French, in Spanish there are two ways of addressing people: the polite form (for people you don't know well or who are older) and the familiar form (for friends, family and children). The polite you is **usted** in the singular, and **ustedes** in the plural. You can see from above that **usted** uses the same verb ending as for he and she; **ustedes** the same ending as for they. Often the words **usted** and **ustedes** are omitted, but the verb ending itself indicates that you are using the polite form. The informal words for you are **tú** (singular) and **vosotros** (plural).

THE VERB 'TO BE'

There are two different Spanish verbs for **to be** – **ser** and **estar**.

Ser is used to describe a permanent state:

soy inglés	I am English
es una playa	it is a beach

Estar is used to describe a temporary state or where something is located:

¿cómo está?	how are you?
¿dónde está la playa?	where is the beach?

	SER	**TO BE**
	soy	I am
	eres	you are
(usted)	**es**	(s)he is/you are
	somos	we are
	sois	you are
(ustedes)	**son**	they are/you are

	ESTAR	**TO BE**
	estoy	I am
	estás	you are
(usted)	**está**	(s)he is/you are
	estamos	we are
	estáis	you are
(ustedes)	**están**	they are/you are

Other common irregular verbs include:

	TENER	TO HAVE
	tengo	I have
	tienes	you have
(usted)	**tiene**	(s)he has/you have
	tenemos	we have
	tenéis	you have
(ustedes)	**tienen**	they have/you have

	IR	TO GO
	voy	I go
	vas	you go
(usted)	**va**	(s)he goes/you go
	vamos	we go
	vais	you go
(ustedes)	**van**	they go/you go

	PODER	TO BE ABLE
	puedo	I can
	puedes	you can
(usted)	**puede**	(s)he can/you can
	podemos	we can
	podéis	you can
(ustedes)	**pueden**	they can/you can

	QUERER	TO WANT
	quiero	I want
	quieres	you want
(usted)	**quiere**	(s)he wants/you want
	queremos	we want
	queréis	you want
(ustedes)	**quieren**	they want/you want

	HACER	TO DO
	hago	I do
	haces	you do
(usted)	**hace**	(s)he does/you do
	hacemos	we do
	hacéis	you do
(ustedes)	**hacen**	they do/you do

	VENIR	TO COME
	vengo	I come
	vienes	you come
(usted)	**viene**	(s)he comes/you come
	venimos	we come
	venís	you come
(ustedes)	**vienen**	they come/you come

PAST TENSE

To form the past tense, for example: I gave/I have given, I finished/I have finished, combine the present tense of the verb **haber** – to have with the past participle of the verb (**cantado**, **comido**, **vivido**):

	HABER	TO HAVE
	he	I have
	has	you have
(usted)	**ha**	(s)he has/you have
	hemos	we have
	habéis	you have
(ustedes)	**han**	they have/you have
e.g.	**he cantado**	I sang/I have sung
	ha comido	he ate/he has eaten
	hemos vivido	we lived/we have lived

To form a negative **no** is placed before all of the verb:

e.g.	**no he cantado**	I haven't sung
	no ha comido	he hasn't eaten
	no hemos vivido	we haven't lived